the
BLACKBURNE
COVENANT ™

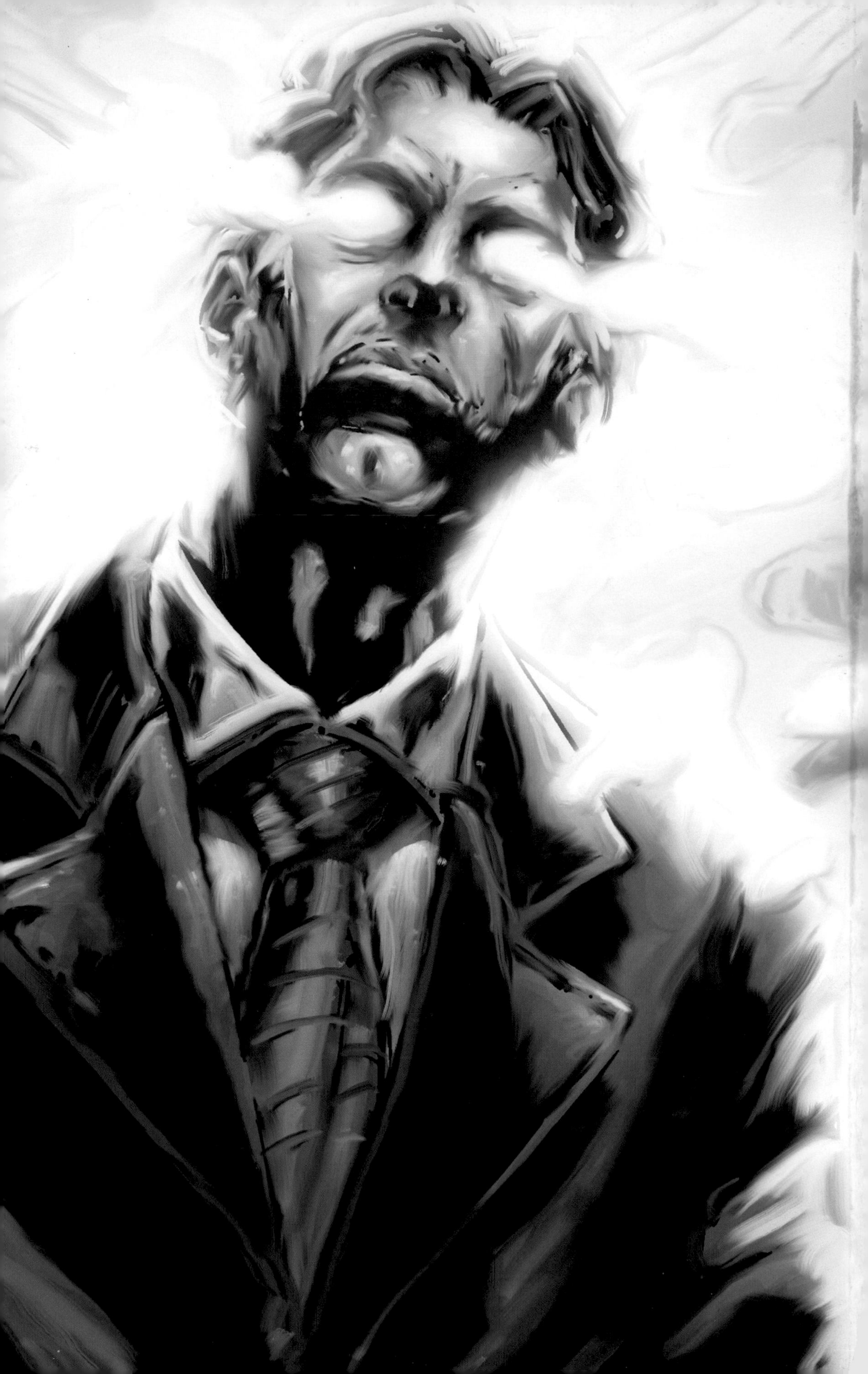

the BLACKBURNE COVENANT™

story | **FABIAN NICIEZA**

art | **STEFANO RAFFAELE**

colors | **ELENA SANJUST**

letters | **MICHAEL HEISLER**

cover art | **STEFANO RAFFAELE** with **DAVID NESTELLE**

chapter break color art | **DAVID NESTELLE**

DARK HORSE BOOKS™

publisher | **MIKE RICHARDSON**

editor | **SCOTT ALLIE** with **MATT DRYER**

designer | **DAVID NESTELLE**

art director | **MARK COX**

Special thanks to Dave Stewart

For Tracey, who was by my side when I had the idea ...
... and is here to see it published.
F.N.

Dedicated to Matteo De Benedittis, 1972-2003. *S.R.*

Published by Dark Horse Books
a division of Dark Horse Comics, Inc.
10956 SE Main Street
Milwaukie, OR 97222

First edition: December 2003
ISBN: 1-56971-889-x

2 4 6 8 10 9 7 5 3 1

Printed in China

The Blackburne Covenant created for Dark Horse Comics by Fabian Nicieza

⋘ *INTRODUCTION* ⋙

The early nineties was a wild time in comics, where money was flowing and the ideas were flowing as well. But...well, let's just say it was so comfortable *inside* the box that there was little need to think outside of it. I broke into the mainstream at that point, and I had the pleasure of cutting my mainstream teeth working with Fabian Nicieza. My first work for Marvel Comics was on *Wolverine #54*, a fill-in issue that he wrote. Then he edited me on the *Wonder Man Annual #1*, which then led to us working closely together on Marvel's *The New Warriors* for two years.

You learn a lot about a person when you read their scripts month after month. It was not unusual for common thinkers to say, "Eh, who cares, it's just a comic-book story." And it showed. By the time 1991 had turned into 1996 it was all over for the comics boom. In five short years readers frustrated by the companies catering to collectors who could care less about what was going on inside their hermetically sealed, triple-mylar-bagged comics, abandoned the industry, and sales sank like the *Titanic*. Like rats from the sinking ship, collectors also abandoned the comics industry to its self-made fate. As things got worse, and jobs disappeared; those that would stay in the business would have to show what they had, and the cream began to rise to the top. Common thinkers found themselves unemployed

Now when I speak of common thinkers, I don't count Fabian Nicieza among them. I never have. I saw better stories in our *New Warriors* than I did in *X-Men* and *Cable*, and mostly it was due to Fabian having more freedom with *New Warriors* than in those more popular and money-making titles The more a comic sells, the more cooks want into the kitchen to mess with the brew. Just like any entertainment form, the more money something makes, the less you see of the real team involved. There's always someone else to please aside from the audience, and usually it's that kind of thinking that leads a title right into the quarter bin.

Fabian was always struggling with boundaries and ideas, and, frustrated by the creative interference from lesser minds more interested in sales figures than art, he eventually left a cozy position at Marvel and at the height of his career, went off to be Editor-in-Chief of Acclaim Comics. The timing wasn't the greatest for new companies. I also had a healthy dose of Vitamin Reality when I saw Malibu's Ultraverse–for which I had created and designed characters–get swallowed up like a small fish by the Marvel whale. I believe that some really good books came out of Acclaim, which showed some very fresh ideas and were rich with quality artwork. Were they ahead of their time? Perhaps. Were they outside of the box? Definitely.

Personally, I had to climb outside the box by working on *Transmetropolitan*, and show that I was capable of doing work more challenging and interesting than straight superhero fare. I had to take chances and risk leaving the mainstream to go with a new imprint that would give me more freedom. With *Blackburne Covenant*, I believe that's what Fabian has done as well.

So when I saw Fabian Nicieza's name in big letters on the cover of *The Blackburne Covenant*, and the compelling cover art of Stefano Raffaele on a Dark Horse book, I bought it. I thought immediately, "This looks like something that I'd expect from the Fabian I know."

See, while I have known Fabian as a friend for years and worked with him as a writer and as an editor, I had always hoped we'd work together on something like this (though ultimately I wouldn't be able to outdo Stefano's art on *Blackburne Covenant*. It's outstanding!) *The Blackburne Covenant* is a compelling story of a writer whose *Matrix*-like reality is shattered when he realizes that he is someone else entirely. There's action, sex, murder, and the thread tying it all together is a very original and unexpected idea.

If you know Fabian Nicieza's work, the mainstream work of the nineties, you only know half of what he's capable of doing. Just like the lead character, there's a lot more to this writer than meets the eye. Personally, I'm looking forward to working with Fabian again in the future, and seeing what we do when we both approach things from this new perspective. In the meantime, I'm going to be enjoying what he's doing now. I think you will too.

The nineties are over. It's a new millennium for comics. Welcome to the outside of the box.

–Darick Robertson

Darick Robertson is a fourteen-year veteran of the comics industry, best known for co-creating Transmetropolitan *for Vertigo Comics and his current run on Marvel Comics' relaunch of* Wolverine. *You can find out more at www.darickr.com*

Act One
THE GOOD LIFE

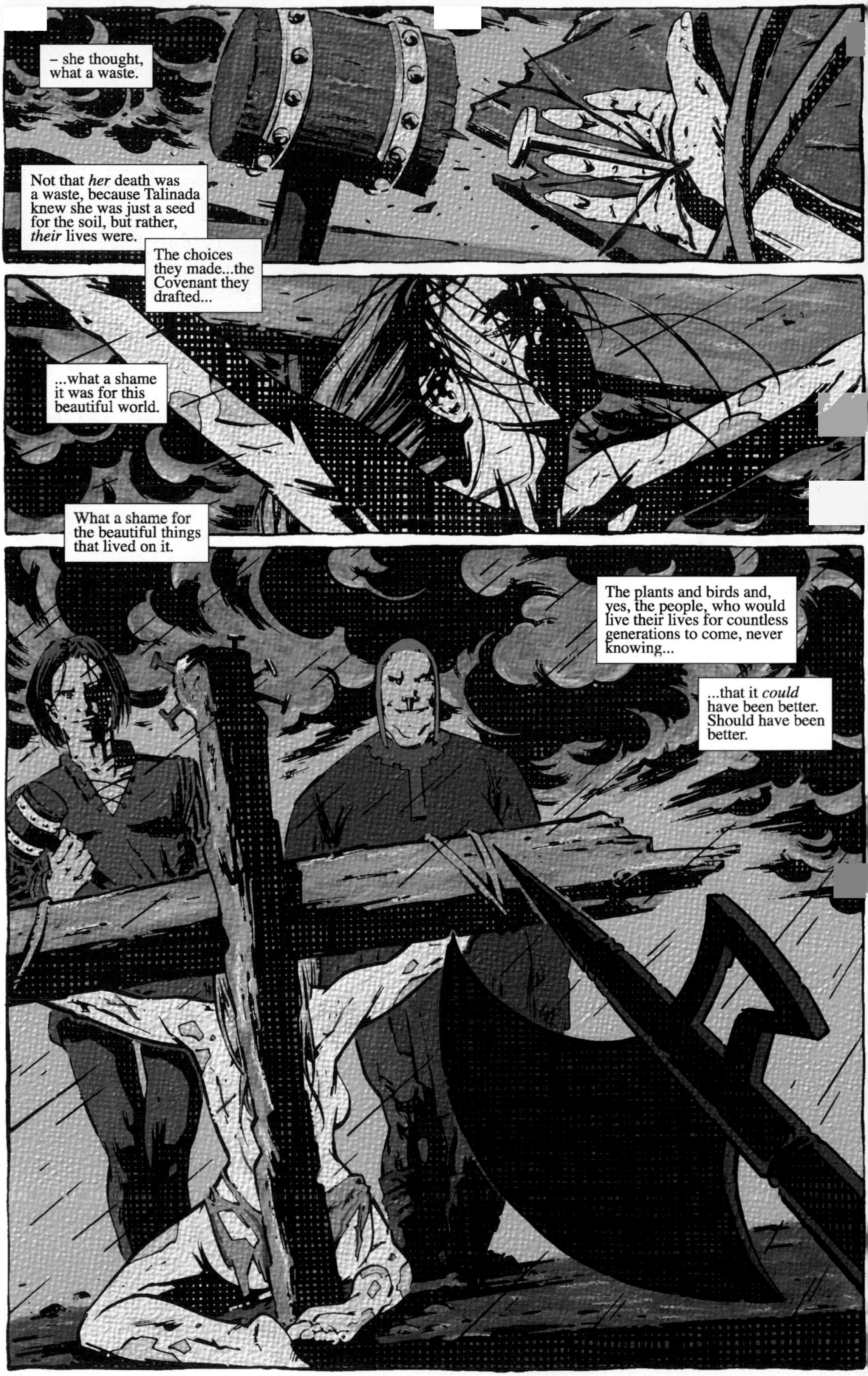
– she thought, what a waste.
Not that *her* death was a waste, because Talinada knew she was just a seed for the soil, but rather, *their* lives were.
The choices they made...the Covenant they drafted...
...what a shame it was for this beautiful world.
What a shame for the beautiful things that lived on it.
The plants and birds and, yes, the people, who would live their lives for countless generations to come, never knowing...
...that it *could* have been better. Should have been better.

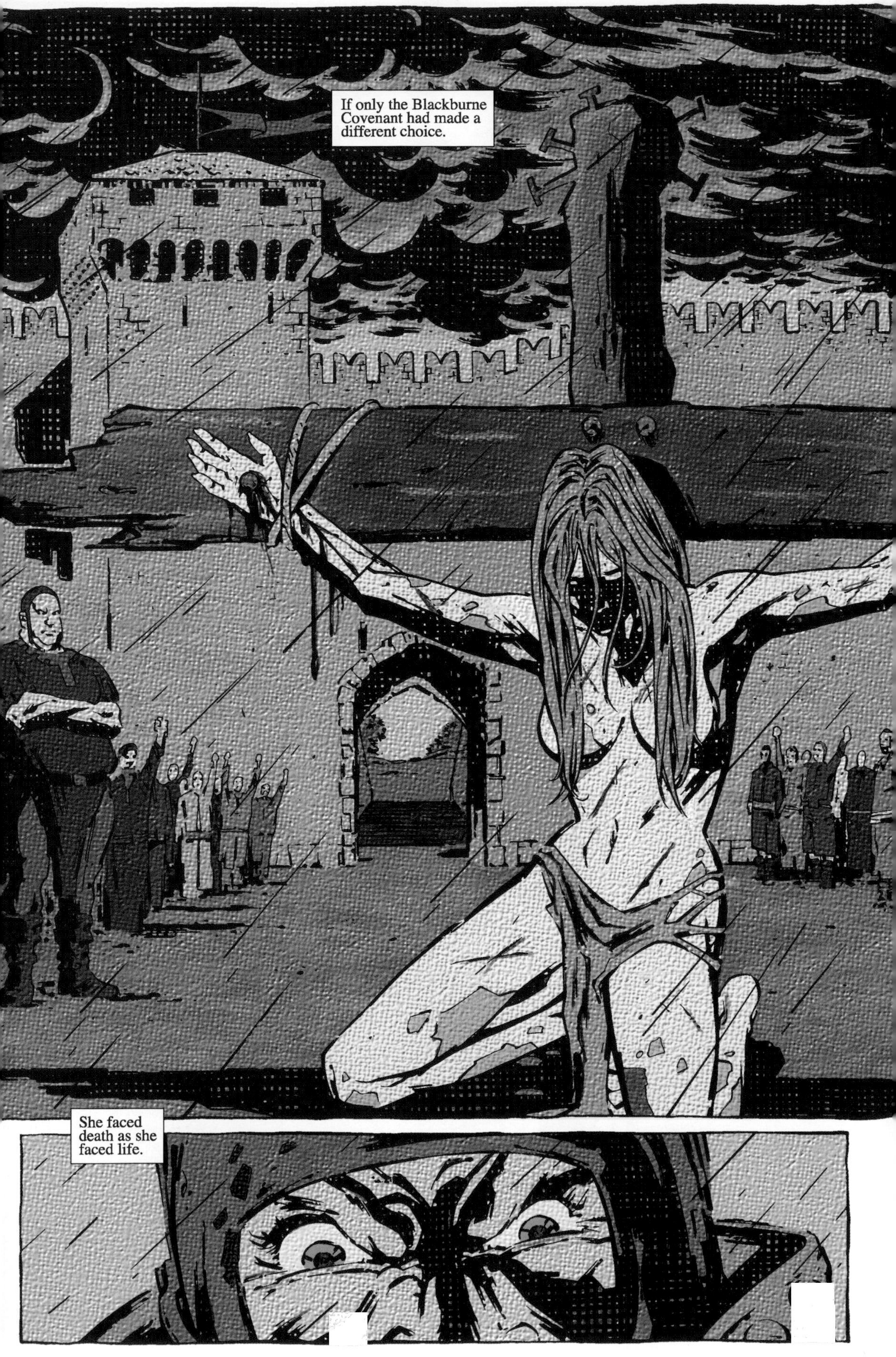
If only the Blackburne Covenant had made a different choice.
She faced death as she faced life.

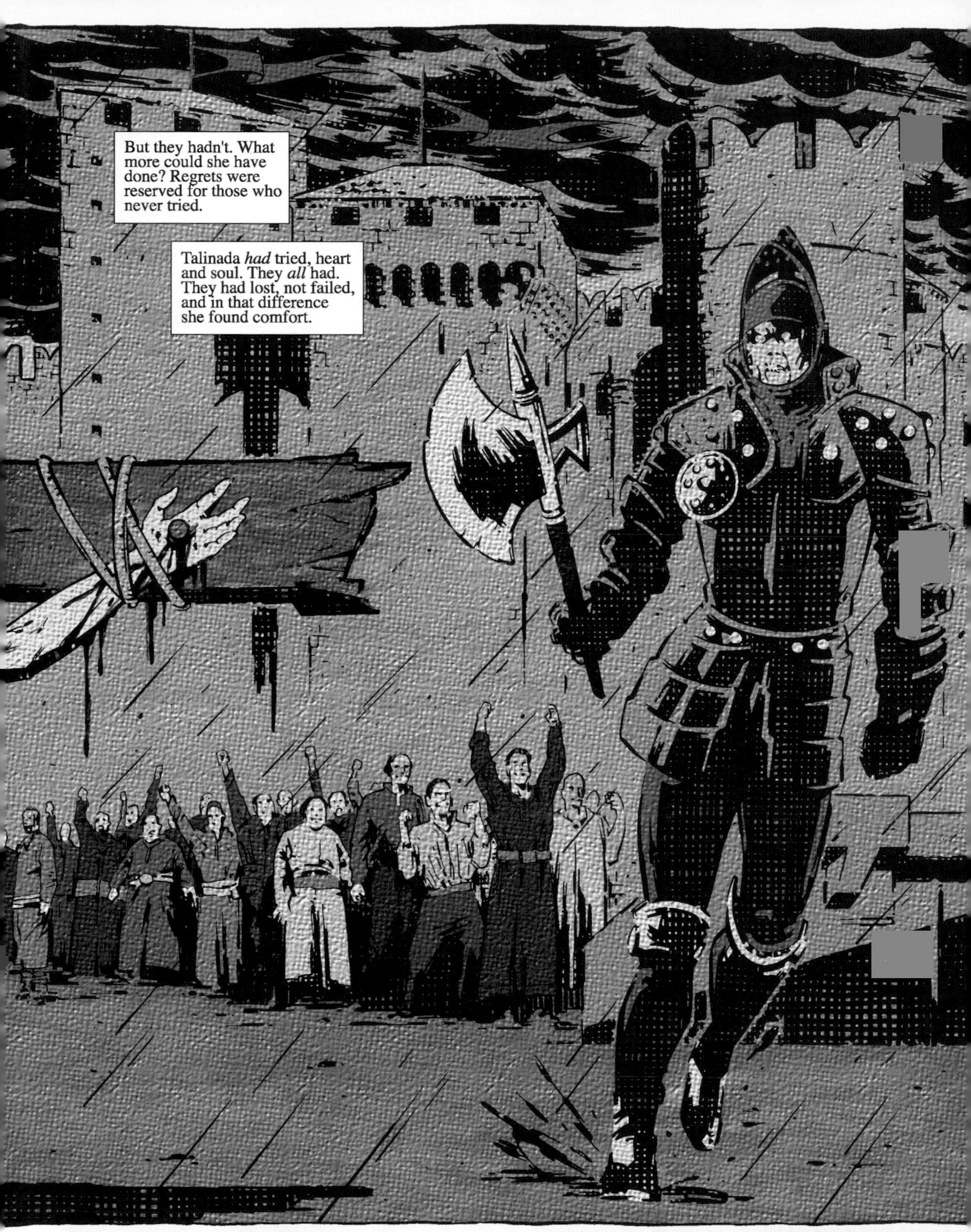
But they hadn't. What more could she have done? Regrets were reserved for those who never tried.
Talinada *had* tried, heart and soul. They *all* had. They had lost, not failed, and in that difference she found comfort.

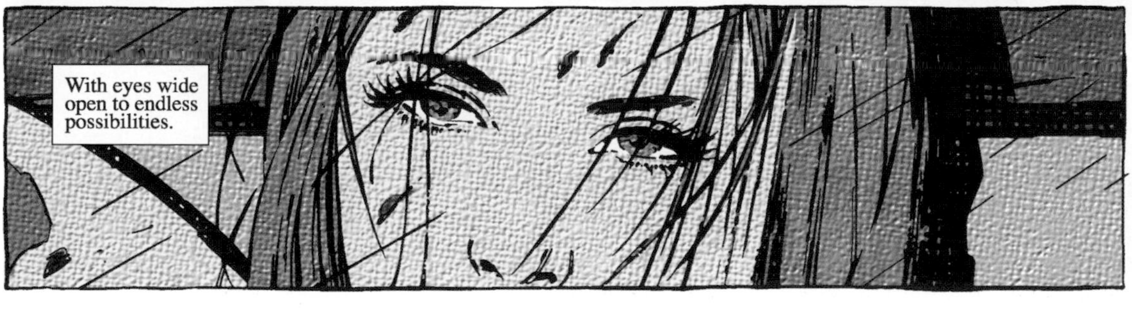
With eyes wide open to endless possibilities.

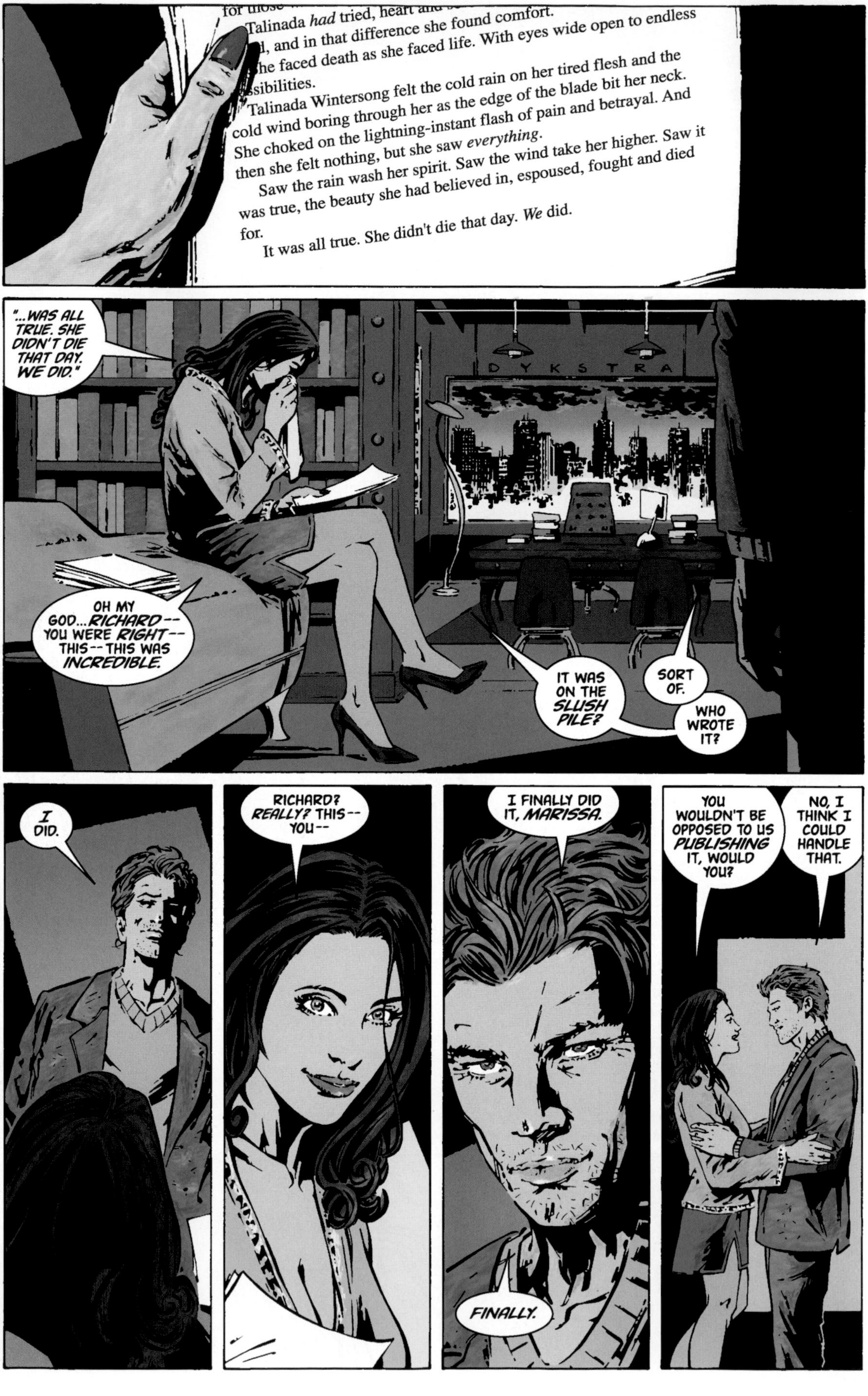

Talinada *had* tried, heart and
and in that difference she found comfort.
he faced death as she faced life. With eyes wide open to endless
ssibilities.
Talinada Wintersong felt the cold rain on her tired flesh and the cold wind boring through her as the edge of the blade bit her neck. She choked on the lightning-instant flash of pain and betrayal. And then she felt nothing, but she saw *everything*.
Saw the rain wash her spirit. Saw the wind take her higher. Saw it was true, the beauty she had believed in, espoused, fought and died for.
It was all true. She didn't die that day. *We* did.
"...WAS ALL TRUE. SHE DIDN'T DIE THAT DAY. WE DID."
OH MY GOD... *RICHARD*-- YOU WERE *RIGHT*-- THIS-- THIS WAS *INCREDIBLE*.
DYKSTRA
IT WAS ON THE *SLUSH PILE?*
SORT OF.
WHO WROTE IT?
I DID.
RICHARD? *REALLY?* THIS-- YOU--
I FINALLY DID IT, *MARISSA*.
FINALLY.
YOU WOULDN'T BE OPPOSED TO US *PUBLISHING* IT, WOULD YOU?
NO, I THINK I COULD HANDLE THAT.

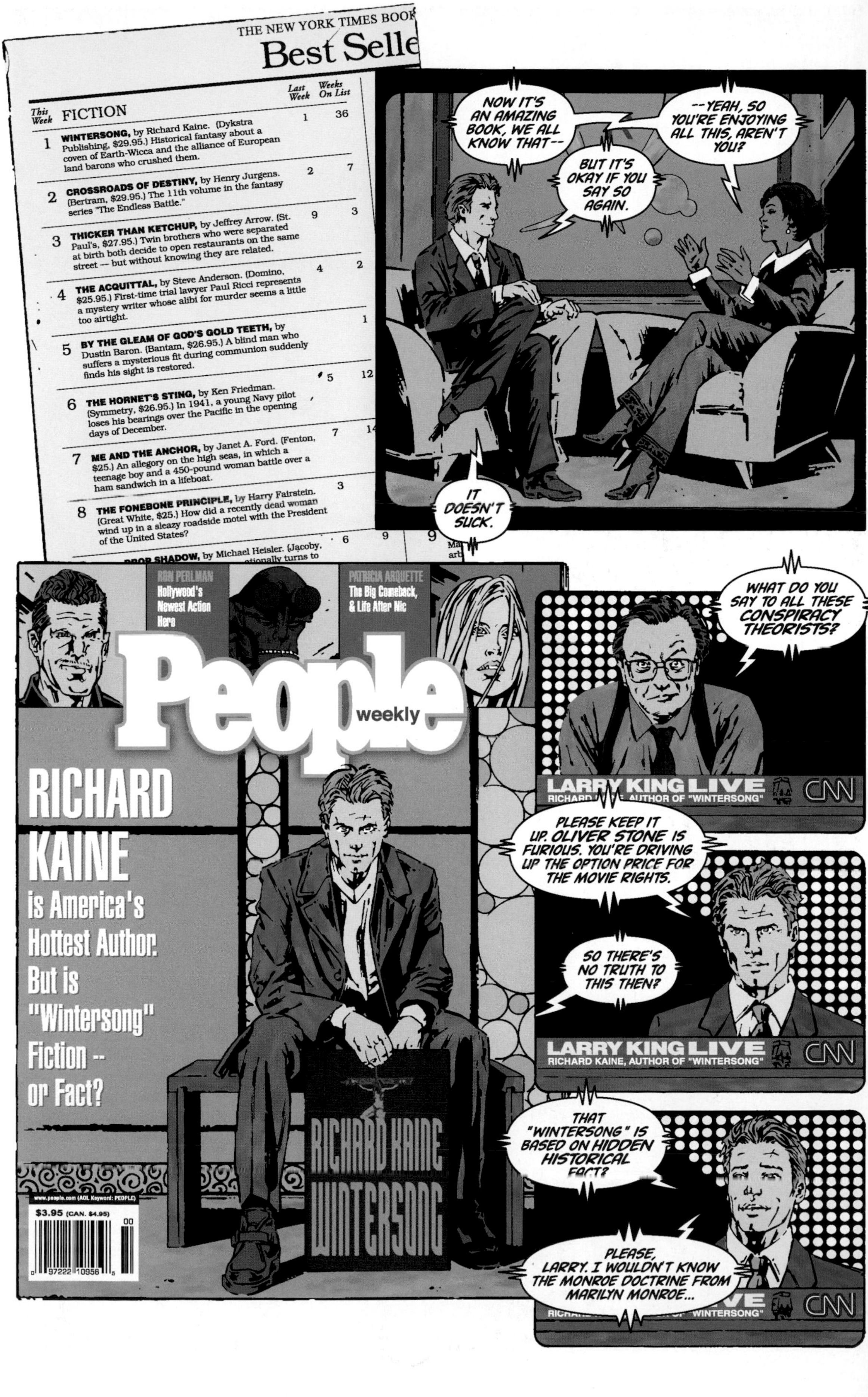
THE NEW YORK TIMES BOOK
Best Selle
This Week
FICTION
Last Week
Weeks On List
1 WINTERSONG, by Richard Kaine. (Dykstra Publishing, $29.95.) Historical fantasy about a coven of Earth-Wicca and the alliance of European land barons who crushed them. 1 36
2 CROSSROADS OF DESTINY, by Henry Jurgens. (Bertram, $29.95.) The 11th volume in the fantasy series "The Endless Battle." 2 7
3 THICKER THAN KETCHUP, by Jeffrey Arrow. (St. Paul's, $27.95.) Twin brothers who were separated at birth both decide to open restaurants on the same street -- but without knowing they are related. 9 3
4 THE ACQUITTAL, by Steve Anderson. (Domino, $25.95.) First-time trial lawyer Paul Ricci represents a mystery writer whose alibi for murder seems a little too airtight. 4 2
5 BY THE GLEAM OF GOD'S GOLD TEETH, by Dustin Baron. (Bantam, $26.95.) A blind man who suffers a mysterious fit during communion suddenly finds his sight is restored. 1
6 THE HORNET'S STING, by Ken Friedman. (Symmetry, $26.95.) In 1941, a young Navy pilot loses his bearings over the Pacific in the opening days of December. 5 12
7 ME AND THE ANCHOR, by Janet A. Ford. (Fenton, $25.) An allegory on the high seas, in which a teenage boy and a 450-pound woman battle over a ham sandwich in a lifeboat. 7
8 THE FONEBONE PRINCIPLE, by Harry Fairstein. (Great White, $25.) How did a recently dead woman wind up in a sleazy roadside motel with the President of the United States? 3
6 9
SHADOW, by Michael Heisler. (Jacoby,
NOW IT'S AN AMAZING BOOK, WE ALL KNOW THAT--
--YEAH, SO YOU'RE ENJOYING ALL THIS, AREN'T YOU?
BUT IT'S OKAY IF YOU SAY SO AGAIN.
IT DOESN'T SUCK.
RON PERLMAN
Hollywood's Newest Action Hero
PATRICIA ARQUETTE
The Big Comeback, & Life After Nic
People weekly
RICHARD KAINE is America's Hottest Author. But is "Wintersong" Fiction -- or Fact?
RICHARD KAINE
WINTERSONG
www.people.com (AOL Keyword: PEOPLE)
$3.95 (CAN. $4.95)
WHAT DO YOU SAY TO ALL THESE CONSPIRACY THEORISTS?
LARRY KING LIVE
CNN
PLEASE KEEP IT UP. OLIVER STONE IS FURIOUS. YOU'RE DRIVING UP THE OPTION PRICE FOR THE MOVIE RIGHTS.
SO THERE'S NO TRUTH TO THIS THEN?
LARRY KING LIVE
RICHARD KAINE, AUTHOR OF "WINTERSONG"
CNN
THAT "WINTERSONG" IS BASED ON HIDDEN HISTORICAL FACT?
PLEASE, LARRY. I WOULDN'T KNOW THE MONROE DOCTRINE FROM MARILYN MONROE...
CNN

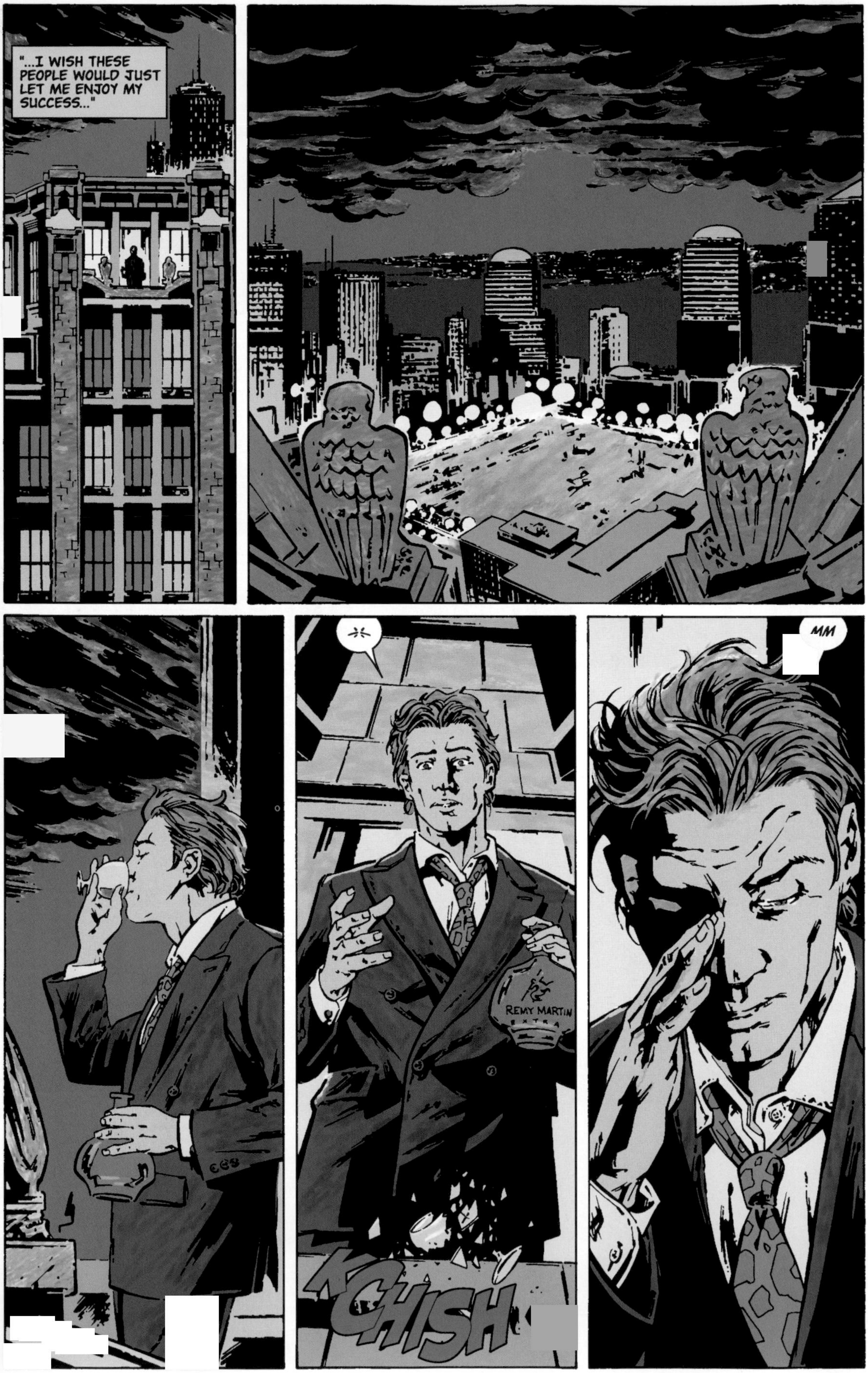
"...I WISH THESE PEOPLE WOULD JUST LET ME ENJOY MY SUCCESS..."
REMY MARTIN
EXTRA
KCHISH
MM

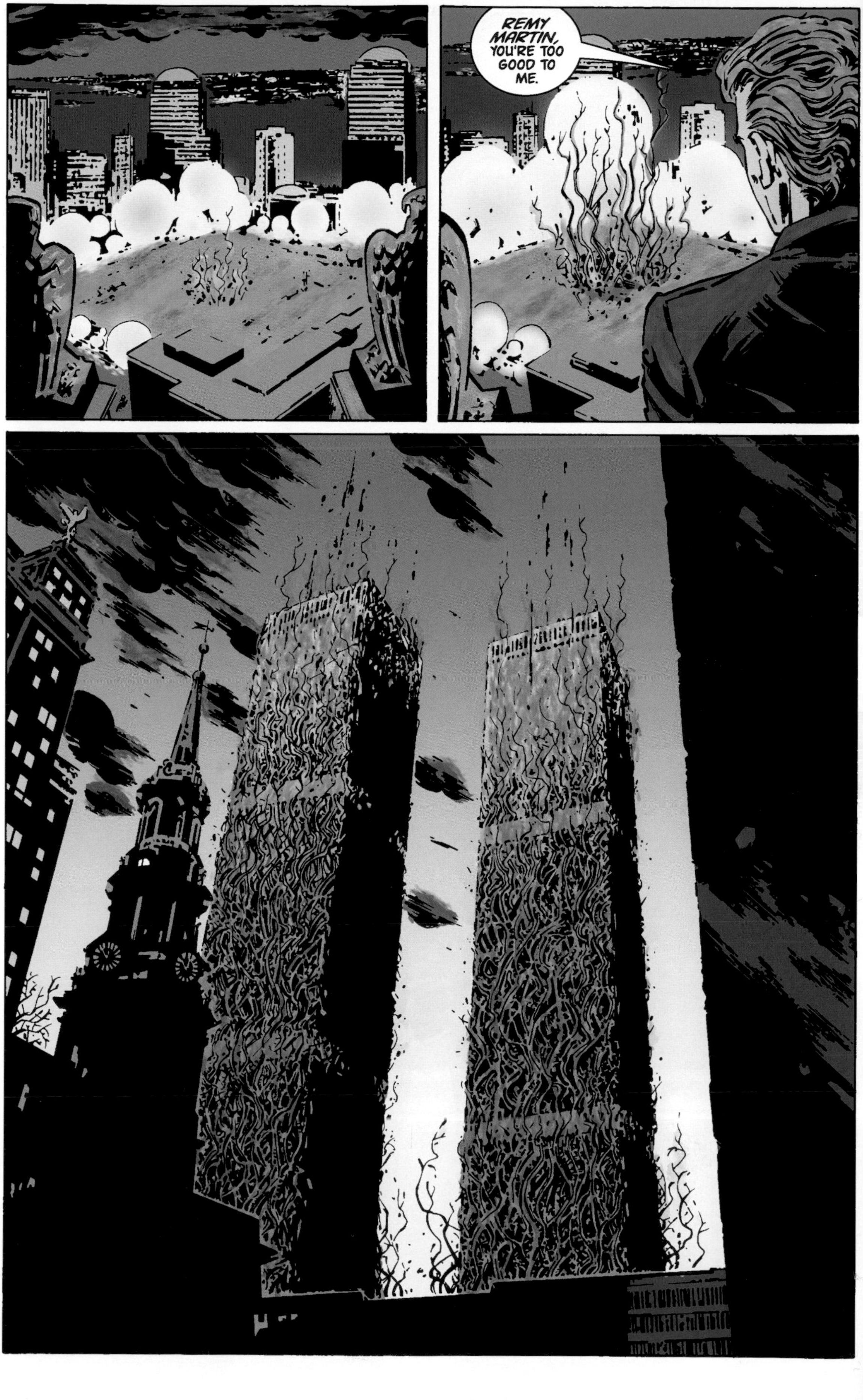
REMY MARTIN, YOU'RE TOO GOOD TO ME.

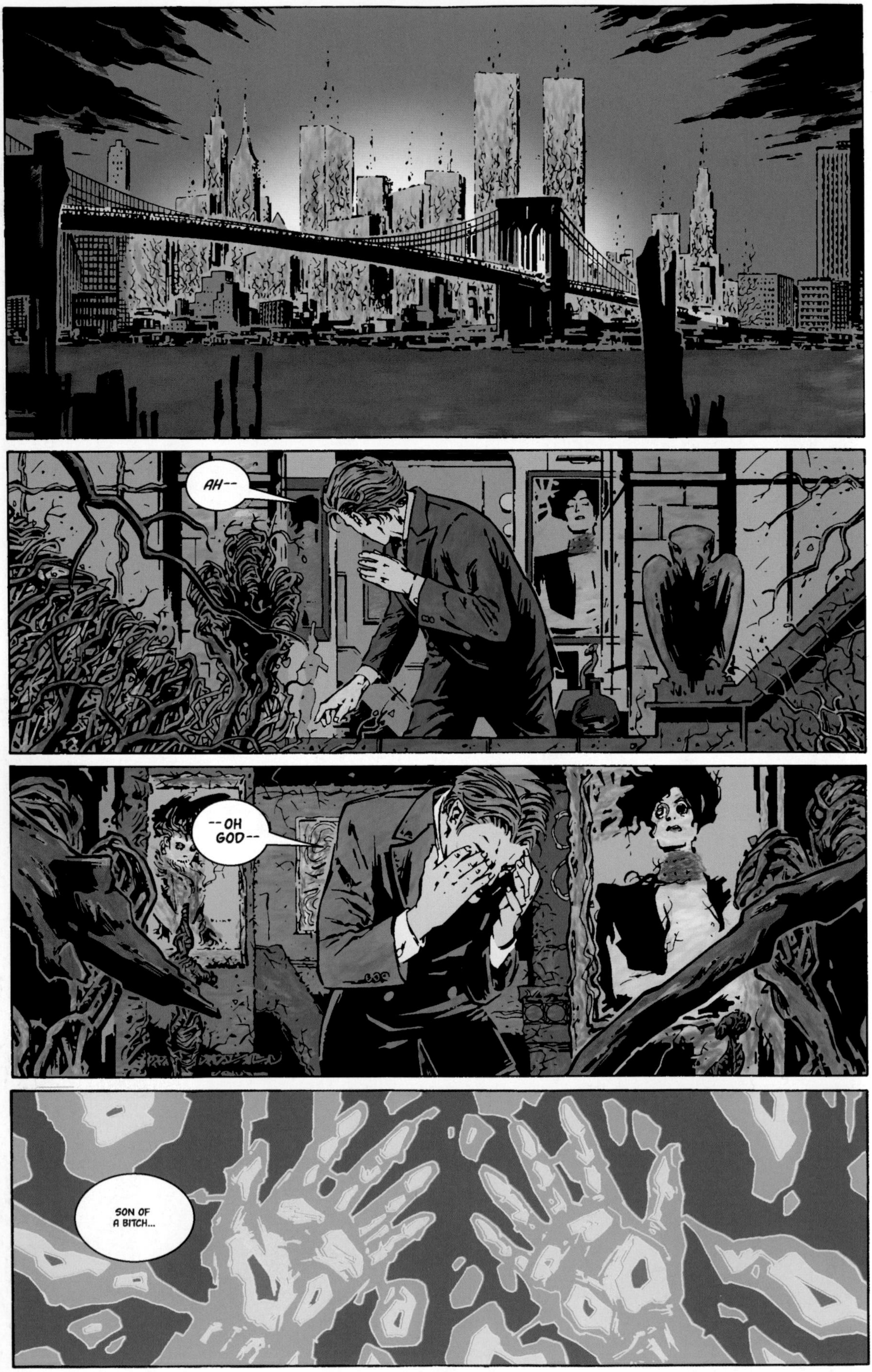
AH--
--OH GOD--
SON OF A BITCH...

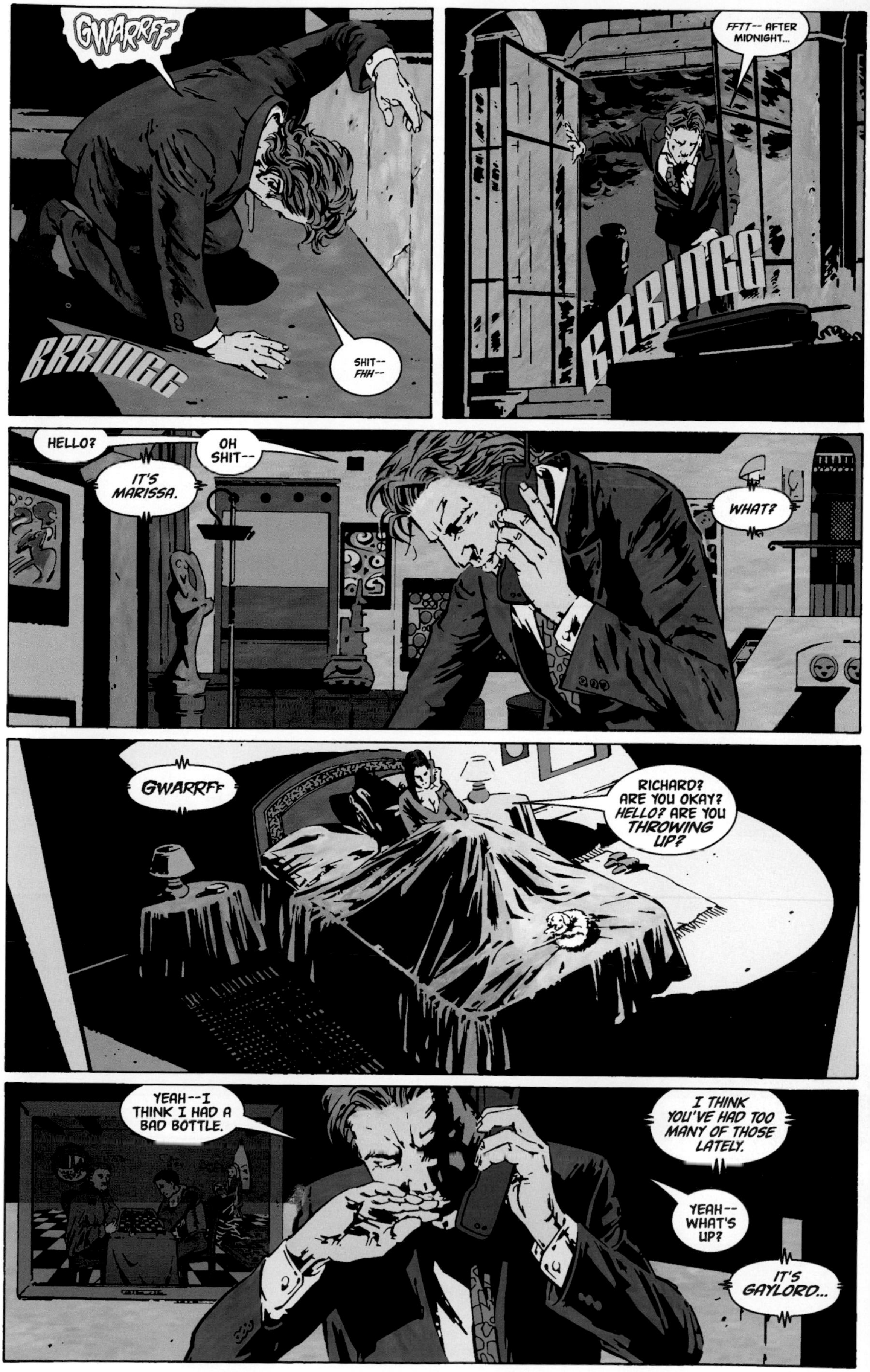
GWARRFF
BRRINGG
SHIT-- FHH--
FFTT-- AFTER MIDNIGHT...
BRRINGG
HELLO?
OH SHIT--
IT'S MARISSA.
WHAT?
GWARRFF
RICHARD? ARE YOU OKAY? HELLO? ARE YOU THROWING UP?
YEAH--I THINK I HAD A BAD BOTTLE.
I THINK YOU'VE HAD TOO MANY OF THOSE LATELY.
YEAH-- WHAT'S UP?
IT'S GAYLORD...

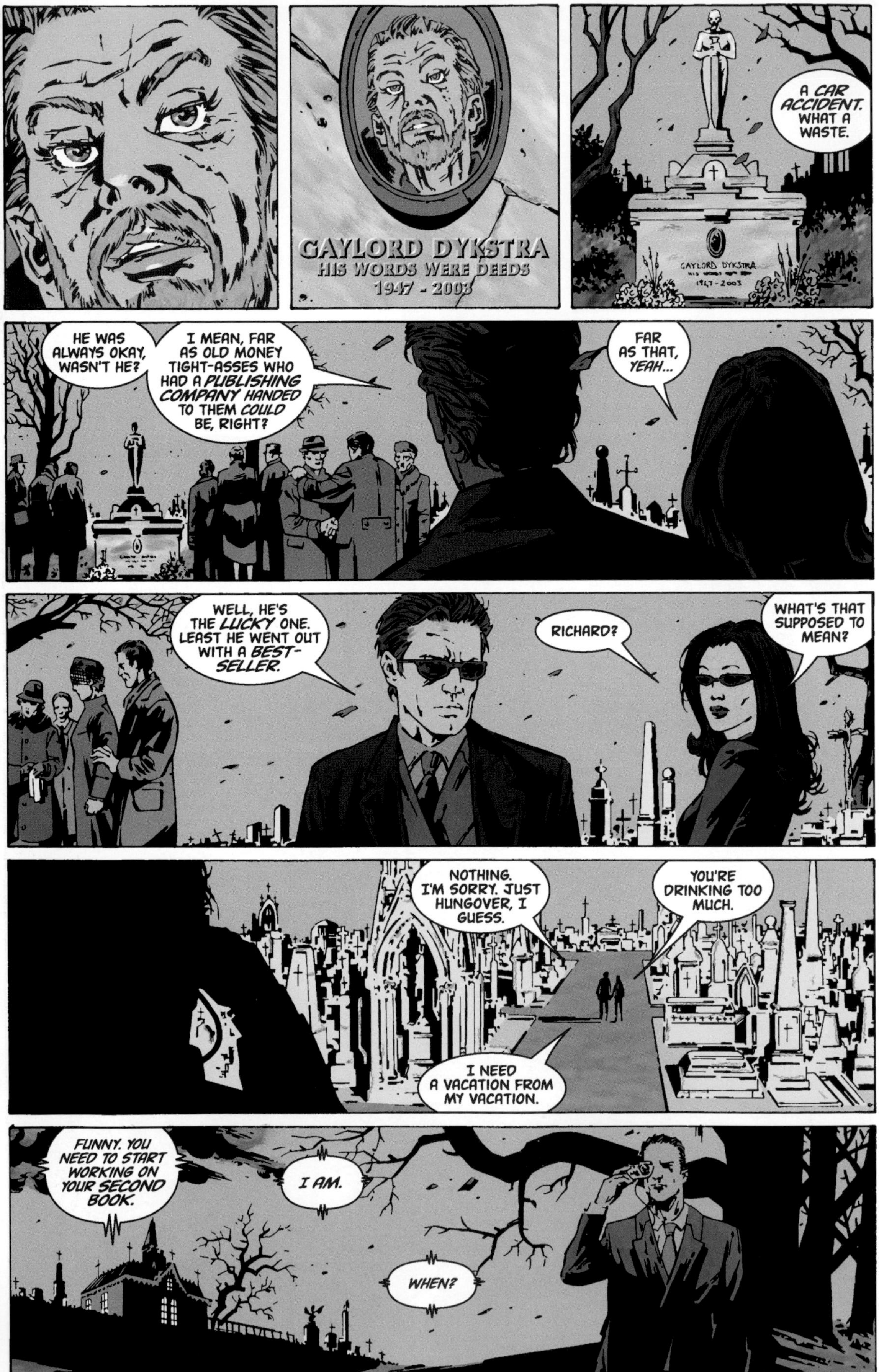
GAYLORD DYKSTRA
HIS WORDS WERE DEEDS
1947 - 2003
A CAR ACCIDENT. WHAT A WASTE.
GAYLORD DYKSTRA
1947 - 2003
HE WAS ALWAYS OKAY, WASN'T HE?
I MEAN, FAR AS OLD MONEY TIGHT-ASSES WHO HAD A PUBLISHING COMPANY HANDED TO THEM COULD BE, RIGHT?
FAR AS THAT, YEAH...
WELL, HE'S THE LUCKY ONE. LEAST HE WENT OUT WITH A BEST-SELLER.
RICHARD?
WHAT'S THAT SUPPOSED TO MEAN?
NOTHING. I'M SORRY. JUST HUNGOVER, I GUESS.
YOU'RE DRINKING TOO MUCH.
I NEED A VACATION FROM MY VACATION.
FUNNY. YOU NEED TO START WORKING ON YOUR SECOND BOOK.
I AM.
WHEN?

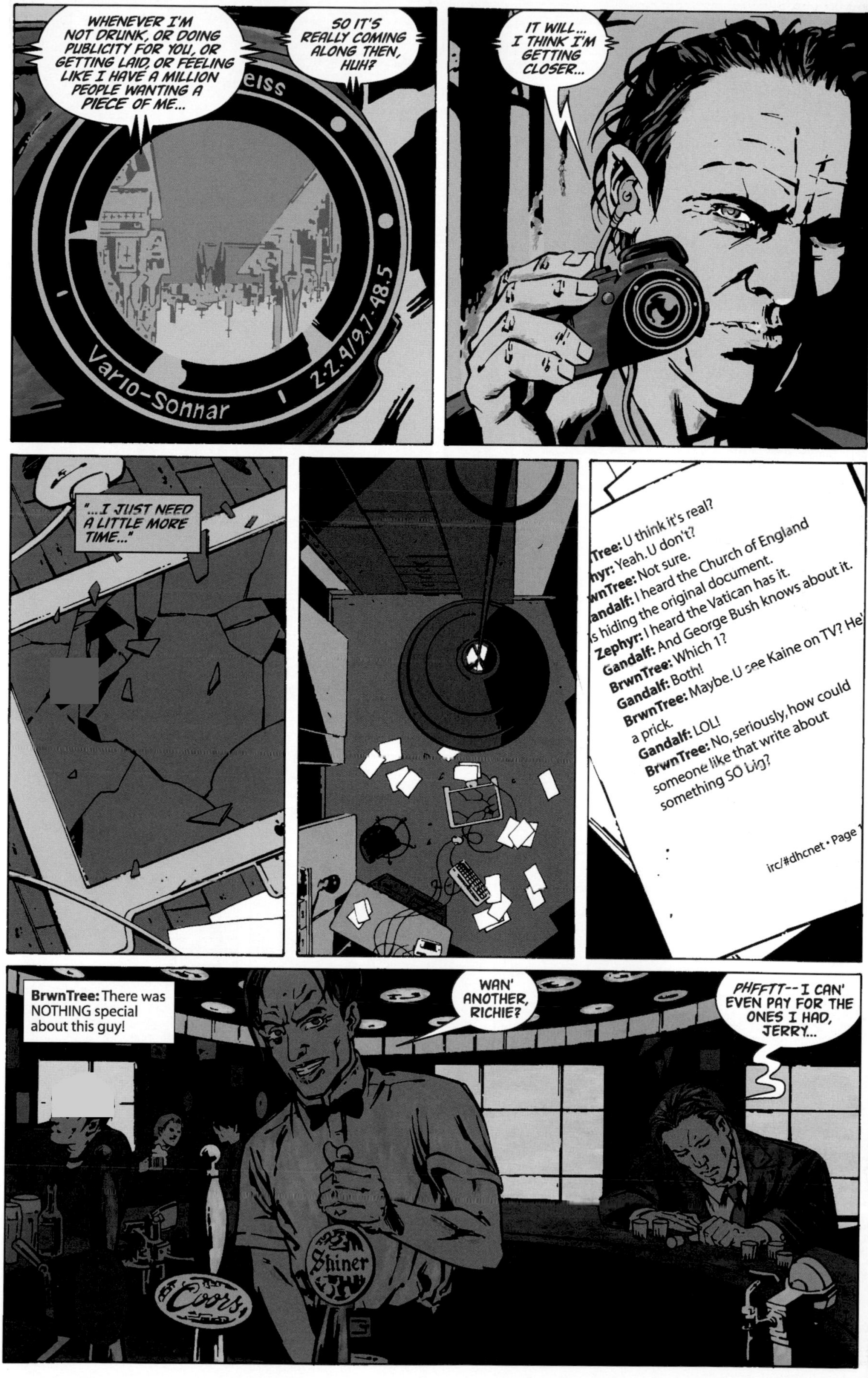

WHENEVER I'M NOT DRUNK, OR DOING PUBLICITY FOR YOU, OR GETTING LAID, OR FEELING LIKE I HAVE A MILLION PEOPLE WANTING A PIECE OF ME...
SO IT'S REALLY COMING ALONG THEN, HUH?
eiss
Vario-Sonnar
2-2.4/9.7-48.5
IT WILL... I THINK I'M GETTING CLOSER...
"...I JUST NEED A LITTLE MORE TIME..."
Tree: U think it's real?
hyr: Yeah. U don't?
wnTree: Not sure.
andalf: I heard the Church of England
s hiding the original document.
Zephyr: I heard the Vatican has it.
Gandalf: And George Bush knows about it.
BrwnTree: Which 1?
Gandalf: Both!
BrwnTree: Maybe. U see Kaine on TV? He'
a prick.
Gandalf: LOL!
BrwnTree: No, seriously, how could
someone like that write about
something SO big?
irc/#dhcnet • Page 1
BrwnTree: There was NOTHING special about this guy!
WAN' ANOTHER, RICHIE?
PHFFTT--I CAN' EVEN PAY FOR THE ONES I HAD, JERRY...
Coors
Shiner

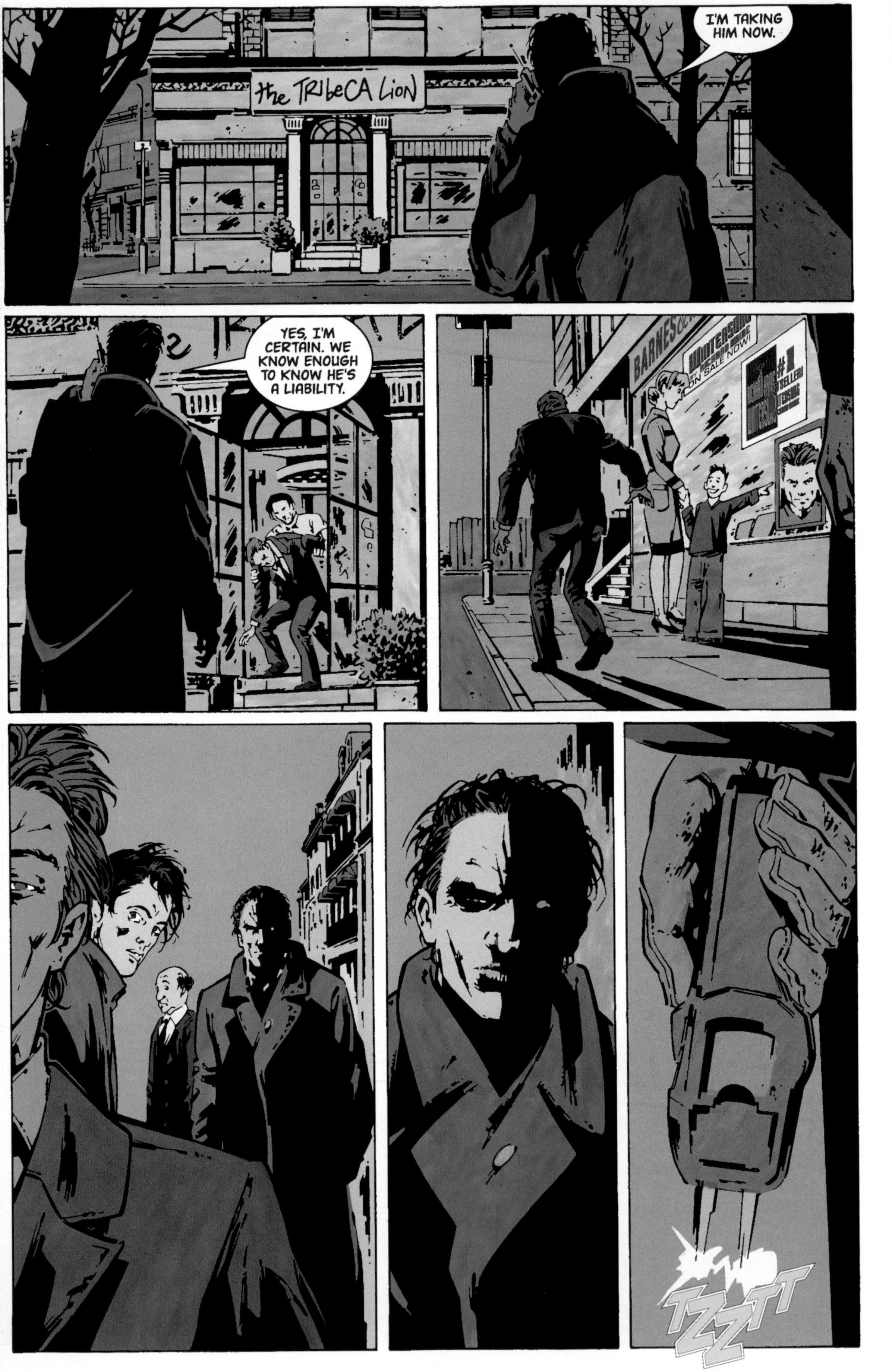
I'M TAKING HIM NOW.
the TRIbeCA Lion
YES, I'M CERTAIN. WE KNOW ENOUGH TO KNOW HE'S A LIABILITY.
ON SALE NOW!
TZZTT

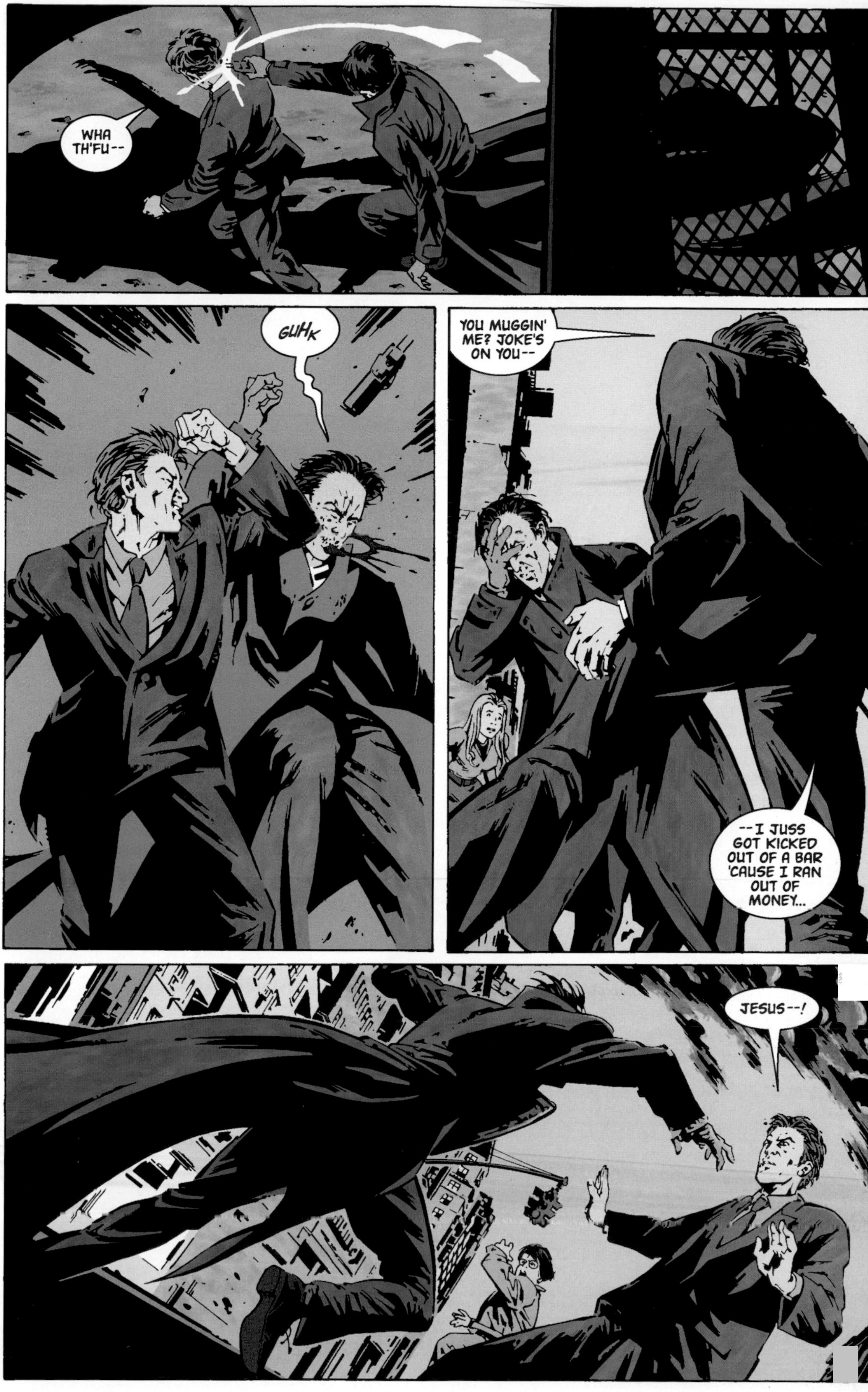
WHA TH'FU--
GUHK
YOU MUGGIN' ME? JOKE'S ON YOU--
--I JUSS GOT KICKED OUT OF A BAR 'CAUSE I RAN OUT OF MONEY...
JESUS--!

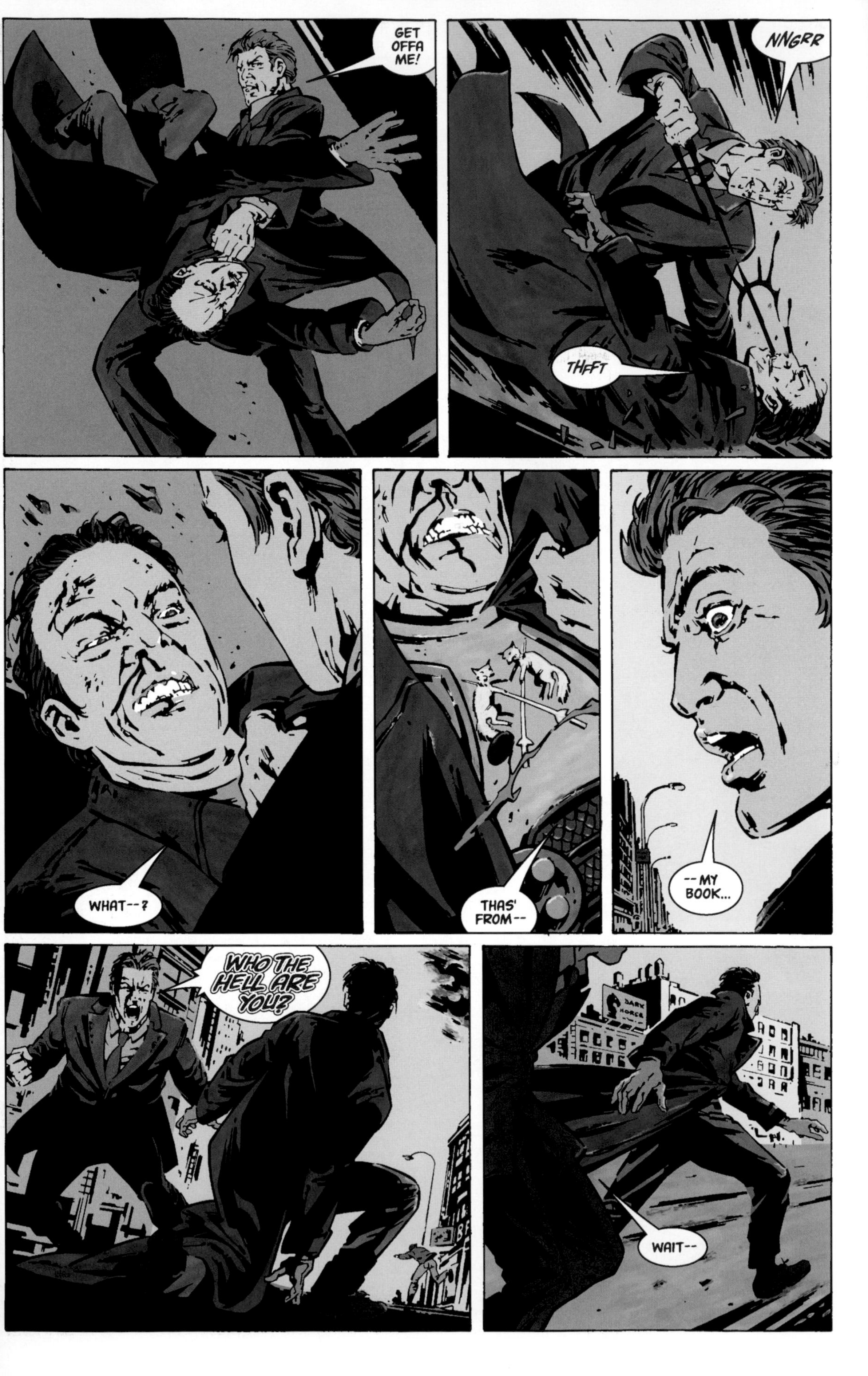
GET OFFA ME!
NNGRR
THFFT
WHAT--?
THAS' FROM--
--MY BOOK...
WHO THE HELL ARE YOU?
WAIT--

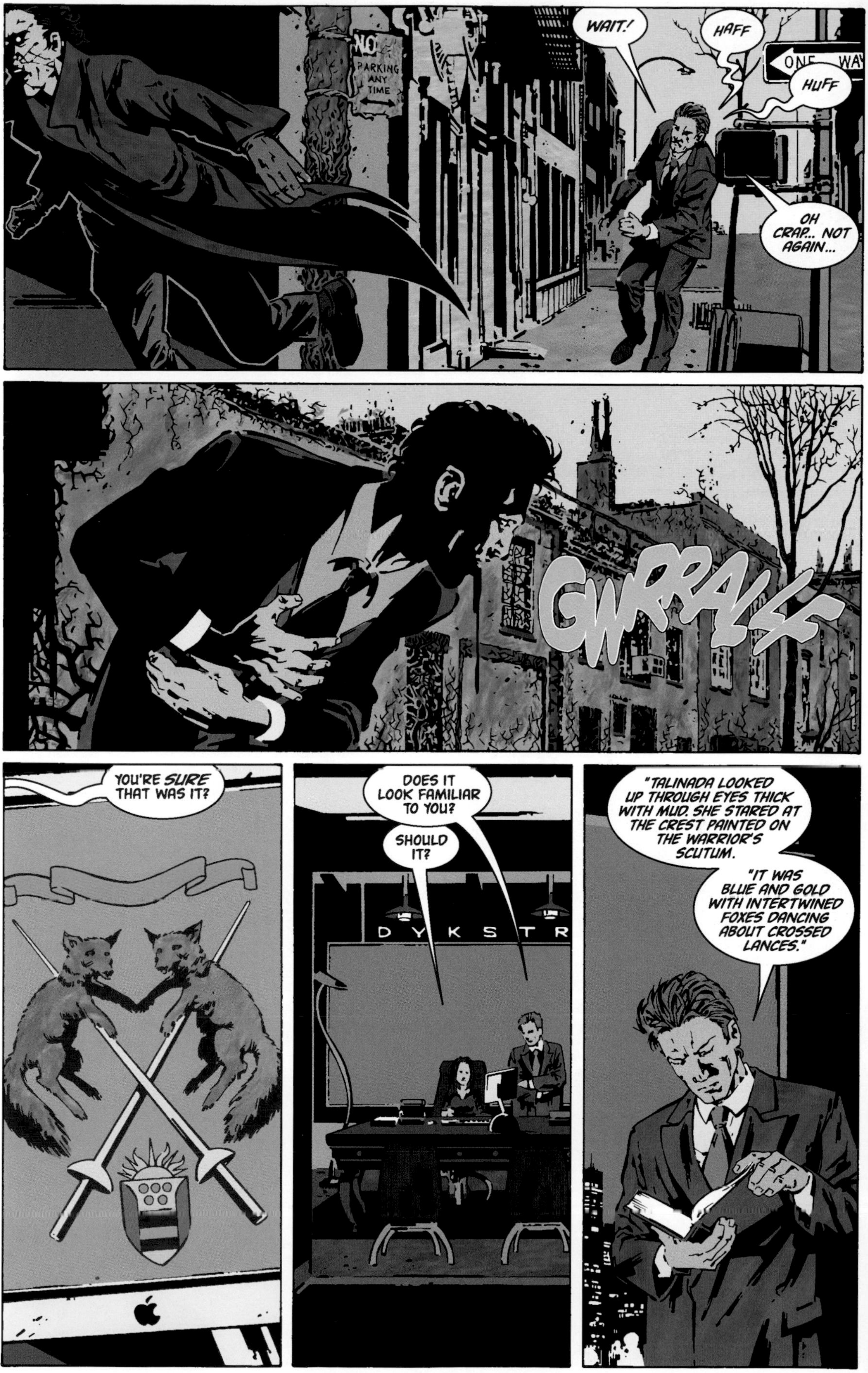
WAIT!
HAFF
ONE WAY
HUFF
OH CRAP... NOT AGAIN...
GWRRALLF
YOU'RE *SURE* THAT WAS IT?
DOES IT LOOK FAMILIAR TO YOU?
SHOULD IT?
DYKSTR
"TALINADA LOOKED UP THROUGH EYES THICK WITH MUD. SHE STARED AT THE CREST PAINTED ON THE WARRIOR'S SCUTUM.
"IT WAS BLUE AND GOLD WITH INTERTWINED FOXES DANCING ABOUT CROSSED LANCES."

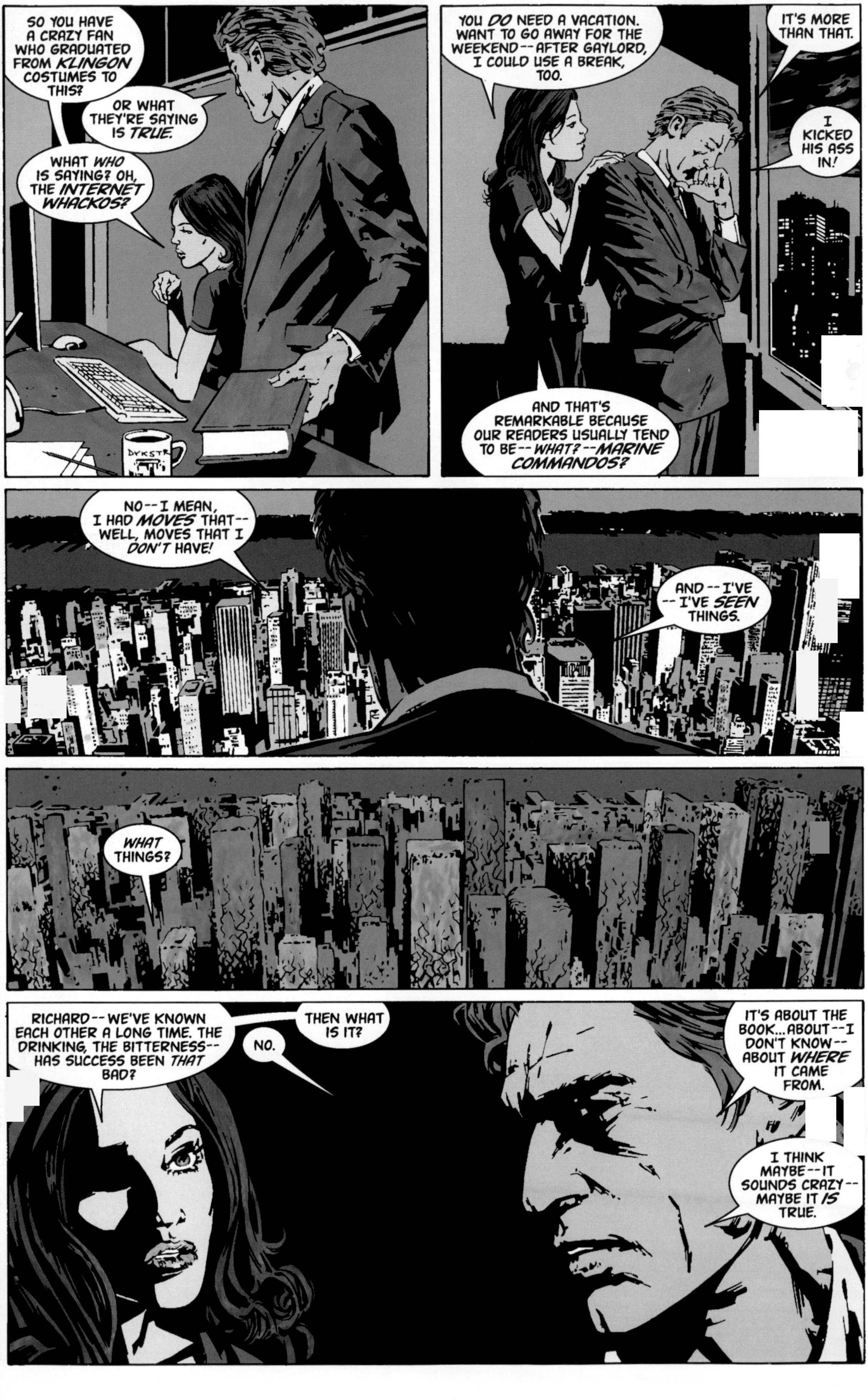
SO YOU HAVE A CRAZY FAN WHO GRADUATED FROM KLINGON COSTUMES TO THIS?
OR WHAT THEY'RE SAYING IS TRUE.
WHAT WHO IS SAYING? OH, THE INTERNET WHACKOS?
DYKSTR
YOU DO NEED A VACATION. WANT TO GO AWAY FOR THE WEEKEND--AFTER GAYLORD, I COULD USE A BREAK, TOO.
IT'S MORE THAN THAT.
I KICKED HIS ASS IN!
AND THAT'S REMARKABLE BECAUSE OUR READERS USUALLY TEND TO BE--WHAT?--MARINE COMMANDOS?
NO--I MEAN, I HAD MOVES THAT--WELL, MOVES THAT I DON'T HAVE!
AND--I'VE--I'VE SEEN THINGS.
WHAT THINGS?
RICHARD--WE'VE KNOWN EACH OTHER A LONG TIME. THE DRINKING, THE BITTERNESS--HAS SUCCESS BEEN THAT BAD?
NO.
THEN WHAT IS IT?
IT'S ABOUT THE BOOK...ABOUT--I DON'T KNOW--ABOUT WHERE IT CAME FROM.
I THINK MAYBE--IT SOUNDS CRAZY--MAYBE IT IS TRUE.

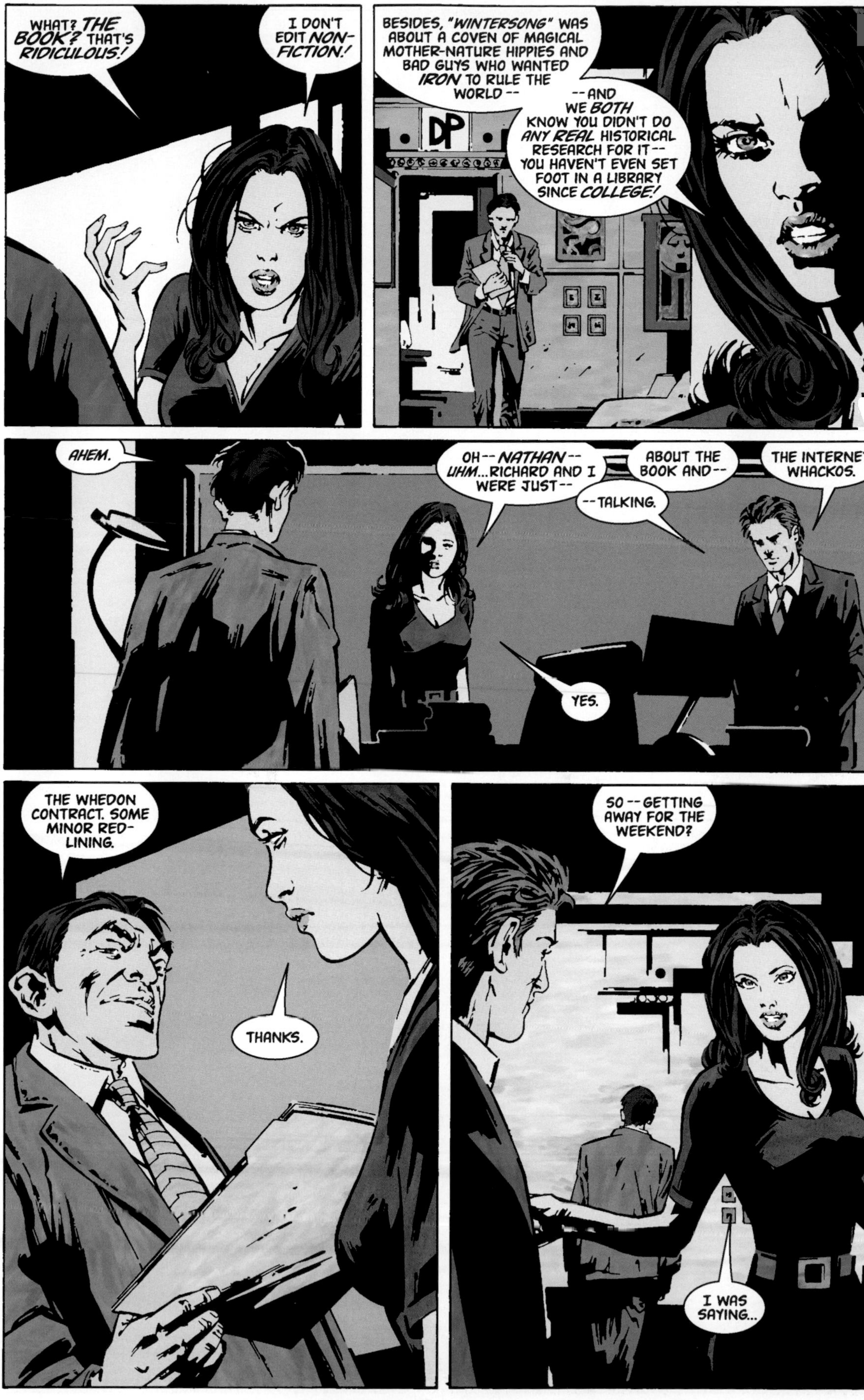
WHAT? THE BOOK? THAT'S RIDICULOUS!
I DON'T EDIT NON-FICTION!
BESIDES, "WINTERSONG" WAS ABOUT A COVEN OF MAGICAL MOTHER-NATURE HIPPIES AND BAD GUYS WHO WANTED IRON TO RULE THE WORLD --
-- AND WE BOTH KNOW YOU DIDN'T DO ANY REAL HISTORICAL RESEARCH FOR IT -- YOU HAVEN'T EVEN SET FOOT IN A LIBRARY SINCE COLLEGE!
DP
AHEM.
OH -- NATHAN -- UHM... RICHARD AND I WERE JUST --
ABOUT THE BOOK AND --
-- TALKING.
THE INTERNET WHACKOS.
YES.
THE WHEDON CONTRACT. SOME MINOR RED-LINING.
THANKS.
SO -- GETTING AWAY FOR THE WEEKEND?
I WAS SAYING...

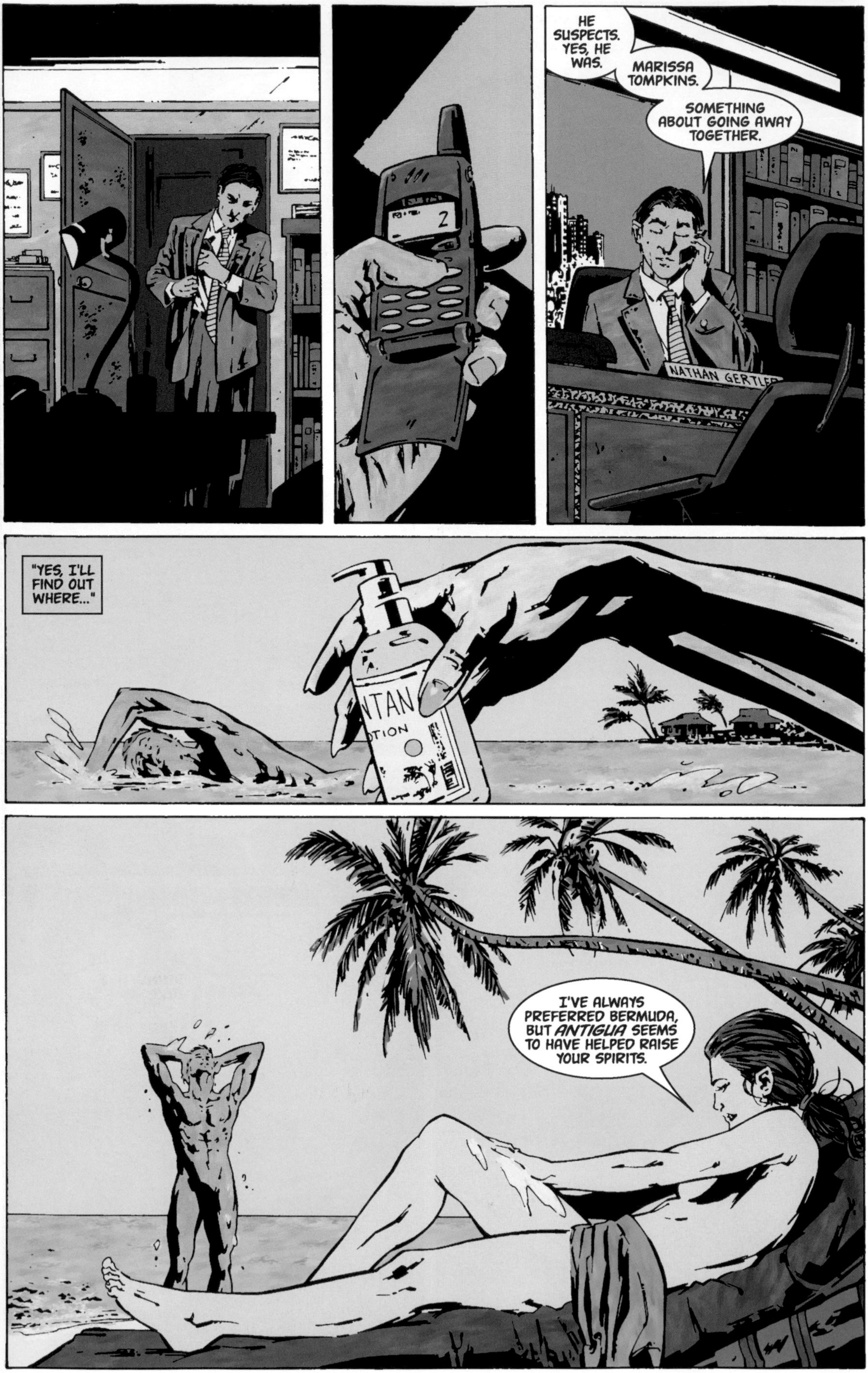
HE SUSPECTS. YES, HE WAS.
MARISSA TOMPKINS.
SOMETHING ABOUT GOING AWAY TOGETHER.
NATHAN GERTLER
"YES, I'LL FIND OUT WHERE..."
I'VE ALWAYS PREFERRED BERMUDA, BUT *ANTIGUA* SEEMS TO HAVE HELPED RAISE YOUR SPIRITS.

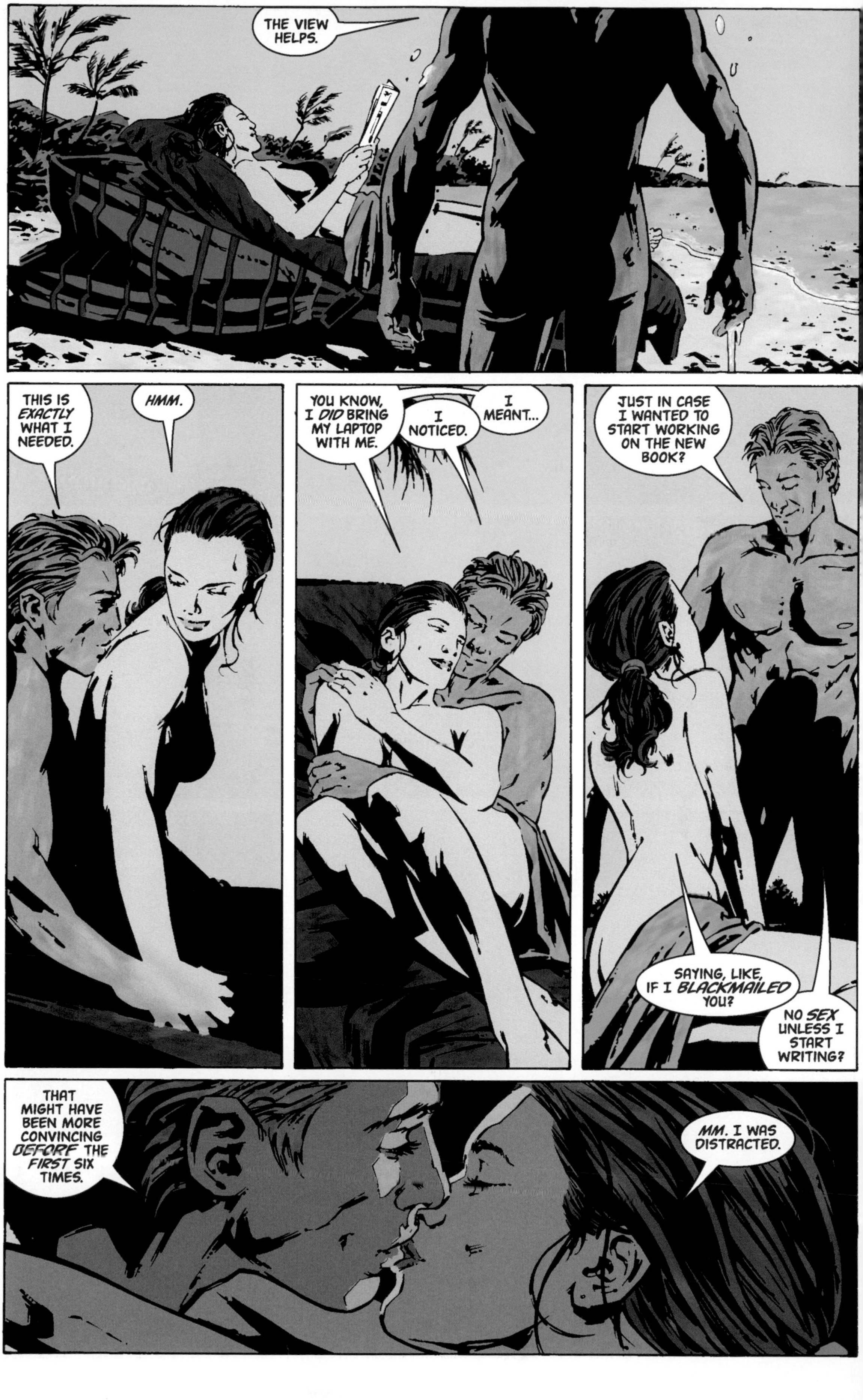
THE VIEW HELPS.
THIS IS EXACTLY WHAT I NEEDED.
HMM.
YOU KNOW, I DID BRING MY LAPTOP WITH ME.
I NOTICED.
I MEANT...
JUST IN CASE I WANTED TO START WORKING ON THE NEW BOOK?
SAYING, LIKE, IF I BLACKMAILED YOU?
NO SEX UNLESS I START WRITING?
THAT MIGHT HAVE BEEN MORE CONVINCING BEFORE THE FIRST SIX TIMES.
MM. I WAS DISTRACTED.

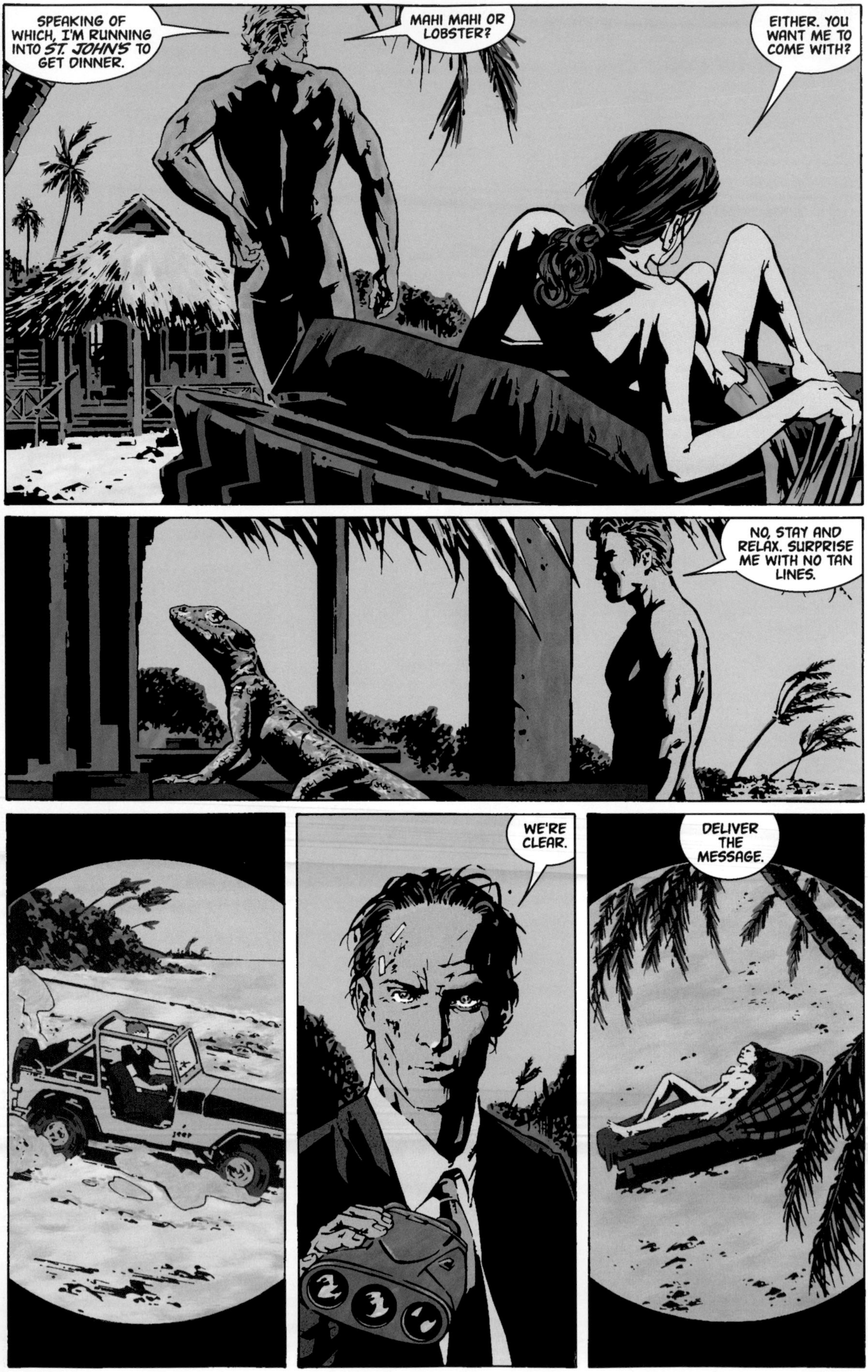

SPEAKING OF WHICH, I'M RUNNING INTO ST. JOHN'S TO GET DINNER.
MAHI MAHI OR LOBSTER?
EITHER. YOU WANT ME TO COME WITH?
NO, STAY AND RELAX. SURPRISE ME WITH NO TAN LINES.
WE'RE CLEAR.
DELIVER THE MESSAGE.

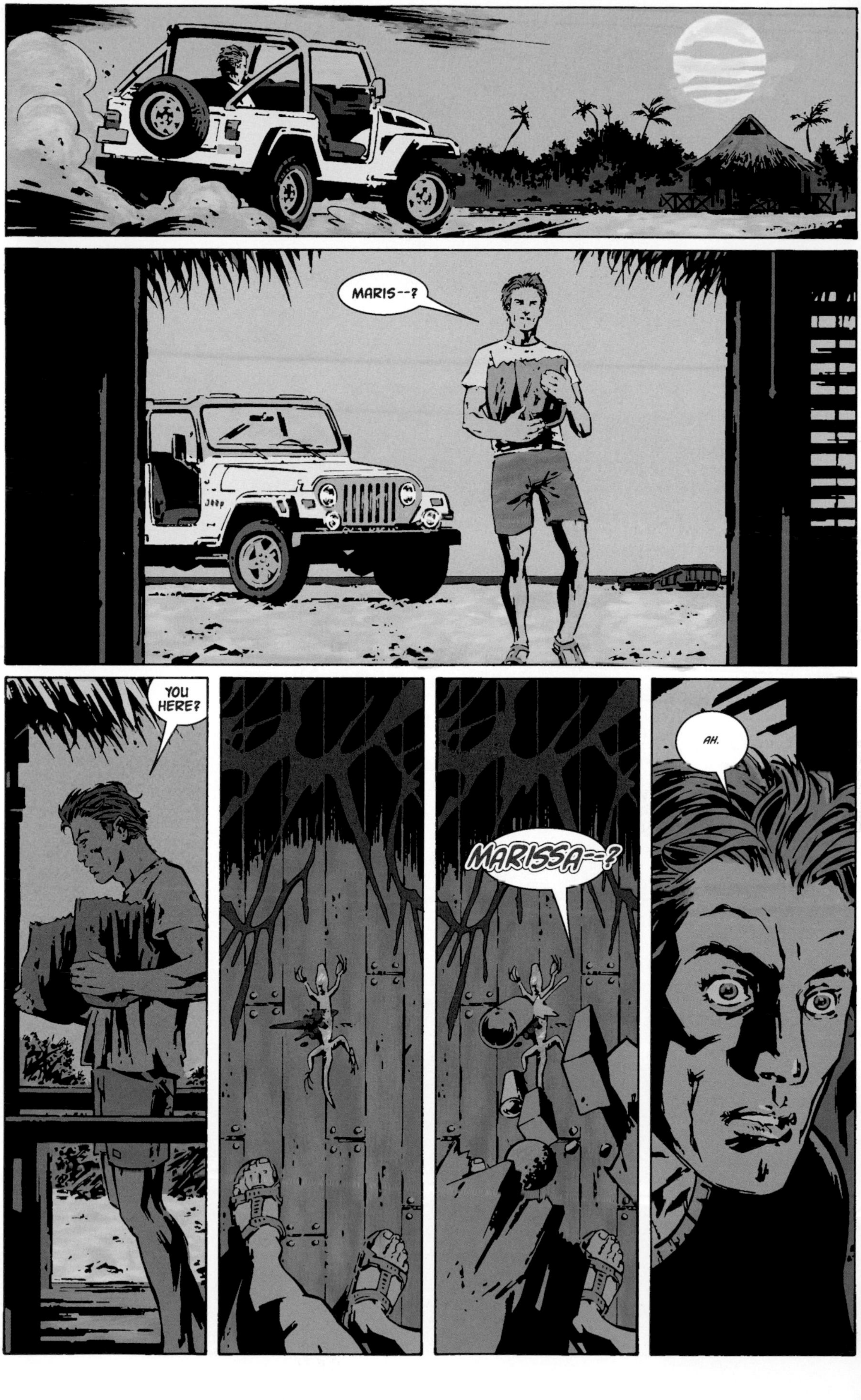
MARIS--?
YOU HERE?
MARISSA--?
AH.

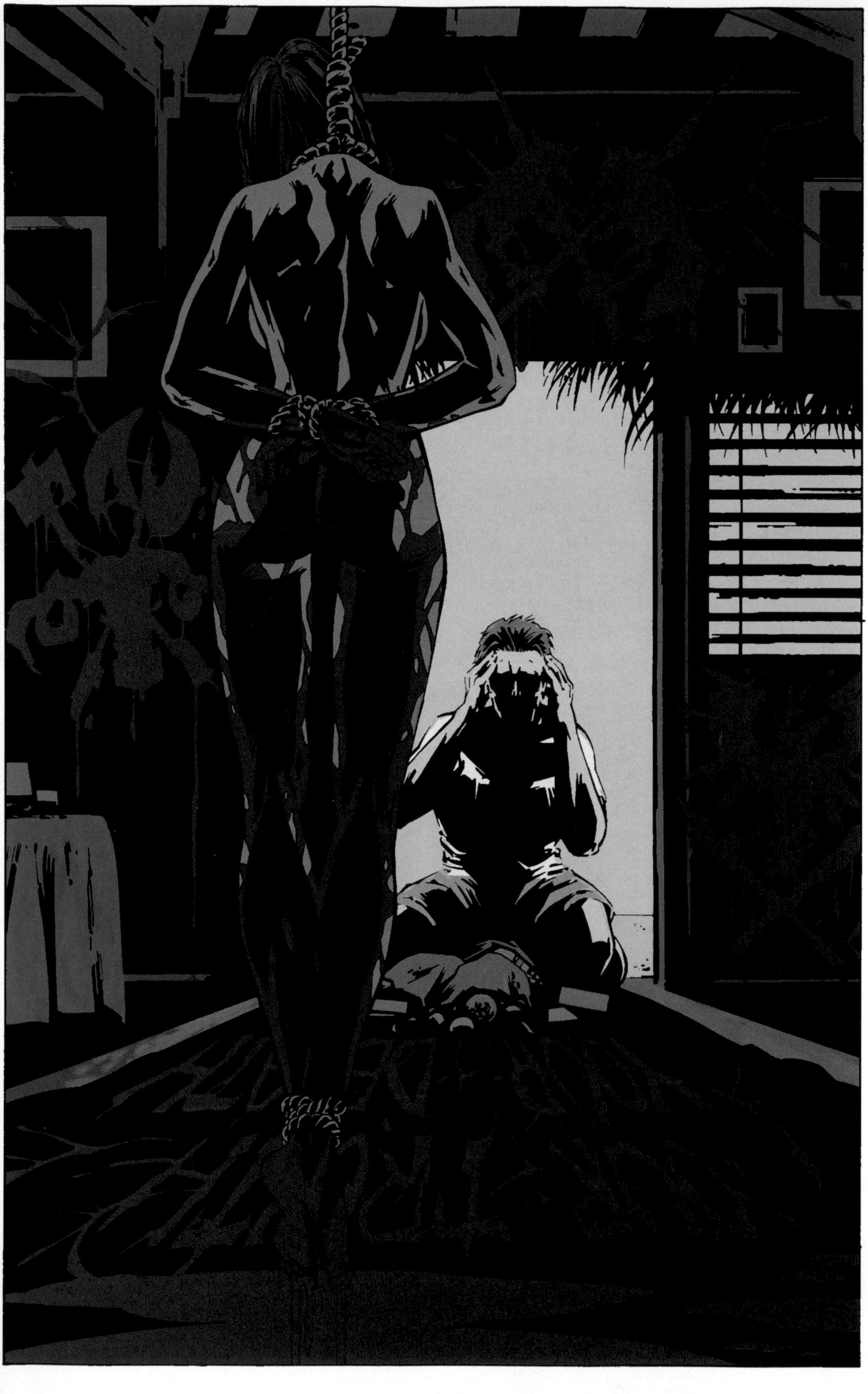

Act Two

THE NOOSE

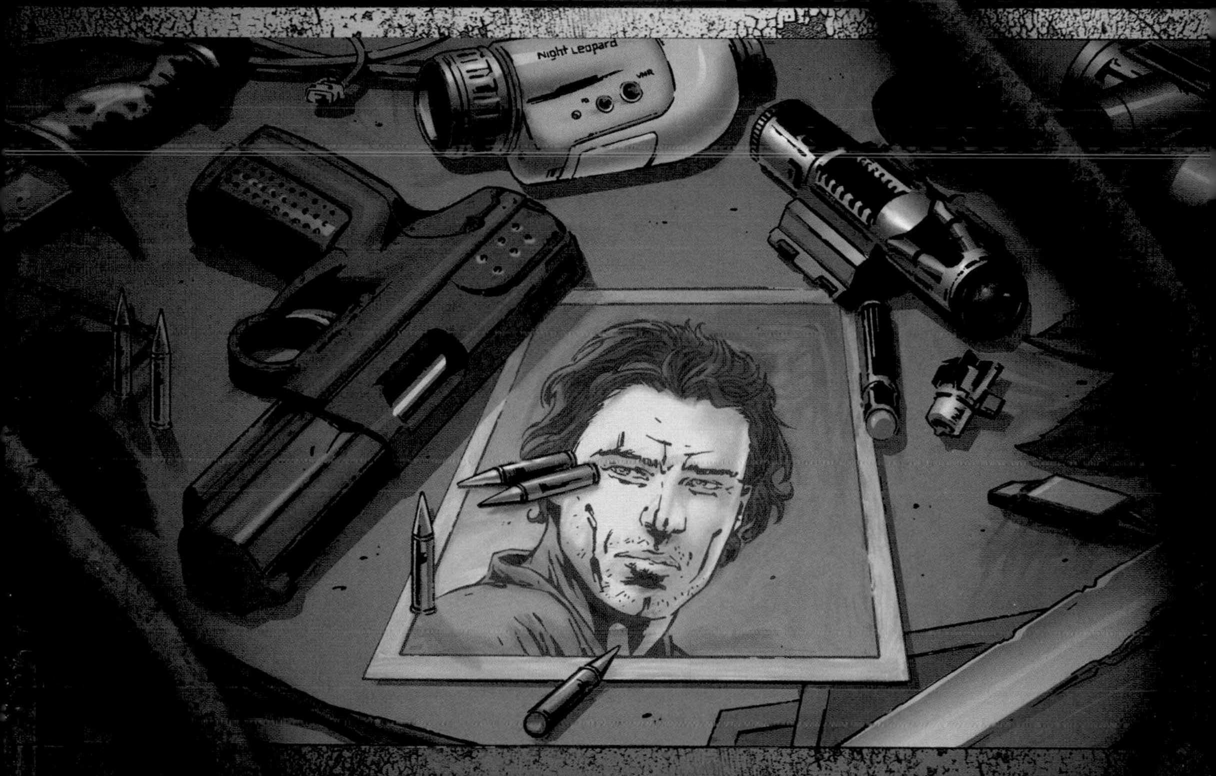
Night Leopard
VNR

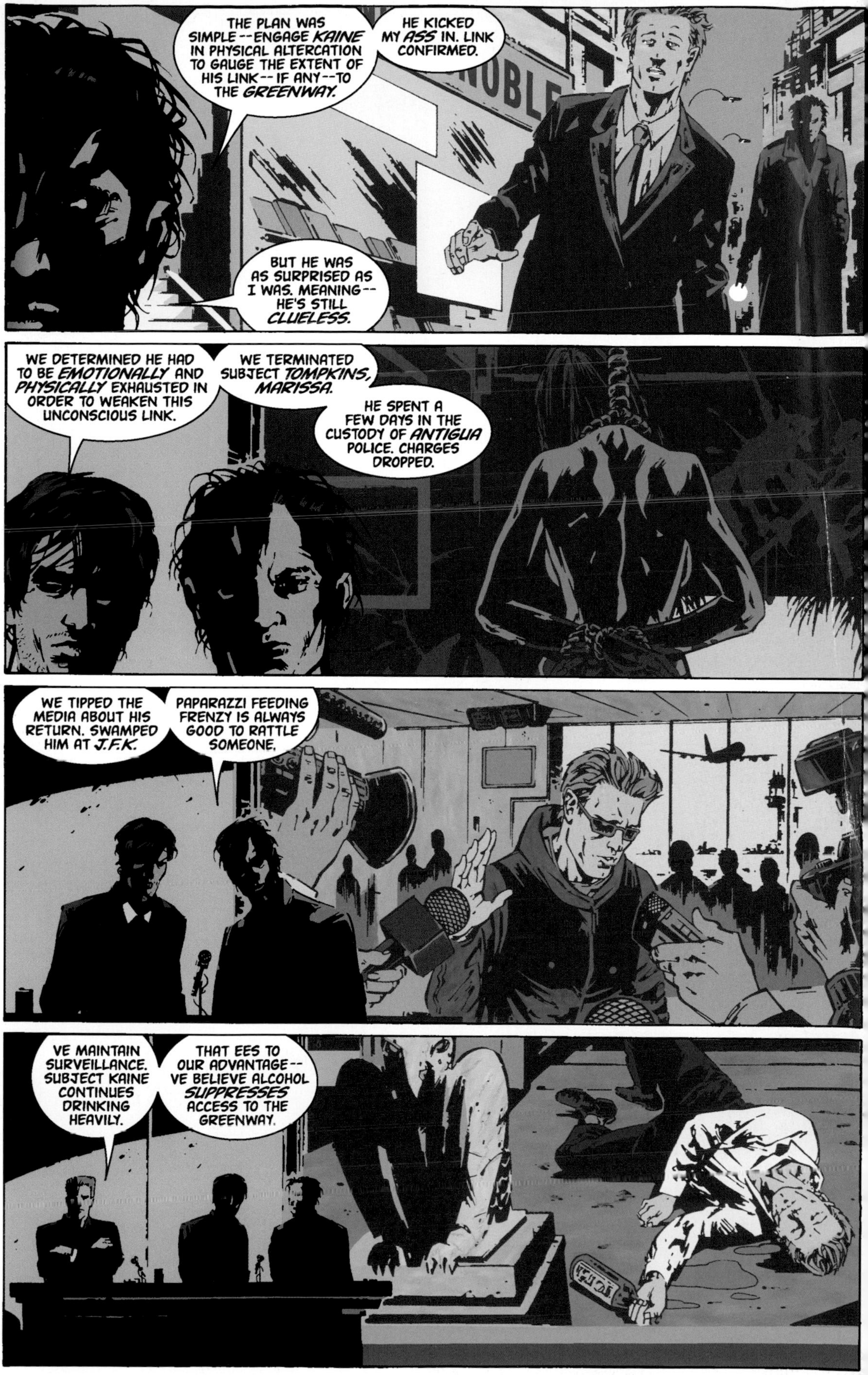
THE PLAN WAS SIMPLE--ENGAGE *KAINE* IN PHYSICAL ALTERCATION TO GAUGE THE EXTENT OF HIS LINK--IF ANY--TO THE *GREENWAY.*
HE KICKED MY *ASS* IN. LINK CONFIRMED.
BUT HE WAS AS SURPRISED AS I WAS. MEANING--HE'S STILL *CLUELESS.*
WE DETERMINED HE HAD TO BE *EMOTIONALLY* AND *PHYSICALLY* EXHAUSTED IN ORDER TO WEAKEN THIS UNCONSCIOUS LINK.
WE TERMINATED SUBJECT *TOMPKINS, MARISSA.*
HE SPENT A FEW DAYS IN THE CUSTODY OF *ANTIGUA* POLICE. CHARGES DROPPED.
WE TIPPED THE MEDIA ABOUT HIS RETURN. SWAMPED HIM AT *J.F.K.*
PAPARAZZI FEEDING FRENZY IS ALWAYS GOOD TO RATTLE SOMEONE.
VE MAINTAIN SURVEILLANCE. SUBJECT KAINE CONTINUES DRINKING HEAVILY.
THAT EES TO OUR ADVANTAGE--VE BELIEVE ALCOHOL *SUPPRESSES* ACCESS TO THE GREENWAY.

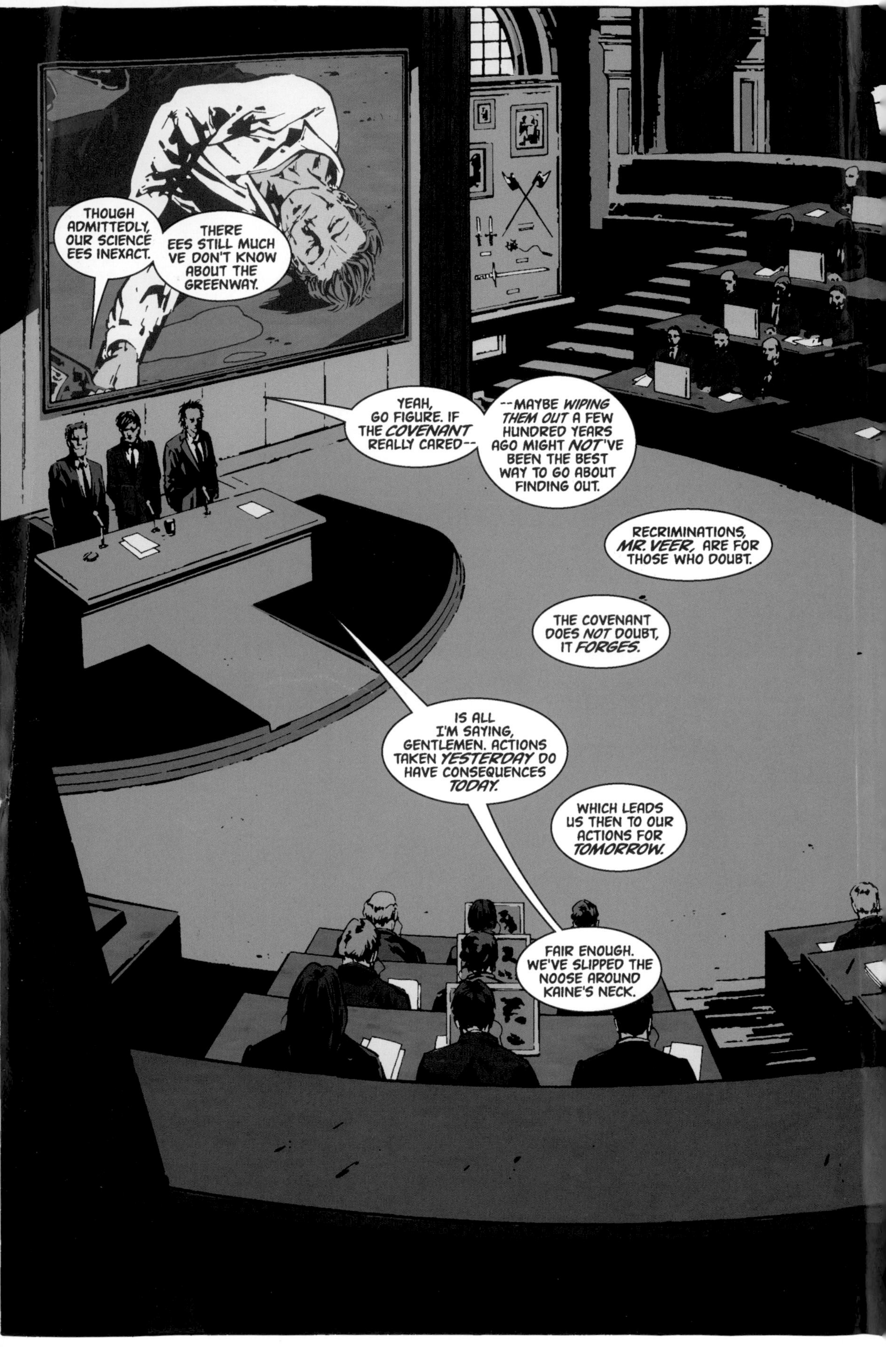
THOUGH ADMITTEDLY, OUR SCIENCE EES INEXACT.
THERE EES STILL MUCH VE DON'T KNOW ABOUT THE GREENWAY.
YEAH, GO FIGURE. IF THE COVENANT REALLY CARED--
--MAYBE WIPING THEM OUT A FEW HUNDRED YEARS AGO MIGHT NOT'VE BEEN THE BEST WAY TO GO ABOUT FINDING OUT.
RECRIMINATIONS, MR. VEER, ARE FOR THOSE WHO DOUBT.
THE COVENANT DOES NOT DOUBT, IT FORGES.
IS ALL I'M SAYING, GENTLEMEN. ACTIONS TAKEN YESTERDAY DO HAVE CONSEQUENCES TODAY.
WHICH LEADS US THEN TO OUR ACTIONS FOR TOMORROW.
FAIR ENOUGH. WE'VE SLIPPED THE NOOSE AROUND KAINE'S NECK.

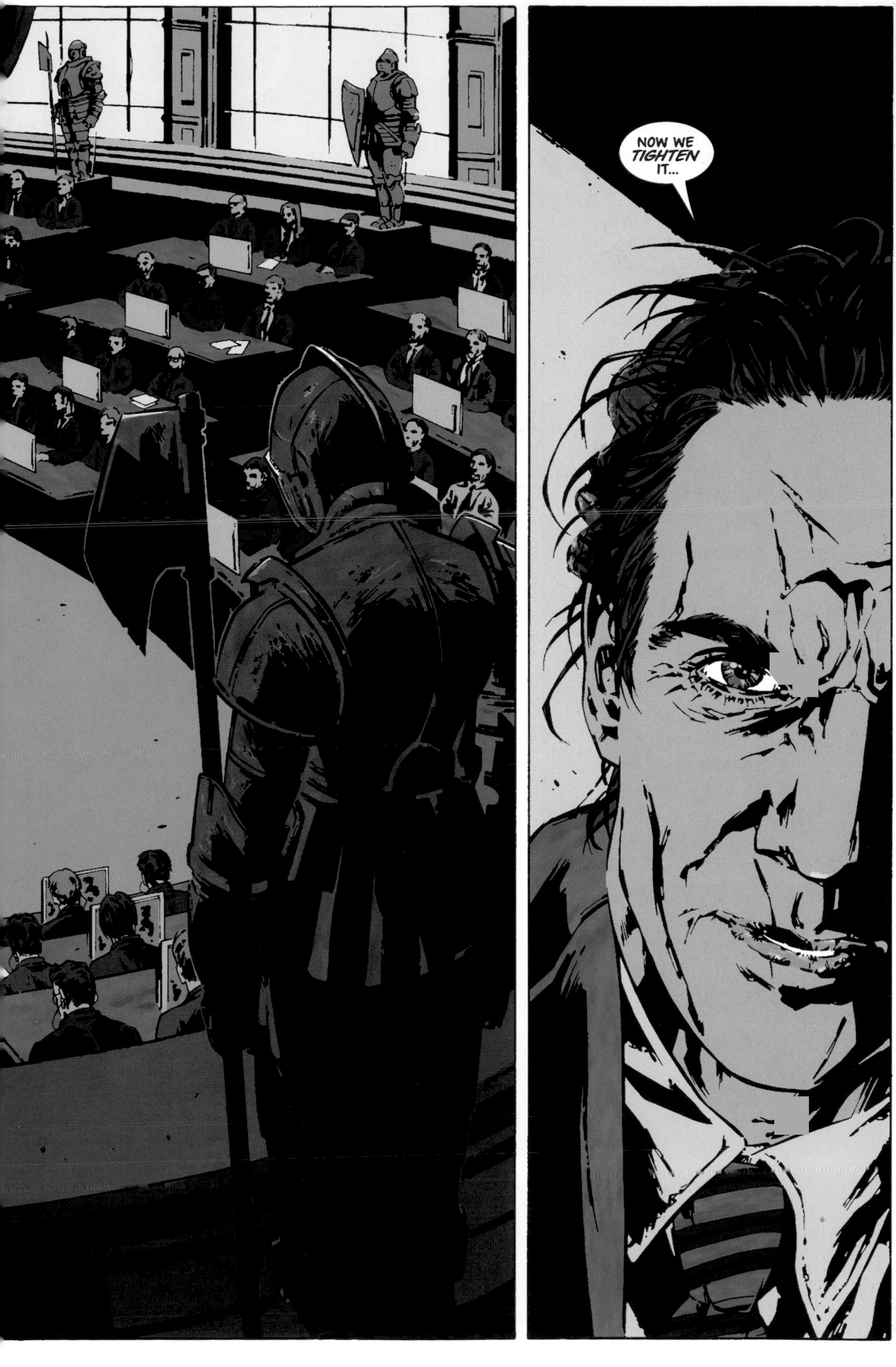
NOW WE *TIGHTEN* IT...

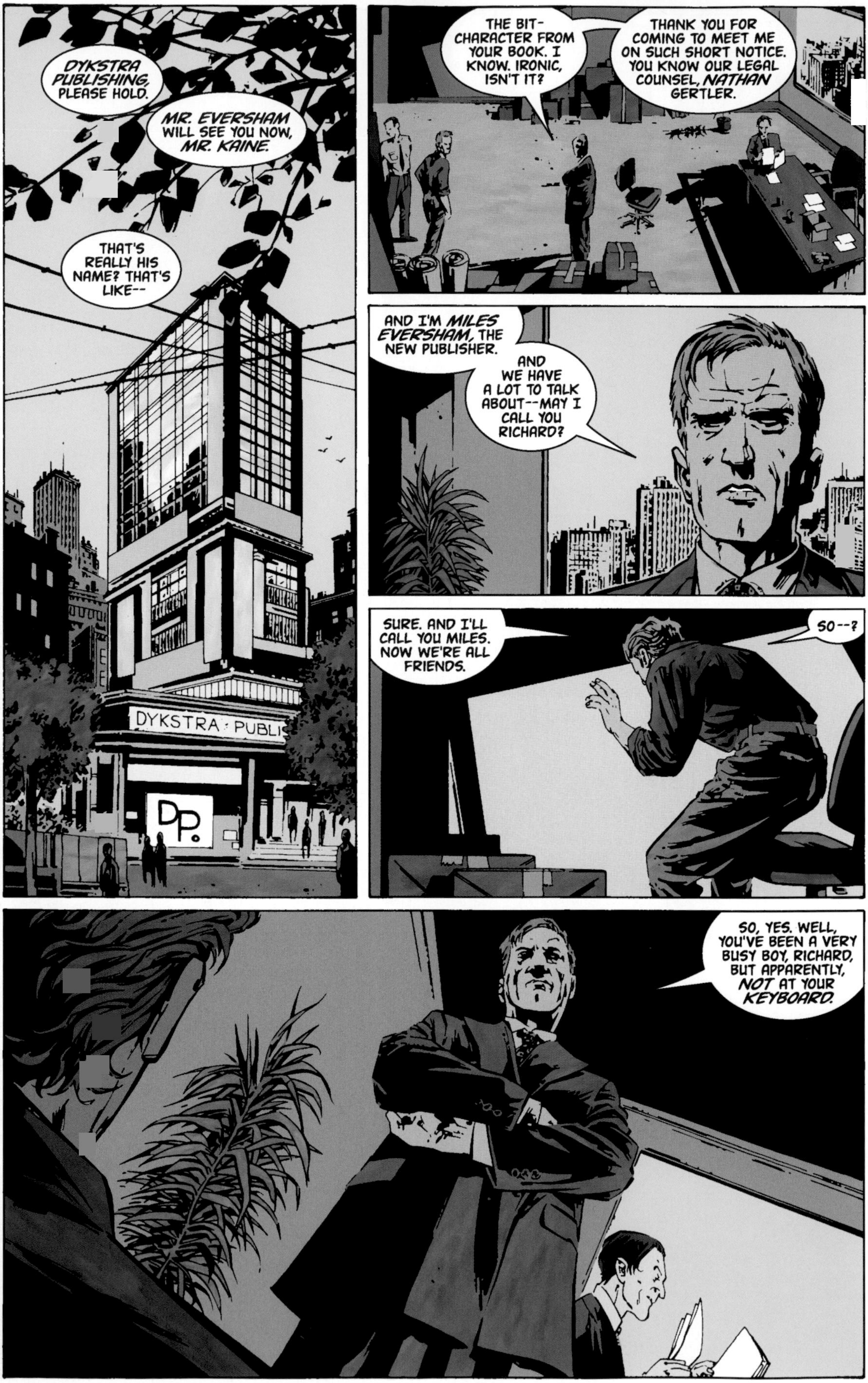
DYKSTRA PUBLISHING, PLEASE HOLD.
MR. EVERSHAM WILL SEE YOU NOW, MR. KAINE.
THAT'S REALLY HIS NAME? THAT'S LIKE--
DYKSTRA PUBLIS
DP.
THE BIT-CHARACTER FROM YOUR BOOK. I KNOW. IRONIC, ISN'T IT?
THANK YOU FOR COMING TO MEET ME ON SUCH SHORT NOTICE. YOU KNOW OUR LEGAL COUNSEL, NATHAN GERTLER.
AND I'M MILES EVERSHAM, THE NEW PUBLISHER.
AND WE HAVE A LOT TO TALK ABOUT--MAY I CALL YOU RICHARD?
SURE. AND I'LL CALL YOU MILES. NOW WE'RE ALL FRIENDS.
SO--?
SO, YES. WELL, YOU'VE BEEN A VERY BUSY BOY, RICHARD, BUT APPARENTLY, NOT AT YOUR KEYBOARD.

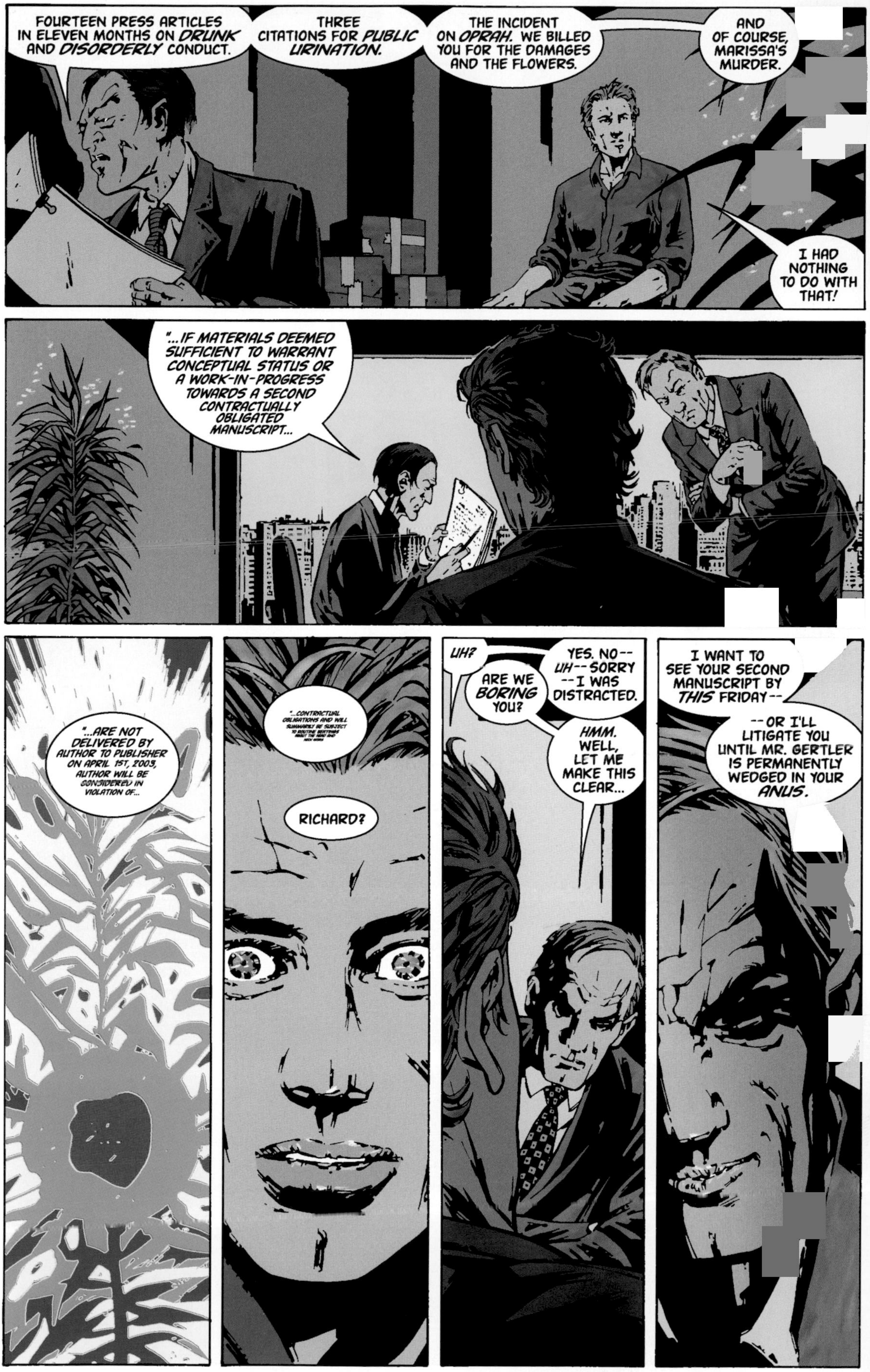
FOURTEEN PRESS ARTICLES IN ELEVEN MONTHS ON *DRUNK* AND *DISORDERLY* CONDUCT.
THREE CITATIONS FOR *PUBLIC URINATION.*
THE INCIDENT ON *OPRAH.* WE BILLED YOU FOR THE DAMAGES AND THE FLOWERS.
AND OF COURSE, MARISSA'S MURDER.
I HAD NOTHING TO DO WITH THAT!
"...IF MATERIALS DEEMED SUFFICIENT TO WARRANT CONCEPTUAL STATUS OR A WORK-IN-PROGRESS TOWARDS A SECOND CONTRACTUALLY OBLIGATED MANUSCRIPT...
"...ARE NOT DELIVERED BY AUTHOR TO PUBLISHER ON APRIL 1ST, 2003, AUTHOR WILL BE CONSIDERED IN VIOLATION OF...
"...CONTRACTUAL OBLIGATIONS AND WILL SUMMARILY BE SUBJECT
RICHARD?
UH?
ARE WE *BORING* YOU?
YES. NO-- *UH*-- SORRY --I WAS DISTRACTED.
HMM. WELL, LET ME MAKE THIS CLEAR...
I WANT TO SEE YOUR SECOND MANUSCRIPT BY *THIS* FRIDAY--
--OR I'LL LITIGATE YOU UNTIL MR. GERTLER IS PERMANENTLY WEDGED IN YOUR *ANUS.*

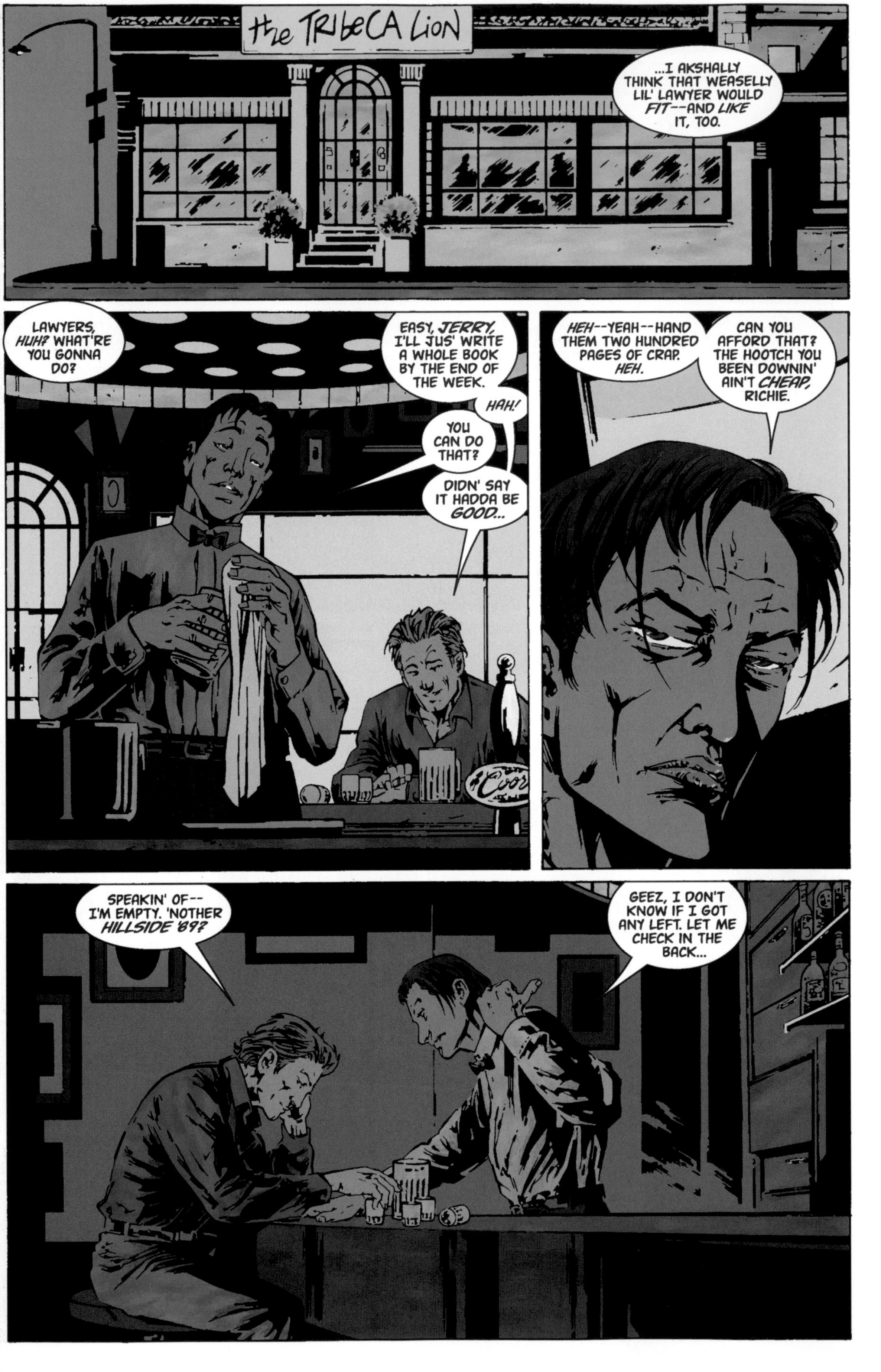
the TRIBeCA Lion
...I AKSHALLY THINK THAT WEASELLY LIL' LAWYER WOULD FIT--AND LIKE IT, TOO.
LAWYERS, HUH? WHAT'RE YOU GONNA DO?
EASY, JERRY, I'LL JUS' WRITE A WHOLE BOOK BY THE END OF THE WEEK.
HAH!
YOU CAN DO THAT?
DIDN' SAY IT HADDA BE GOOD...
HEH--YEAH--HAND THEM TWO HUNDRED PAGES OF CRAP. HEH.
CAN YOU AFFORD THAT? THE HOOTCH YOU BEEN DOWNIN' AIN'T CHEAP, RICHIE.
SPEAKIN' OF--I'M EMPTY. 'NOTHER HILLSIDE '89?
GEEZ, I DON'T KNOW IF I GOT ANY LEFT. LET ME CHECK IN THE BACK...

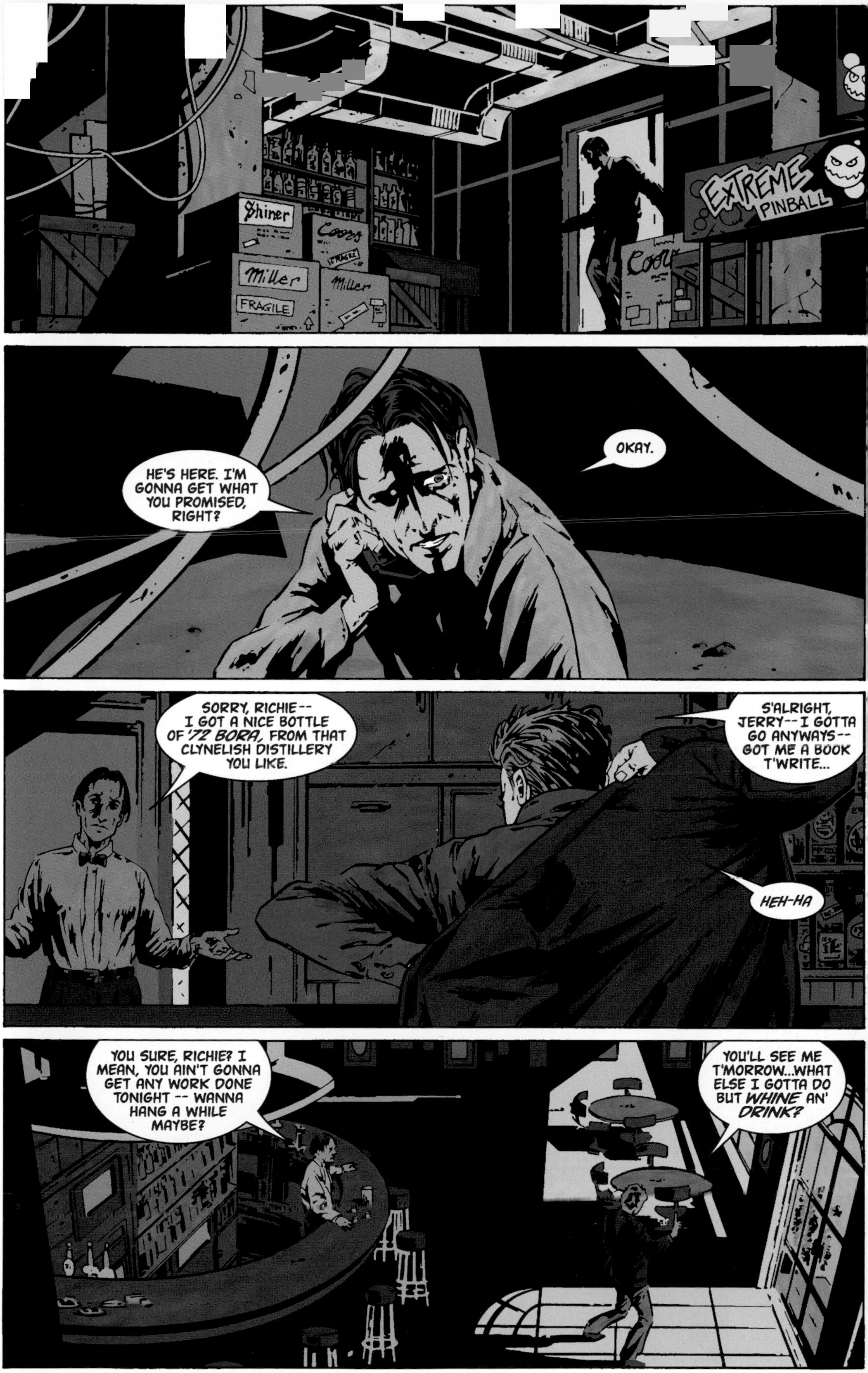
Shiner
Coors
Miller
FRAGILE
Miller
Coors
EXTREME PINBALL
HE'S HERE. I'M GONNA GET WHAT YOU PROMISED, RIGHT?
OKAY.
SORRY, RICHIE-- I GOT A NICE BOTTLE OF '72 BORA, FROM THAT CLYNELISH DISTILLERY YOU LIKE.
S'ALRIGHT, JERRY-- I GOTTA GO ANYWAYS-- GOT ME A BOOK T'WRITE...
HEH-HA
YOU SURE, RICHIE? I MEAN, YOU AIN'T GONNA GET ANY WORK DONE TONIGHT -- WANNA HANG A WHILE MAYBE?
YOU'LL SEE ME T'MORROW...WHAT ELSE I GOTTA DO BUT WHINE AN' DRINK?

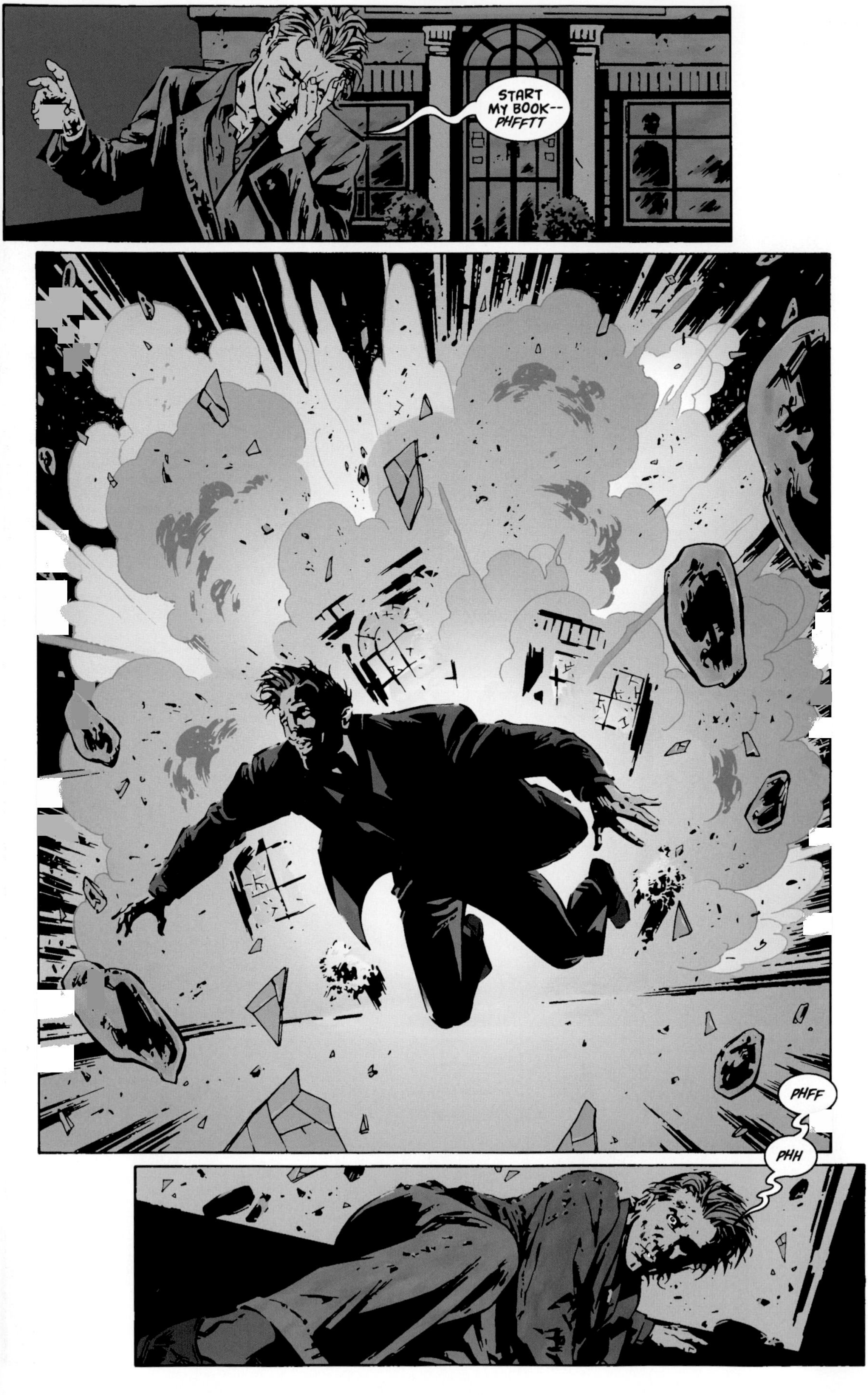
START MY BOOK-- PHFFTT
PHFF
PHH

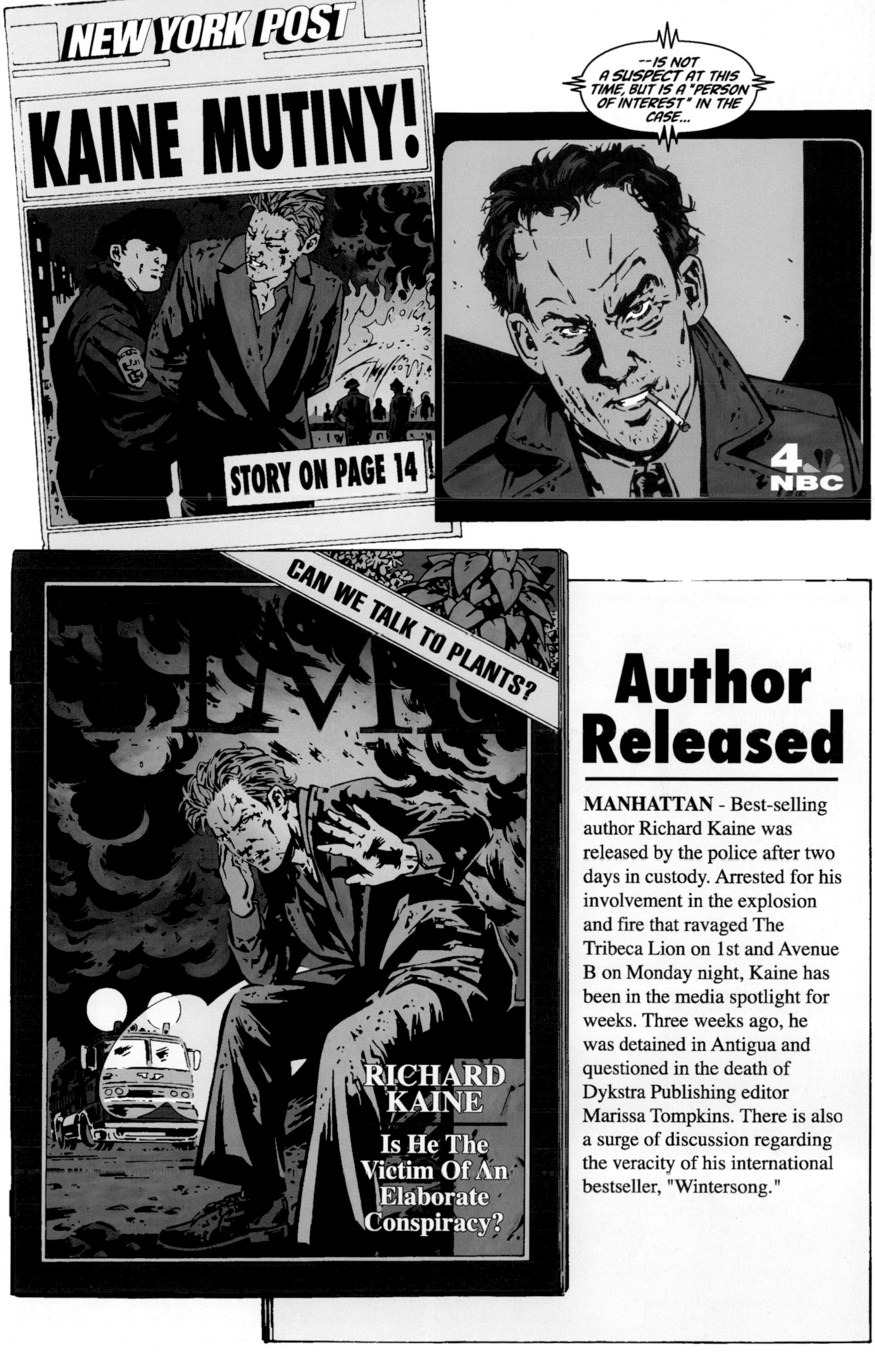
NEW YORK POST
KAINE MUTINY!
STORY ON PAGE 14
--IS NOT A SUSPECT AT THIS TIME, BUT IS A "PERSON OF INTEREST" IN THE CASE...
4 NBC
CAN WE TALK TO PLANTS?
RICHARD KAINE
Is He The Victim Of An Elaborate Conspiracy?
Author Released
MANHATTAN - Best-selling author Richard Kaine was released by the police after two days in custody. Arrested for his involvement in the explosion and fire that ravaged The Tribeca Lion on 1st and Avenue B on Monday night, Kaine has been in the media spotlight for weeks. Three weeks ago, he was detained in Antigua and questioned in the death of Dykstra Publishing editor Marissa Tompkins. There is also a surge of discussion regarding the veracity of his international bestseller, "Wintersong."

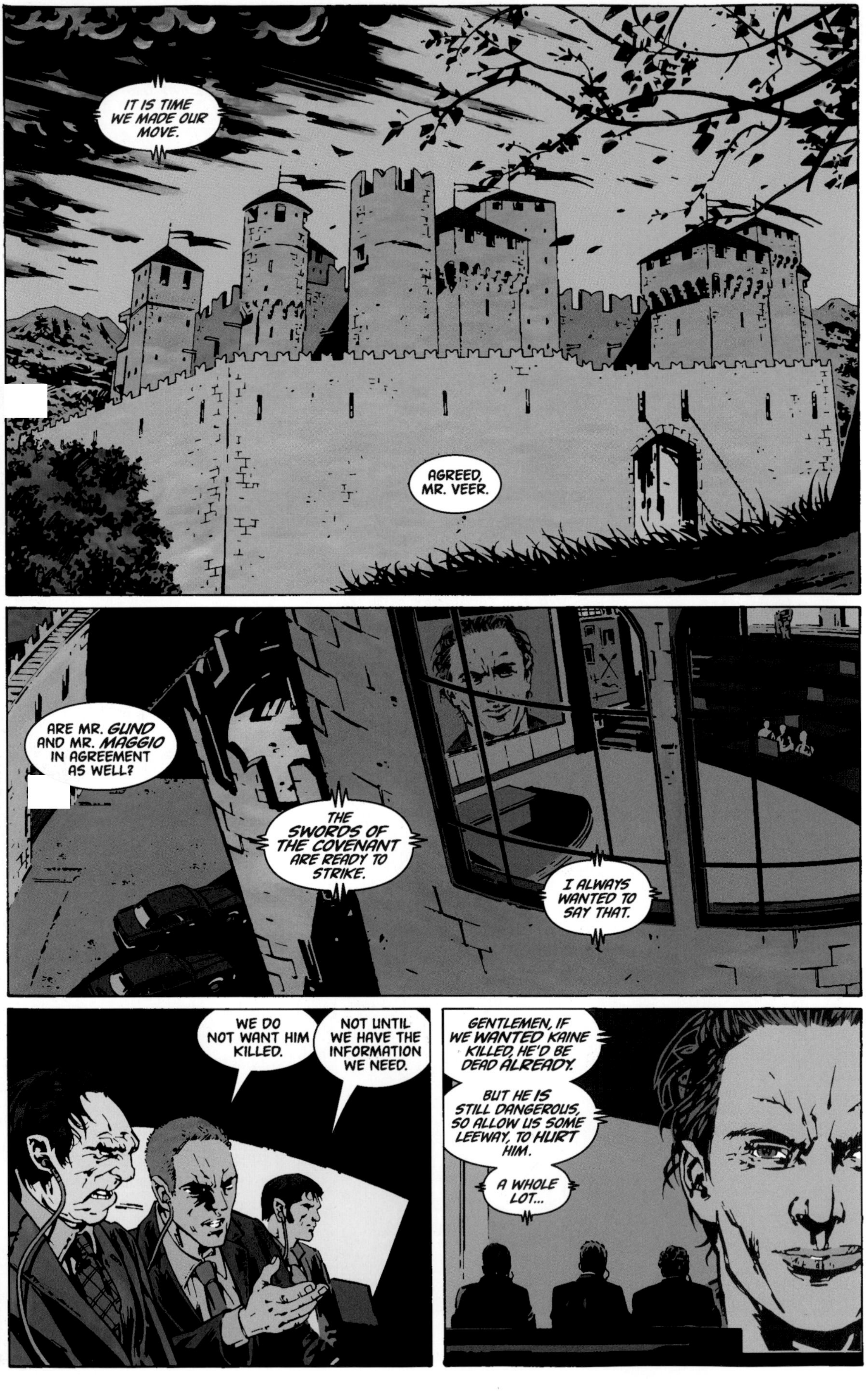
IT IS TIME WE MADE OUR MOVE.
AGREED, MR. VEER.
ARE MR. GUND AND MR. MAGGIO IN AGREEMENT AS WELL?
THE SWORDS OF THE COVENANT ARE READY TO STRIKE.
I ALWAYS WANTED TO SAY THAT.
WE DO NOT WANT HIM KILLED.
NOT UNTIL WE HAVE THE INFORMATION WE NEED.
GENTLEMEN, IF WE WANTED KAINE KILLED, HE'D BE DEAD ALREADY.
BUT HE IS STILL DANGEROUS, SO ALLOW US SOME LEEWAY, TO HURT HIM.
A WHOLE LOT...

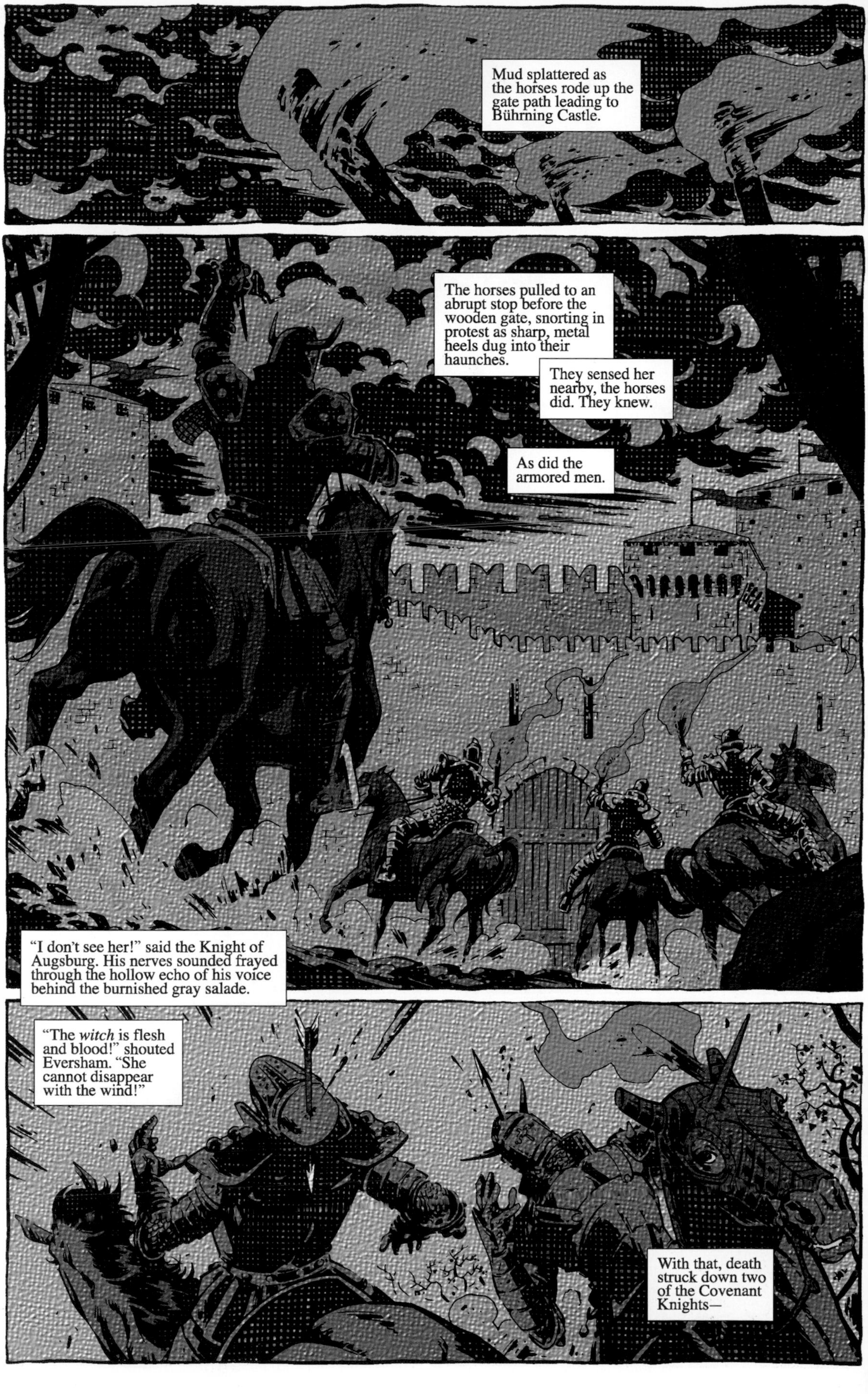
Mud splattered as the horses rode up the gate path leading to Bührning Castle.
The horses pulled to an abrupt stop before the wooden gate, snorting in protest as sharp, metal heels dug into their haunches.
They sensed her nearby, the horses did. They knew.
As did the armored men.
"I don't see her!" said the Knight of Augsburg. His nerves sounded frayed through the hollow echo of his voice behind the burnished gray salade.
"The *witch* is flesh and blood!" shouted Eversham. "She cannot disappear with the wind!"
With that, death struck down two of the Covenant Knights—

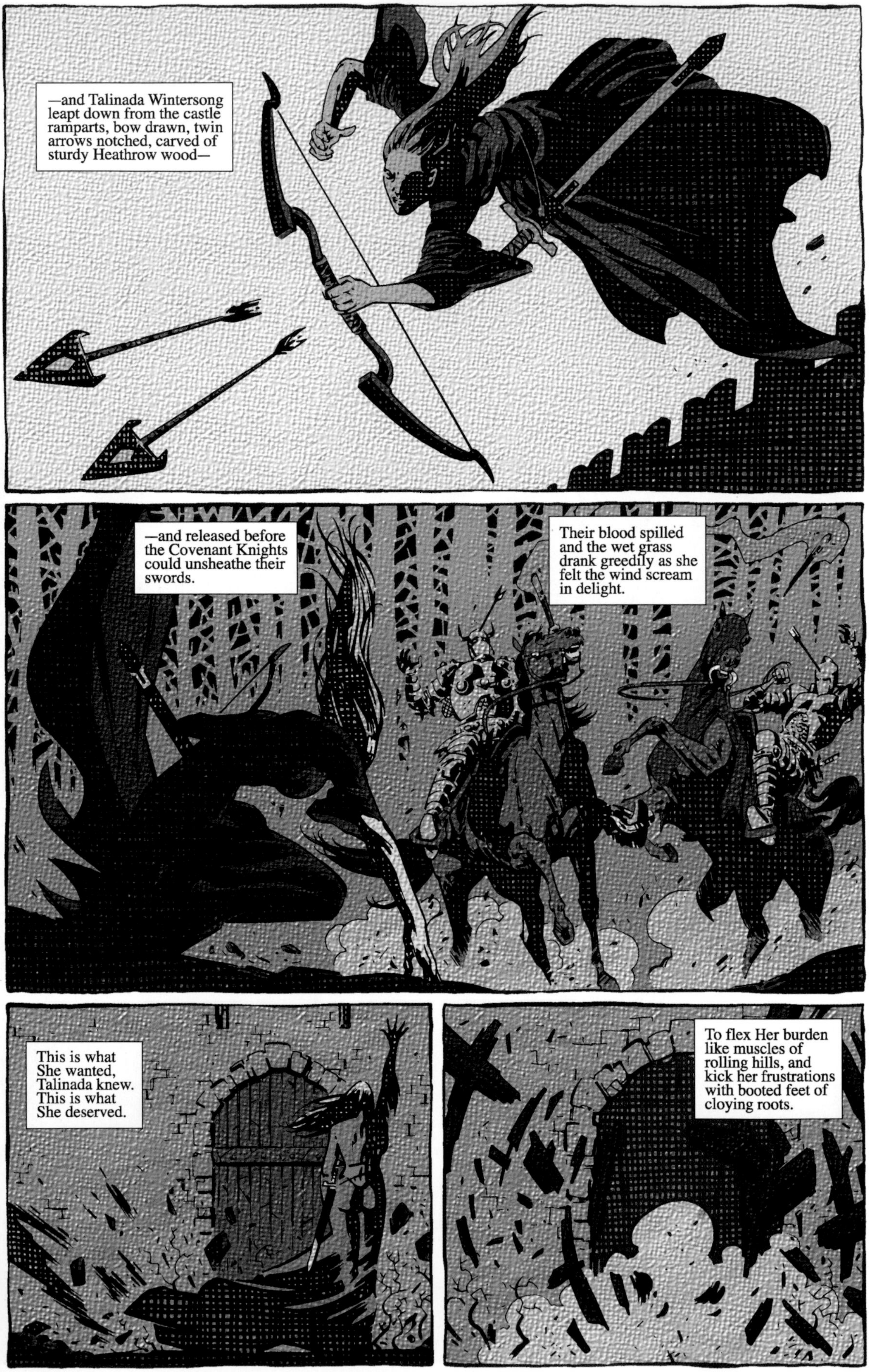
—and Talinada Wintersong leapt down from the castle ramparts, bow drawn, twin arrows notched, carved of sturdy Heathrow wood—
—and released before the Covenant Knights could unsheathe their swords.
Their blood spilled and the wet grass drank greedily as she felt the wind scream in delight.
This is what She wanted, Talinada knew. This is what She deserved.
To flex Her burden like muscles of rolling hills, and kick her frustrations with booted feet of cloying roots.

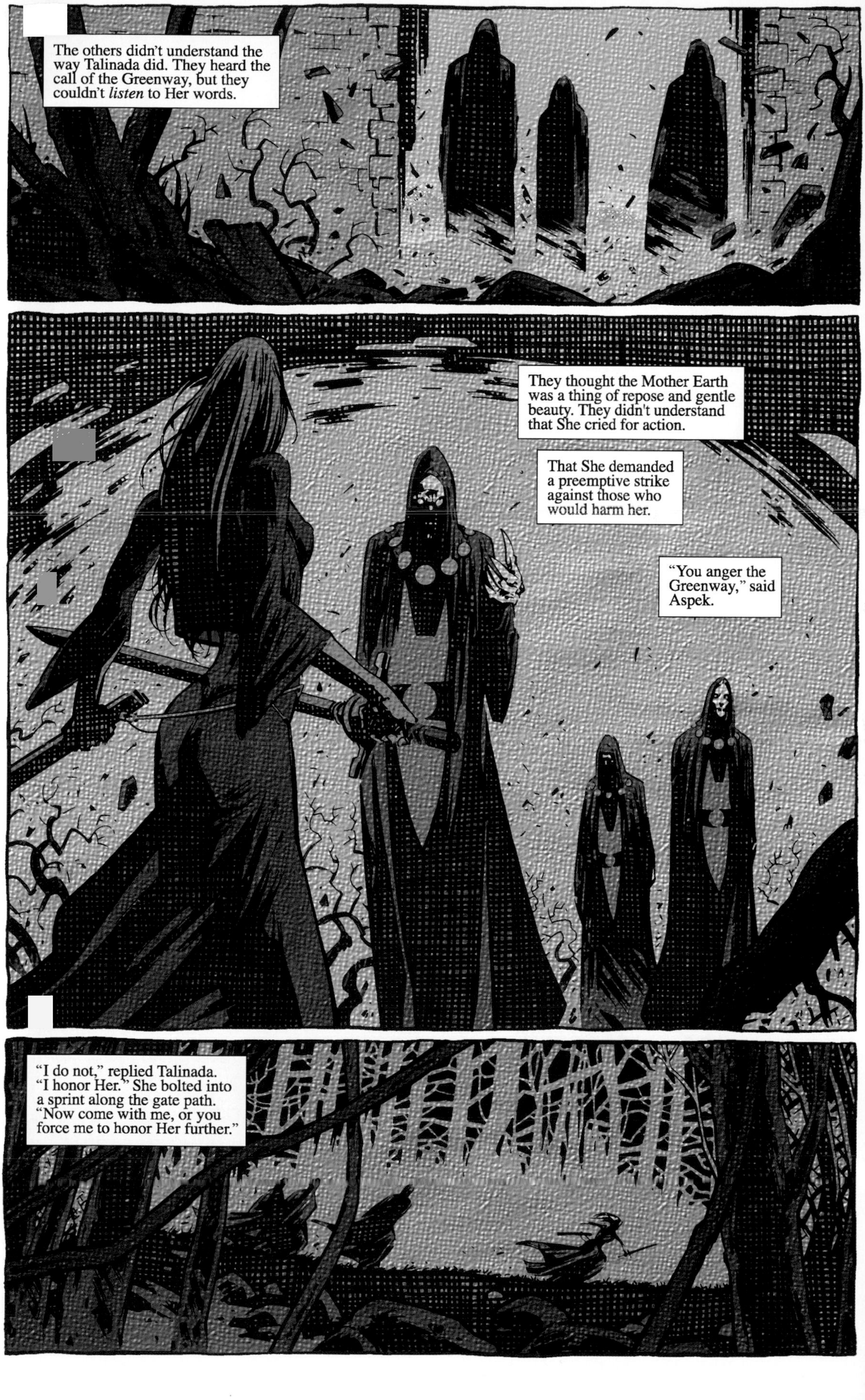

The others didn't understand the way Talinada did. They heard the call of the Greenway, but they couldn't *listen* to Her words.
They thought the Mother Earth was a thing of repose and gentle beauty. They didn't understand that She cried for action.
That She demanded a preemptive strike against those who would harm her.
"You anger the Greenway," said Aspek.
"I do not," replied Talinada. "I honor Her." She bolted into a sprint along the gate path. "Now come with me, or you force me to honor Her further."

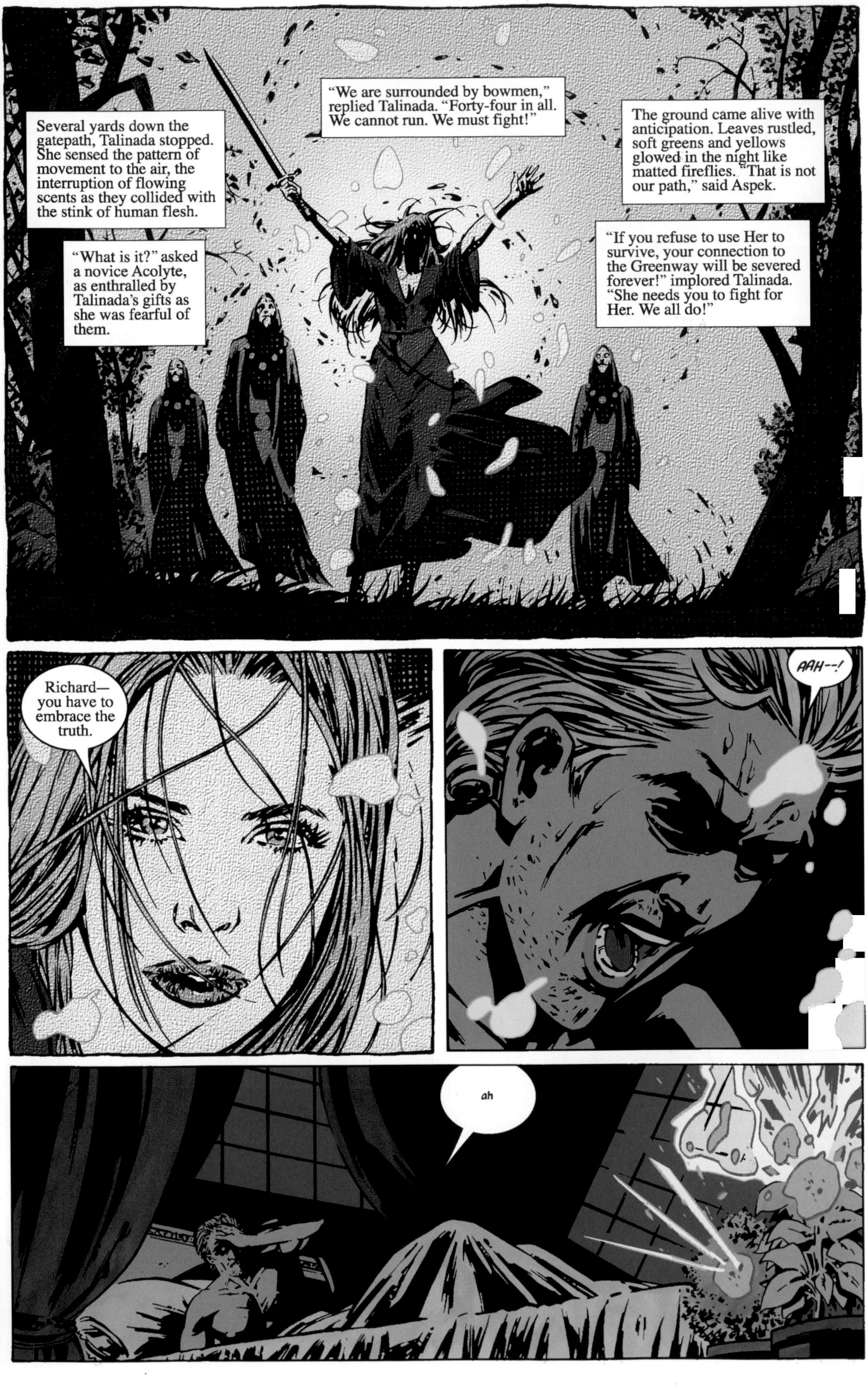
Several yards down the gatepath, Talinada stopped. She sensed the pattern of movement to the air, the interruption of flowing scents as they collided with the stink of human flesh.
"We are surrounded by bowmen," replied Talinada. "Forty-four in all. We cannot run. We must fight!"
The ground came alive with anticipation. Leaves rustled, soft greens and yellows glowed in the night like matted fireflies. "That is not our path," said Aspek.
"What is it?" asked a novice Acolyte, as enthralled by Talinada's gifts as she was fearful of them.
"If you refuse to use Her to survive, your connection to the Greenway will be severed forever!" implored Talinada. "She needs you to fight for Her. We all do!"
Richard—you have to embrace the truth.
AAH--!
ah

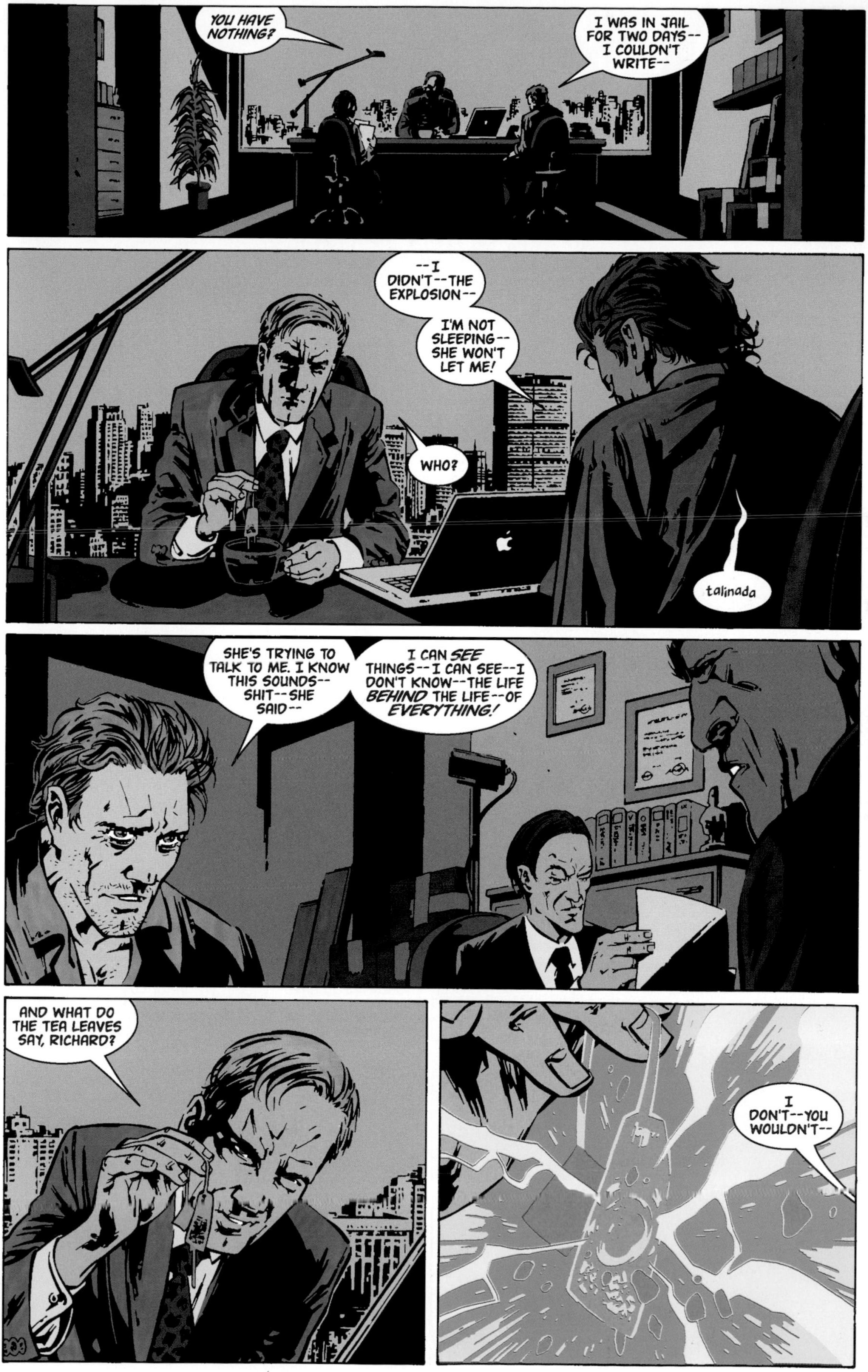
YOU HAVE NOTHING?
I WAS IN JAIL FOR TWO DAYS-- I COULDN'T WRITE--
--I DIDN'T--THE EXPLOSION--
I'M NOT SLEEPING-- SHE WON'T LET ME!
WHO?
talinada
SHE'S TRYING TO TALK TO ME. I KNOW THIS SOUNDS-- SHIT--SHE SAID--
I CAN SEE THINGS--I CAN SEE--I DON'T KNOW--THE LIFE BEHIND THE LIFE--OF EVERYTHING!
AND WHAT DO THE TEA LEAVES SAY, RICHARD?
I DON'T--YOU WOULDN'T--

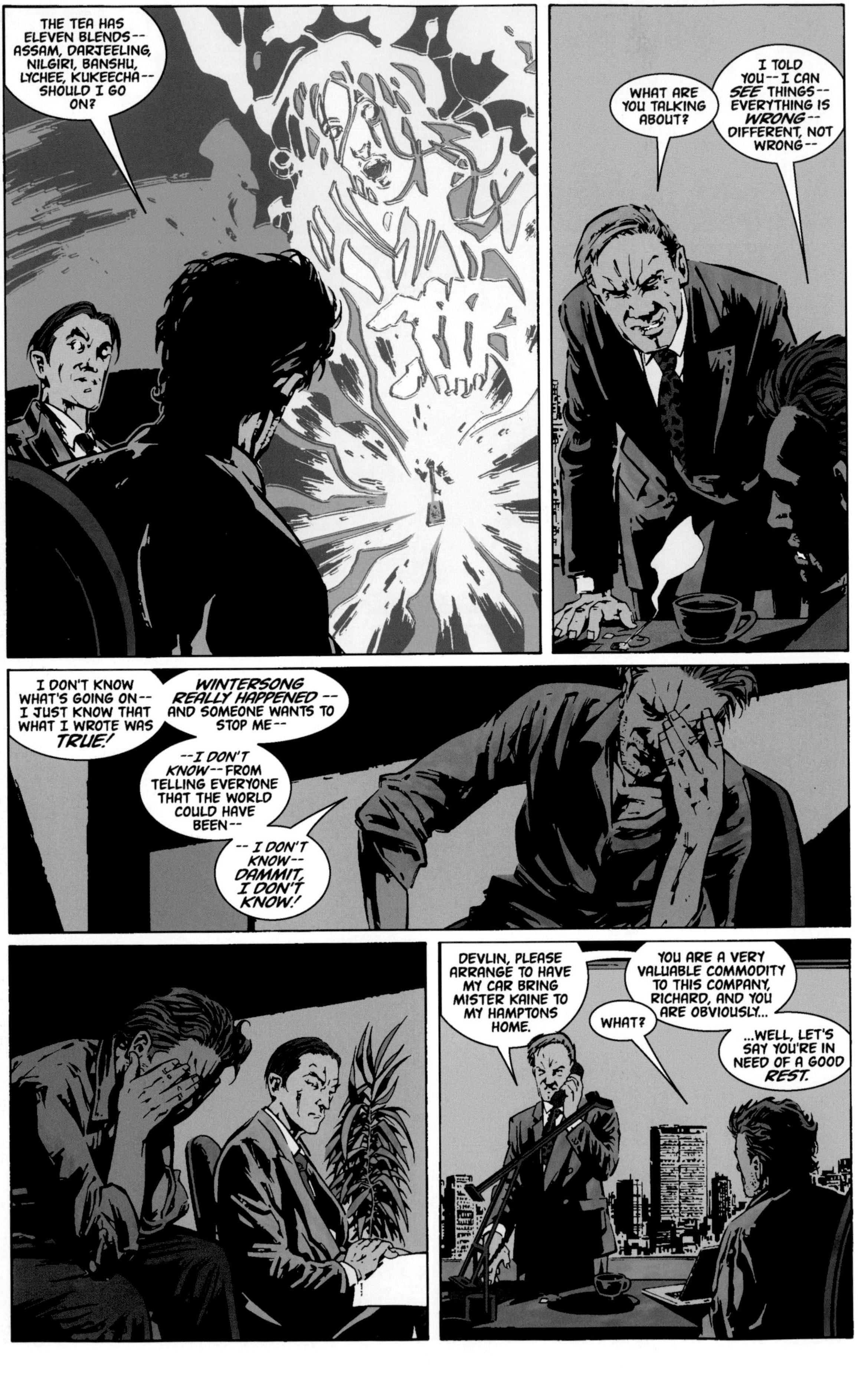
THE TEA HAS ELEVEN BLENDS-- ASSAM, DARJEELING, NILGIRI, BANSHU, LYCHEE, KUKEECHA-- SHOULD I GO ON?
WHAT ARE YOU TALKING ABOUT?
I TOLD YOU-- I CAN SEE THINGS-- EVERYTHING IS WRONG-- DIFFERENT, NOT WRONG--
I DON'T KNOW WHAT'S GOING ON-- I JUST KNOW THAT WHAT I WROTE WAS TRUE!
WINTERSONG REALLY HAPPENED-- AND SOMEONE WANTS TO STOP ME--
--I DON'T KNOW--FROM TELLING EVERYONE THAT THE WORLD COULD HAVE BEEN--
-- I DON'T KNOW-- DAMMIT, I DON'T KNOW!
DEVLIN, PLEASE ARRANGE TO HAVE MY CAR BRING MISTER KAINE TO MY HAMPTONS HOME.
YOU ARE A VERY VALUABLE COMMODITY TO THIS COMPANY, RICHARD, AND YOU ARE OBVIOUSLY...
WHAT?
...WELL, LET'S SAY YOU'RE IN NEED OF A GOOD REST.

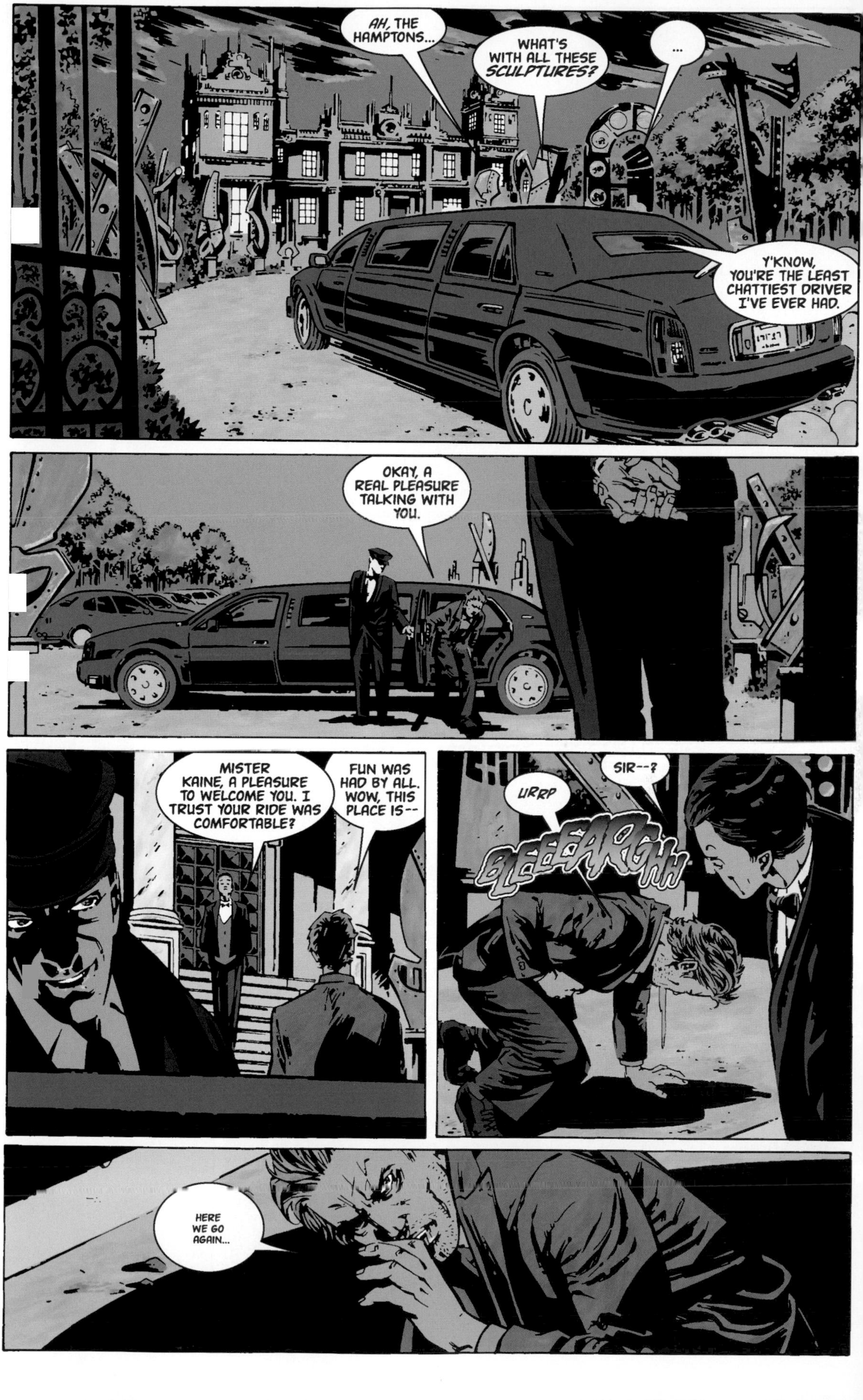
AH, THE HAMPTONS...
WHAT'S WITH ALL THESE SCULPTURES?
...
Y'KNOW, YOU'RE THE LEAST CHATTIEST DRIVER I'VE EVER HAD.
OKAY, A REAL PLEASURE TALKING WITH YOU.
MISTER KAINE, A PLEASURE TO WELCOME YOU. I TRUST YOUR RIDE WAS COMFORTABLE?
FUN WAS HAD BY ALL. WOW, THIS PLACE IS--
SIR--?
URRP
BLEEEARGHH
HERE WE GO AGAIN...

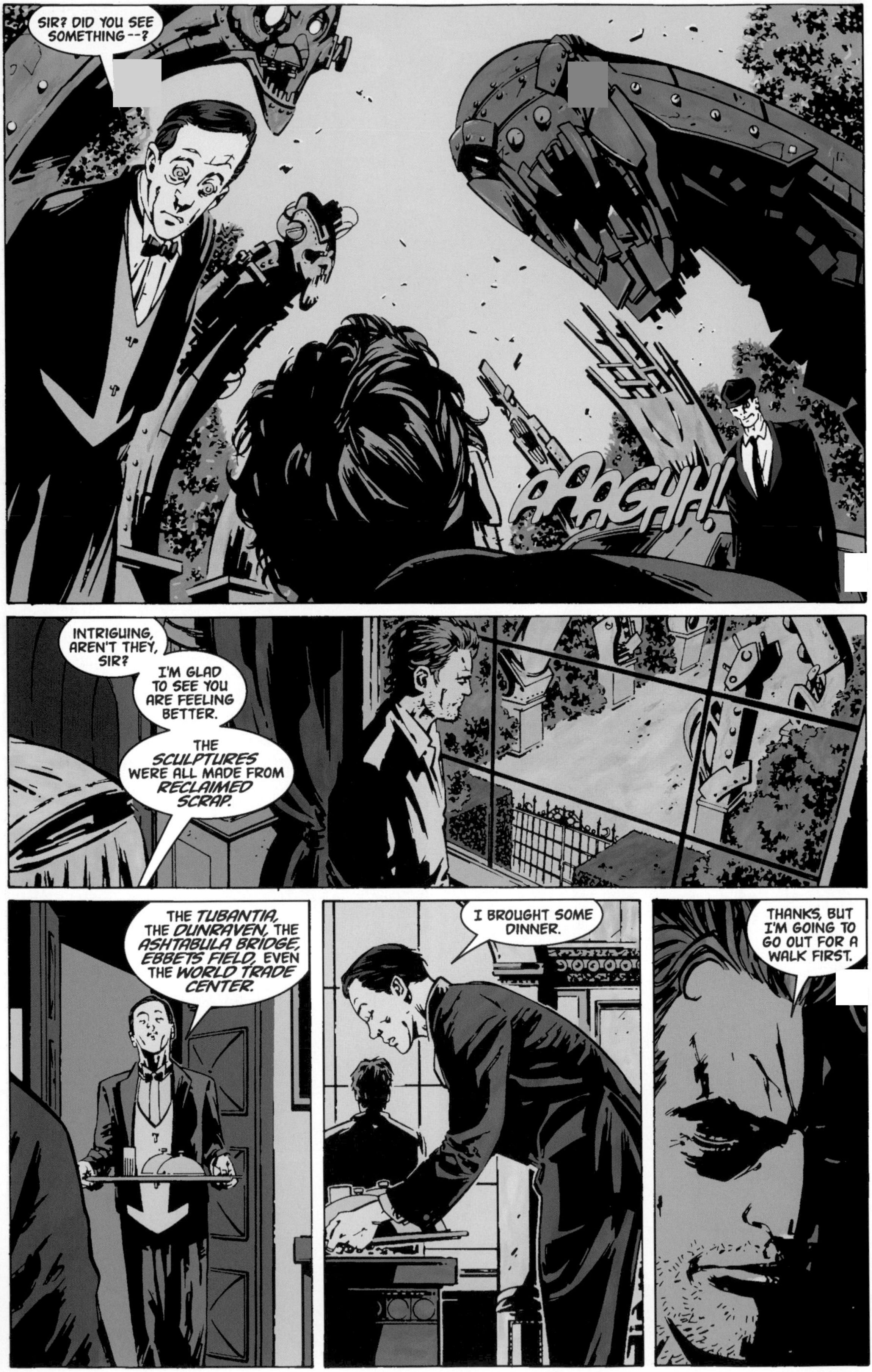

SIR? DID YOU SEE SOMETHING--?
AAAGHH!
INTRIGUING, AREN'T THEY, SIR?
I'M GLAD TO SEE YOU ARE FEELING BETTER.
THE SCULPTURES WERE ALL MADE FROM RECLAIMED SCRAP.
THE TUBANTIA, THE DUNRAVEN, THE ASHTABULA BRIDGE, EBBETS FIELD, EVEN THE WORLD TRADE CENTER.
I BROUGHT SOME DINNER.
THANKS, BUT I'M GOING TO GO OUT FOR A WALK FIRST.

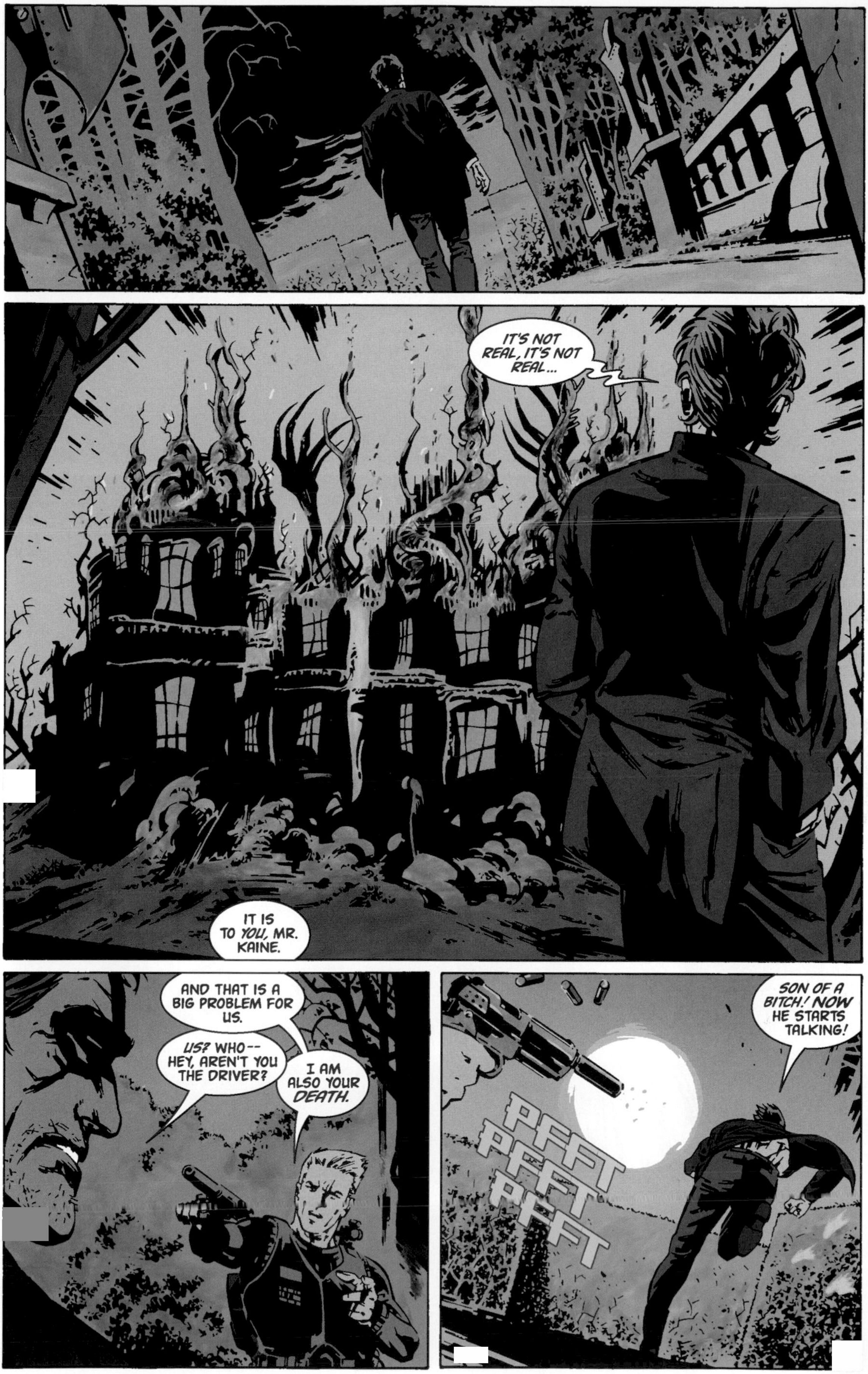
IT'S NOT REAL, IT'S NOT REAL...
IT IS TO YOU, MR. KAINE.
AND THAT IS A BIG PROBLEM FOR US.
US? WHO-- HEY, AREN'T YOU THE DRIVER?
I AM ALSO YOUR DEATH.
SON OF A BITCH! NOW HE STARTS TALKING!
PFFT PFFT PFFT

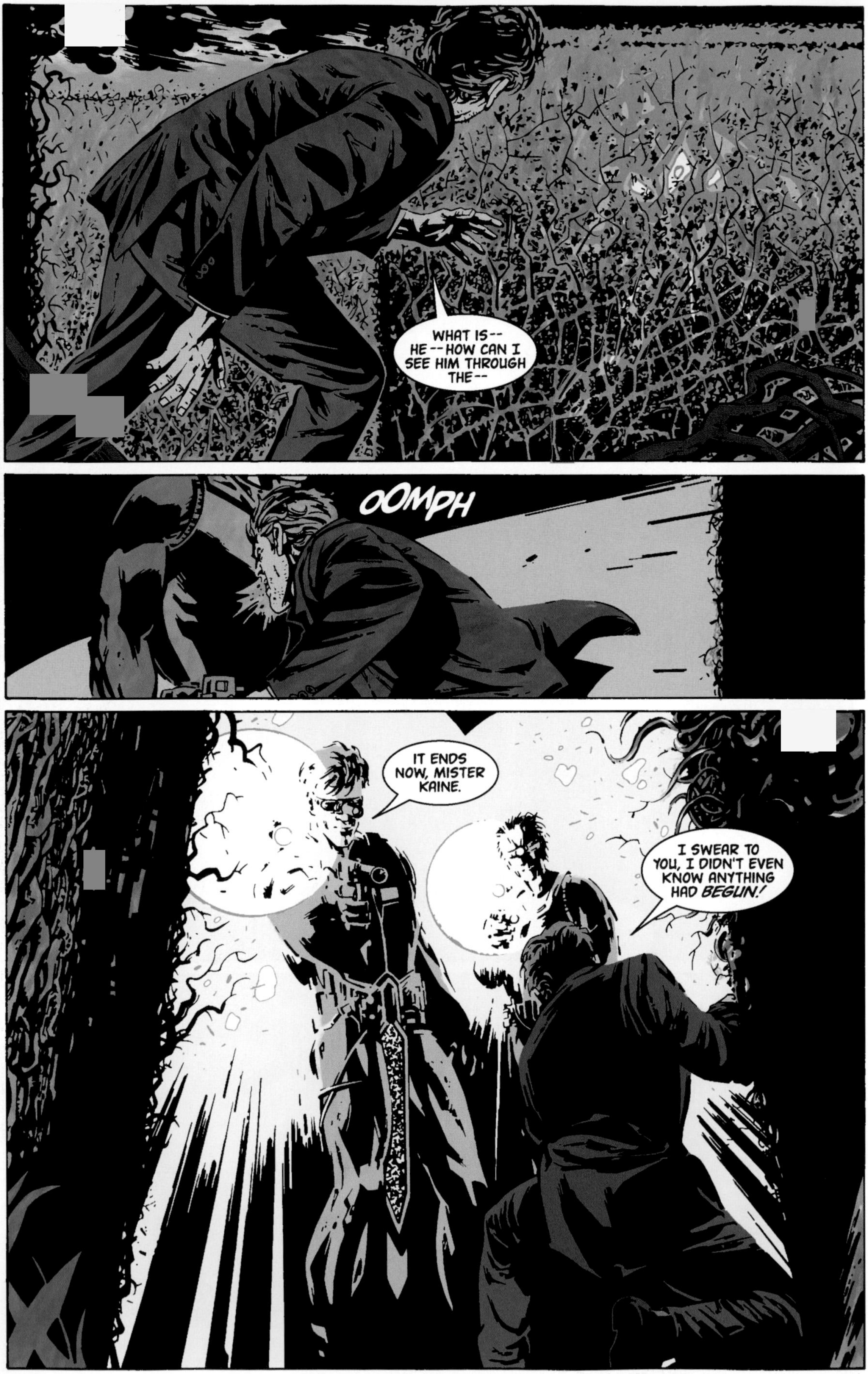
WHAT IS-- HE--HOW CAN I SEE HIM THROUGH THE--
OOMPH
IT ENDS NOW, MISTER KAINE.
I SWEAR TO YOU, I DIDN'T EVEN KNOW ANYTHING HAD *BEGUN!*

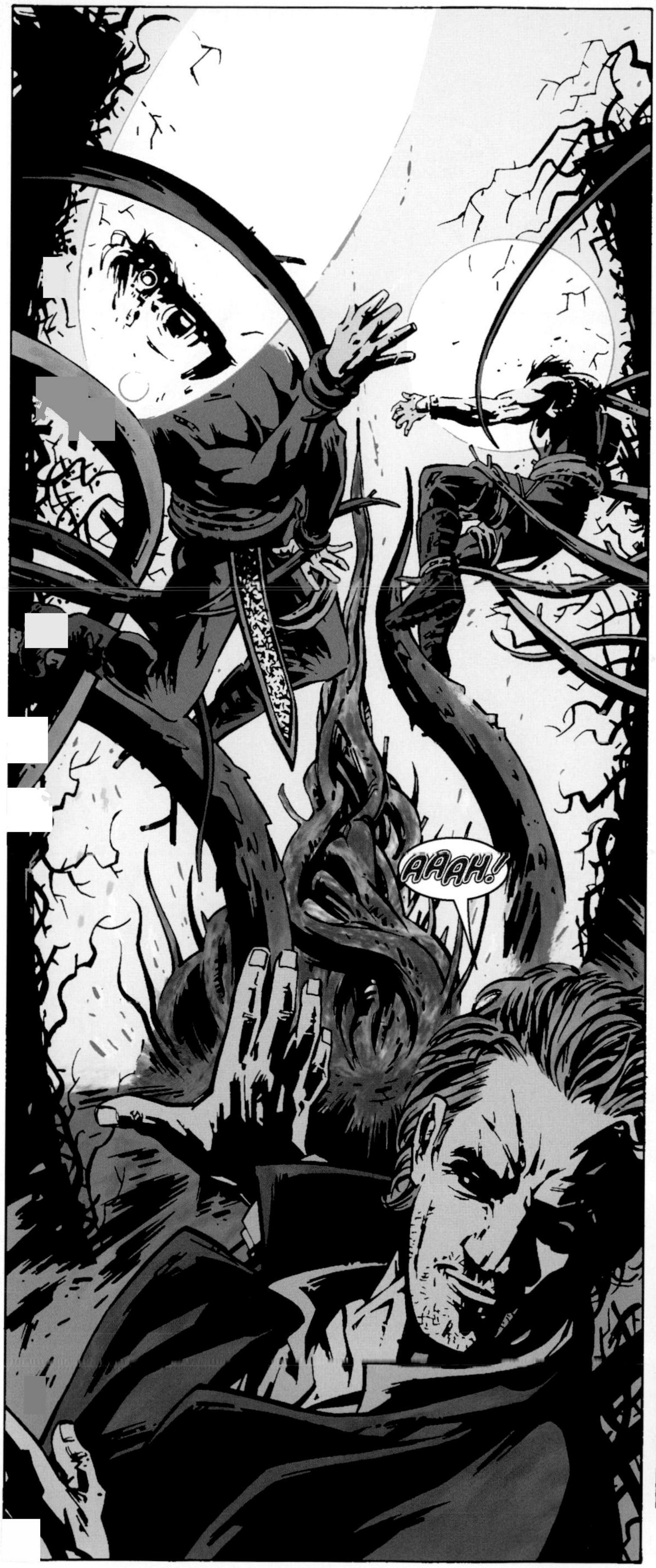
AAAH!

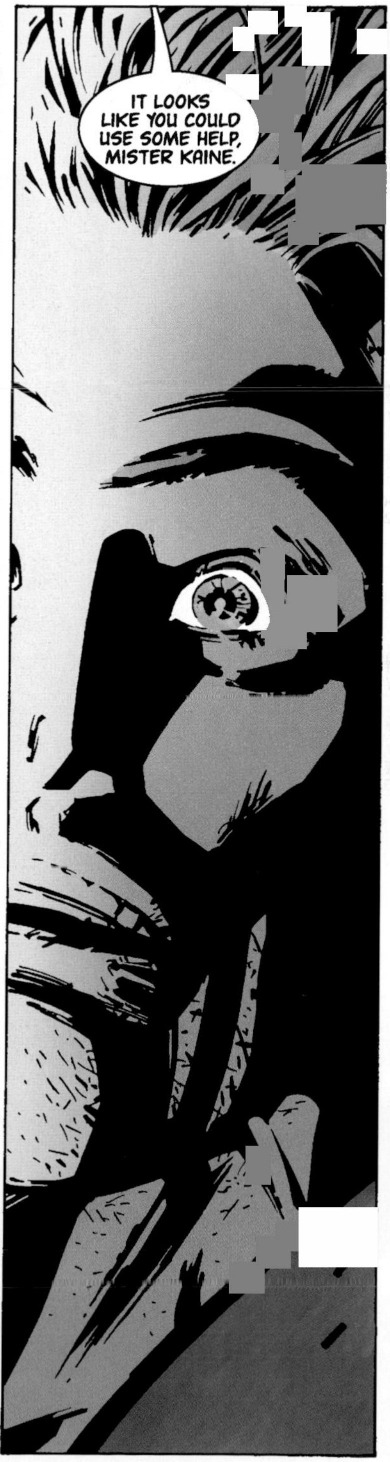
IT LOOKS LIKE YOU COULD USE SOME HELP, MISTER KAINE.

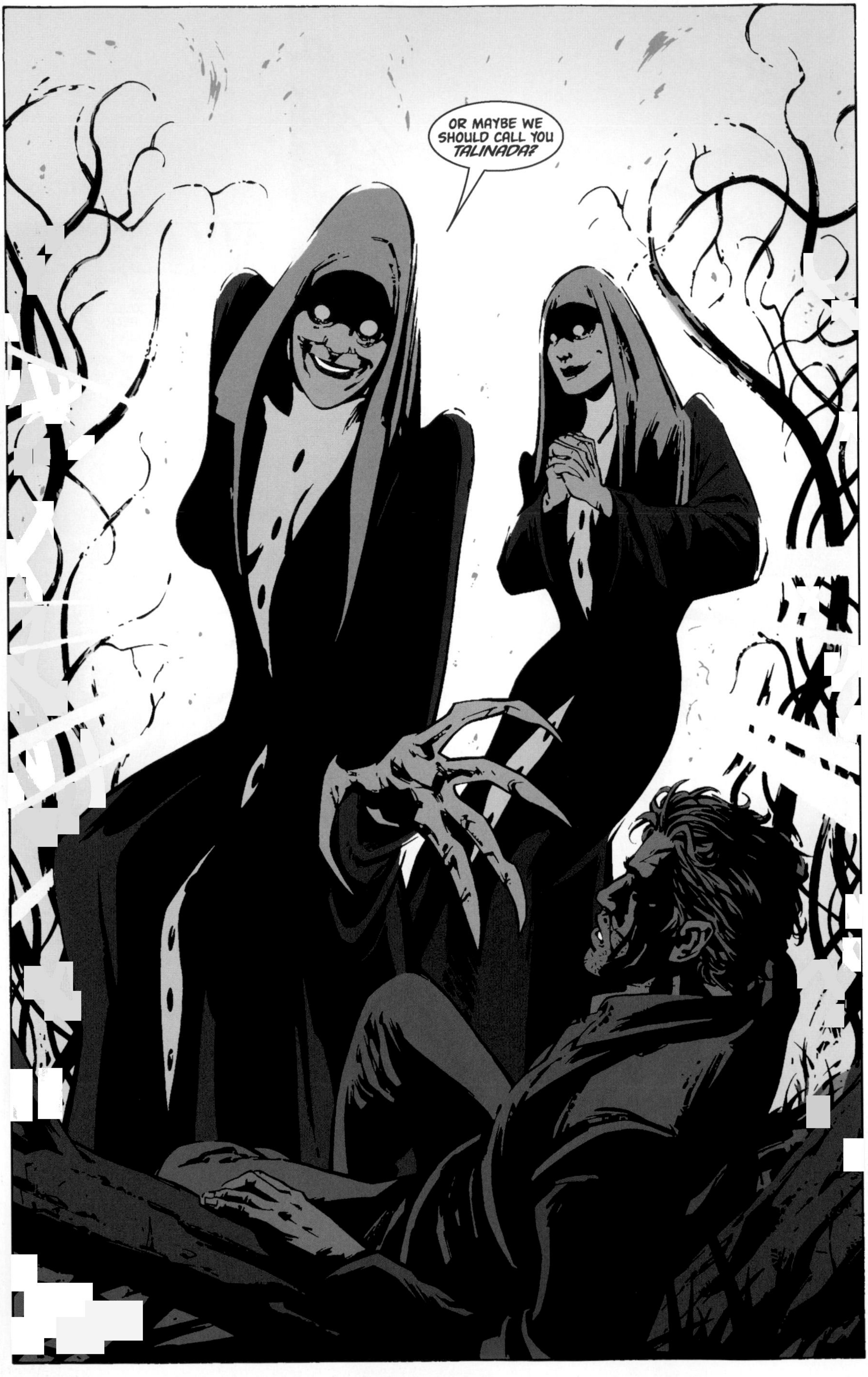
OR MAYBE WE SHOULD CALL YOU TALINADA?

Act Three
BORN TO BE WILD

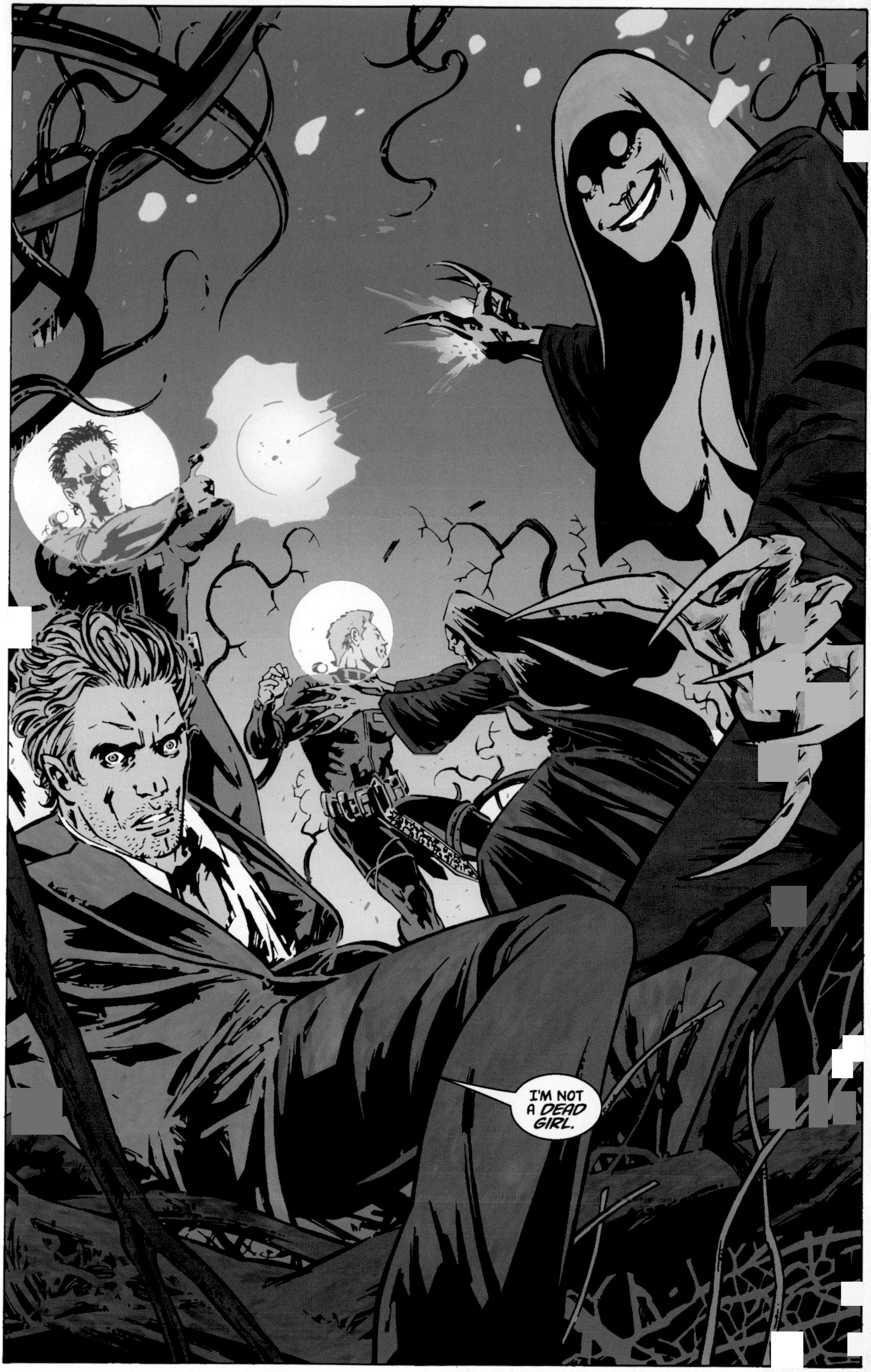
I'M NOT A DEAD GIRL.

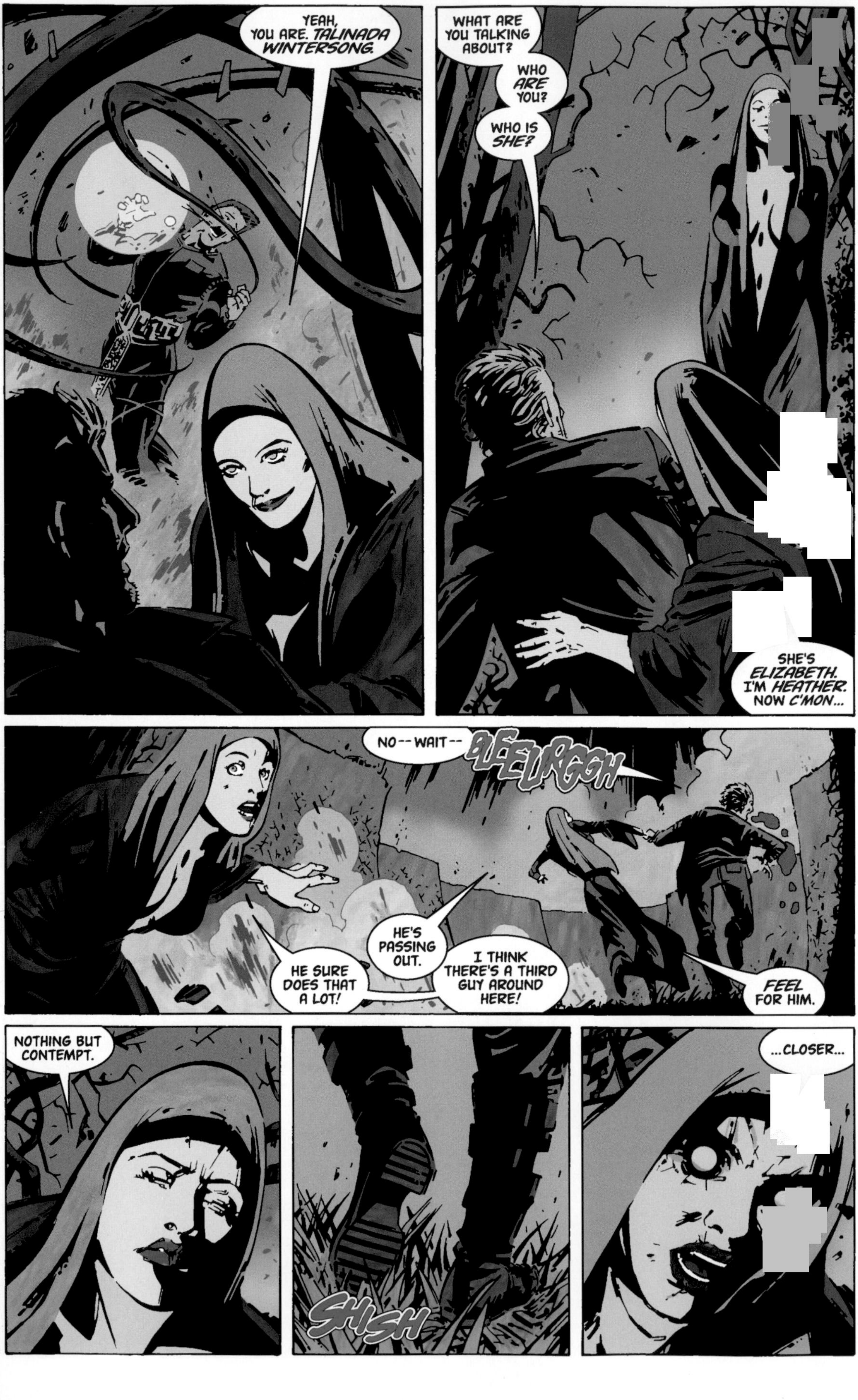
YEAH, YOU ARE. TALINADA WINTERSONG.
WHAT ARE YOU TALKING ABOUT?
WHO ARE YOU?
WHO IS SHE?
SHE'S ELIZABETH. I'M HEATHER. NOW C'MON...
NO--WAIT--
BLEEURGGH
HE SURE DOES THAT A LOT!
HE'S PASSING OUT.
I THINK THERE'S A THIRD GUY AROUND HERE!
FEEL FOR HIM.
NOTHING BUT CONTEMPT.
SHISH
...CLOSER...

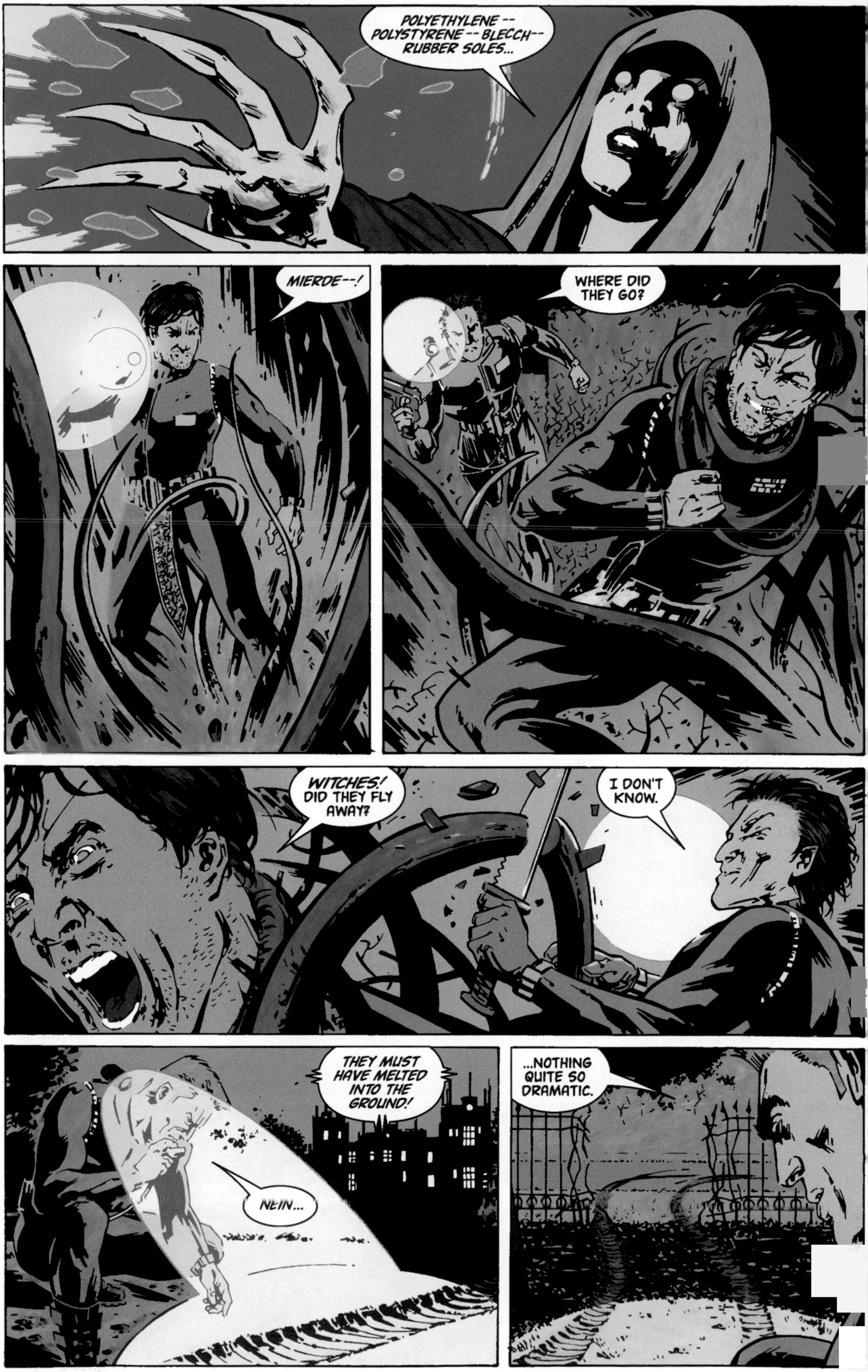
POLYETHYLENE -- POLYSTYRENE -- BLECCH-- RUBBER SOLES...
MIERDE--!
WHERE DID THEY GO?
WITCHES! DID THEY FLY AWAY?
I DON'T KNOW.
THEY MUST HAVE MELTED INTO THE GROUND!
NEIN...
...NOTHING QUITE SO DRAMATIC.

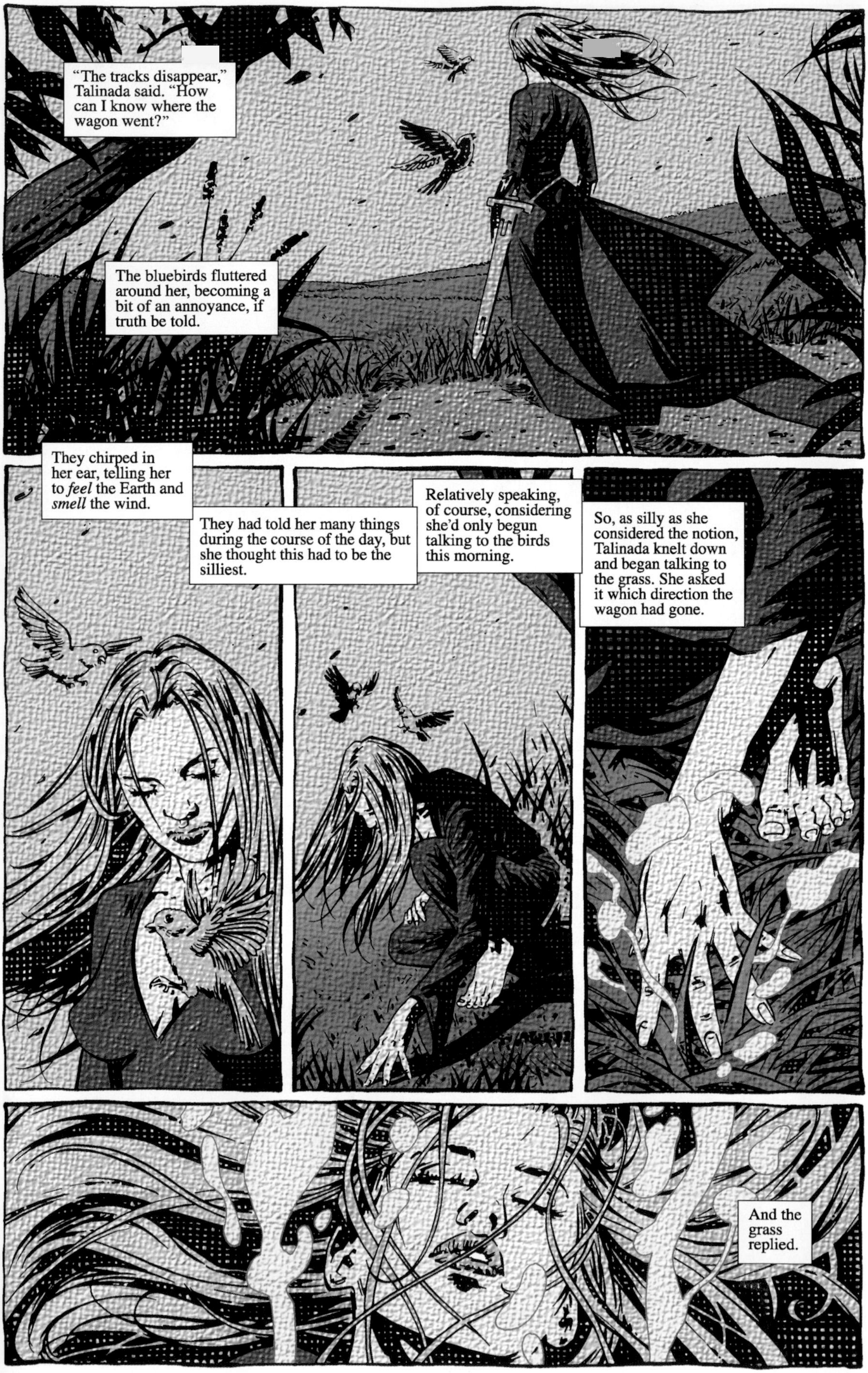
"The tracks disappear," Talinada said. "How can I know where the wagon went?"
The bluebirds fluttered around her, becoming a bit of an annoyance, if truth be told.
They chirped in her ear, telling her to *feel* the Earth and *smell* the wind.
They had told her many things during the course of the day, but she thought this had to be the silliest.
Relatively speaking, of course, considering she'd only begun talking to the birds this morning.
So, as silly as she considered the notion, Talinada knelt down and began talking to the grass. She asked it which direction the wagon had gone.
And the grass replied.

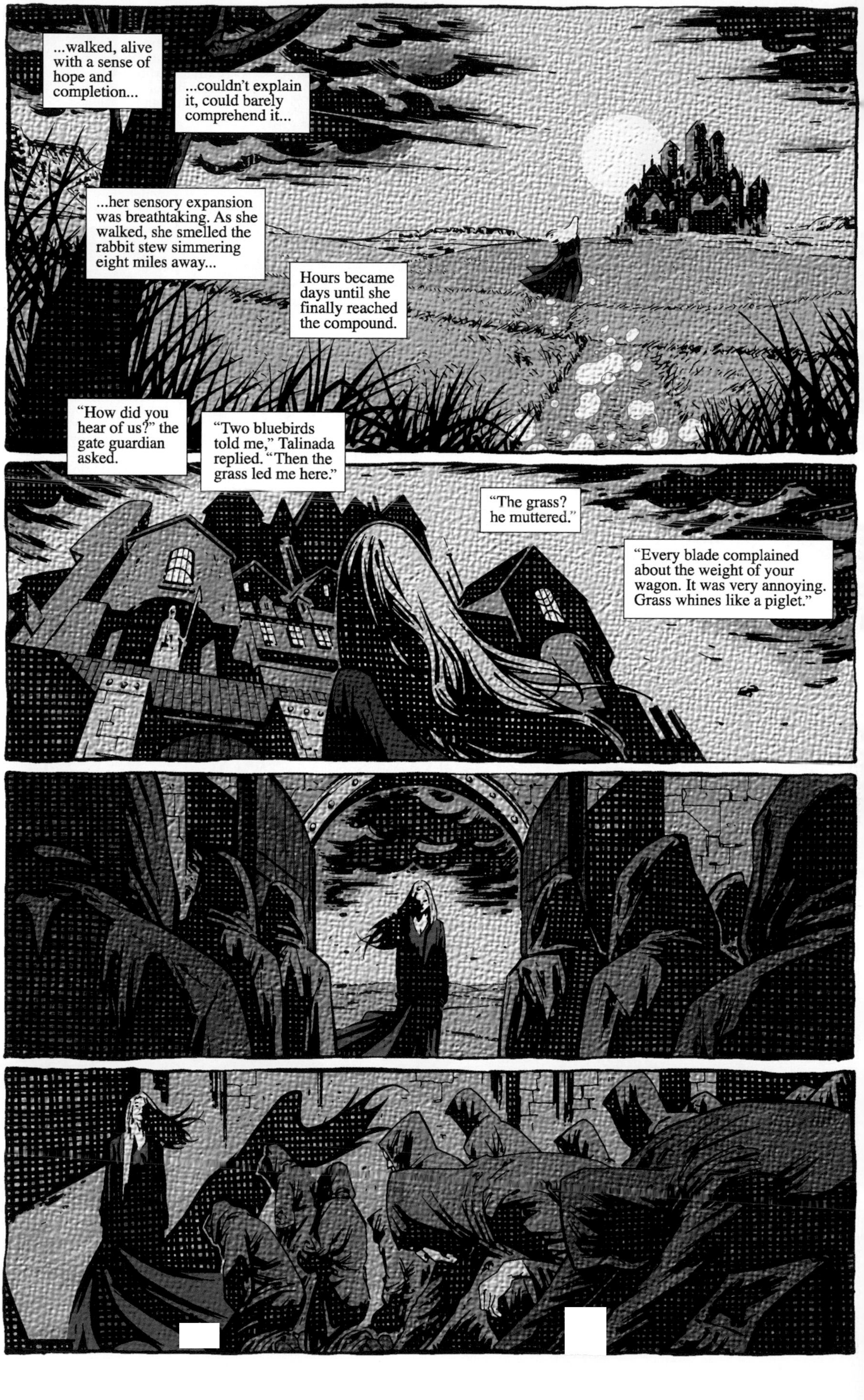
...walked, alive with a sense of hope and completion...
...couldn't explain it, could barely comprehend it...
...her sensory expansion was breathtaking. As she walked, she smelled the rabbit stew simmering eight miles away...
Hours became days until she finally reached the compound.
"How did you hear of us?" the gate guardian asked.
"Two bluebirds told me," Talinada replied. "Then the grass led me here."
"The grass? he muttered."
"Every blade complained about the weight of your wagon. It was very annoying. Grass whines like a piglet."

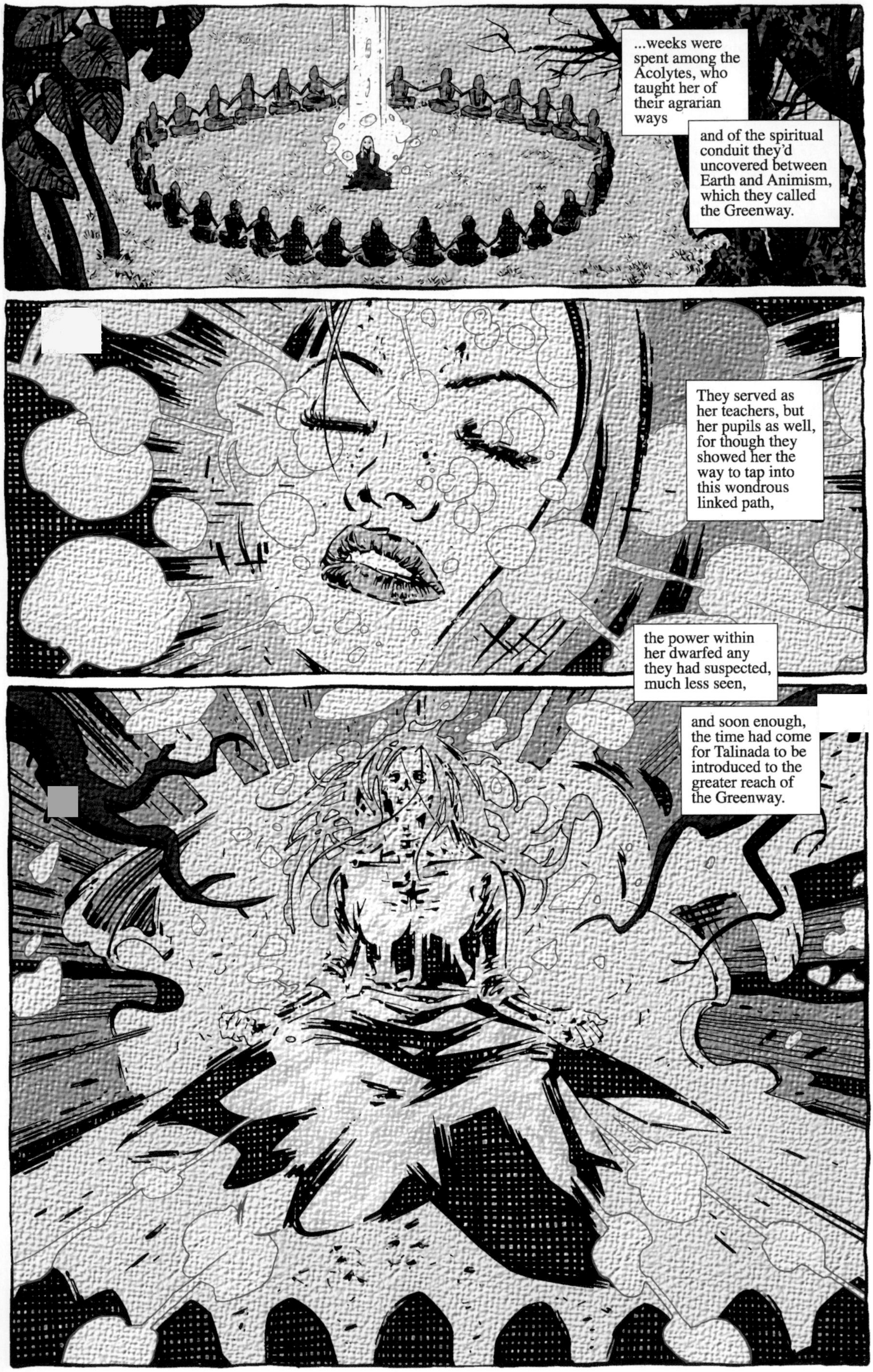
...weeks were spent among the Acolytes, who taught her of their agrarian ways
and of the spiritual conduit they'd uncovered between Earth and Animism, which they called the Greenway.
They served as her teachers, but her pupils as well, for though they showed her the way to tap into this wondrous linked path,
the power within her dwarfed any they had suspected, much less seen,
and soon enough, the time had come for Talinada to be introduced to the greater reach of the Greenway.

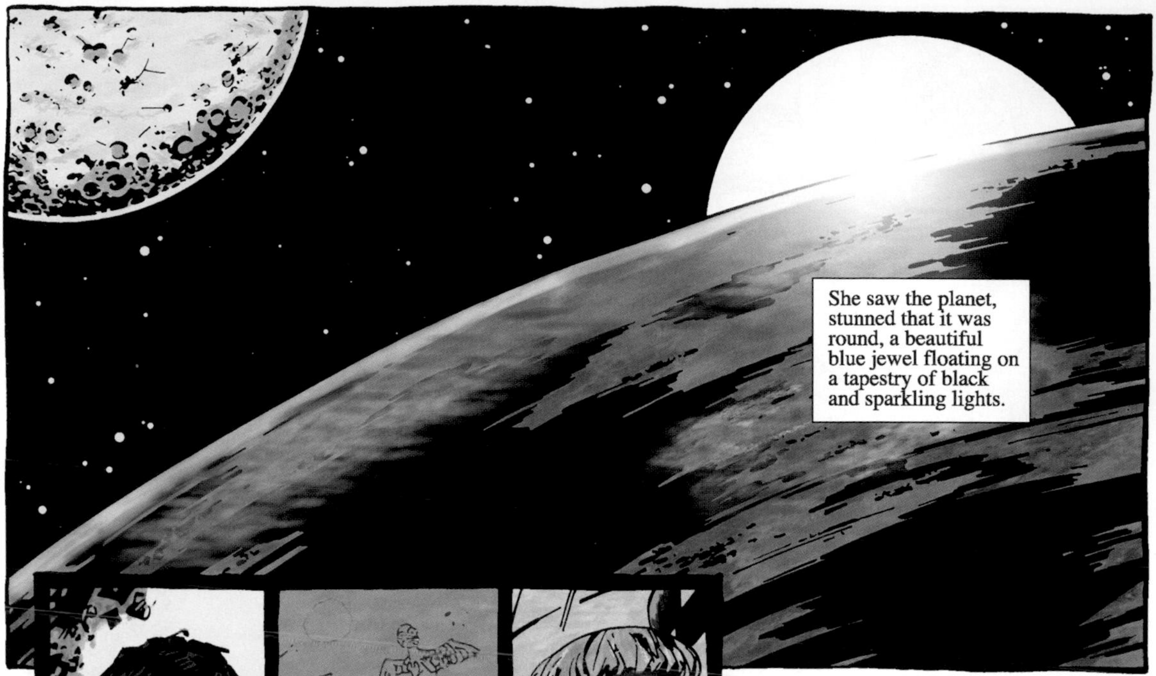
She saw the planet, stunned that it was round, a beautiful blue jewel floating on a tapestry of black and sparkling lights.

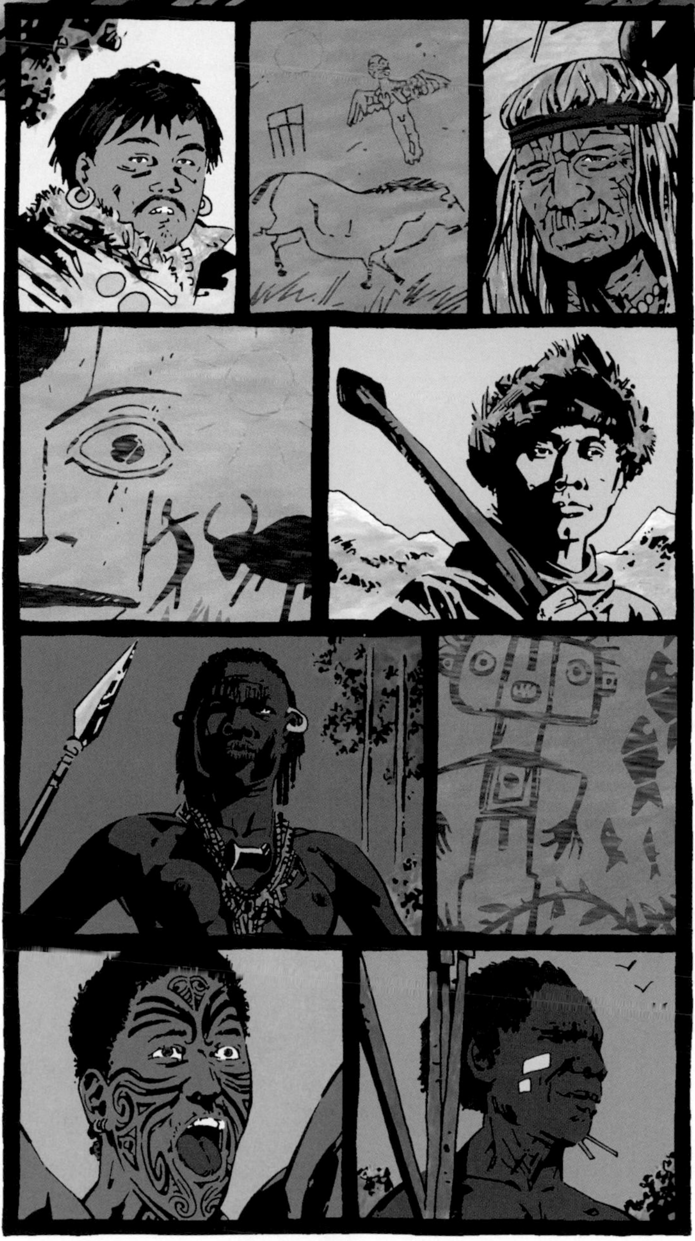

Talinada grit her teeth, feeling a sudden rush of chatter flood through her mind. Nearly all of the spoken languages were unknown to her, some guttural, all clicking consonants, others lilting like a song or a breeze. People from all over the world, she realized, specific kinds of people.

They were vibrant tribes and cultures that understood, far better than she'd ever been taught, how to appreciate the bounty of the planet. People who lived in harmony with Mother Earth. People who respected Her and accepted their responsibility to Her.

And, Talinada realized she could understand their words, communicate with them through the planet itself. She could see them through the eyes of insects buzzing in a field, smell them through the petals of a blooming flower, taste them through salt in the air.

She could hear them and they all said the same thing: Help us save this world from the blight of the Forging Ways.

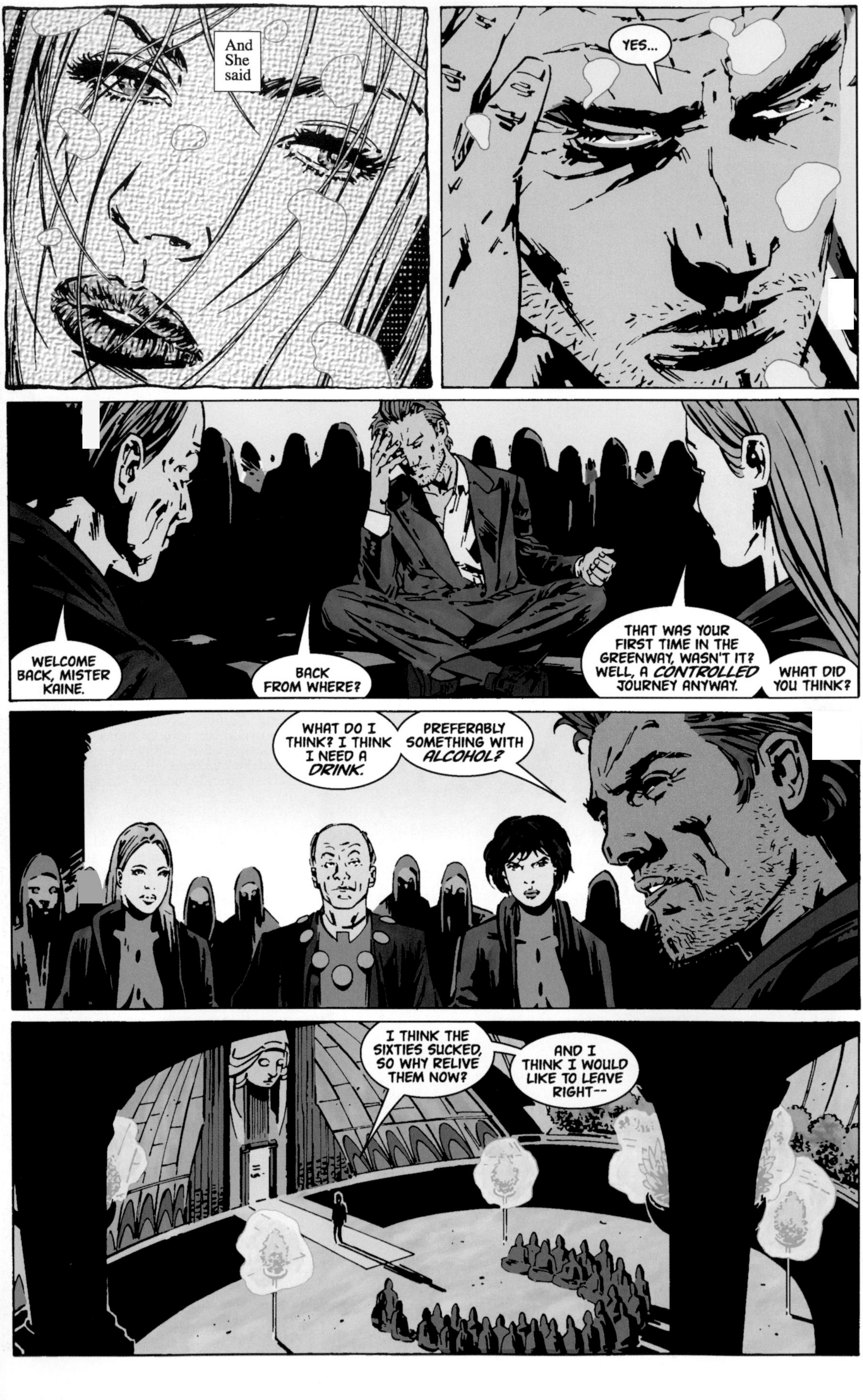
And She said
YES...
WELCOME BACK, MISTER KAINE.
BACK FROM WHERE?
THAT WAS YOUR FIRST TIME IN THE GREENWAY, WASN'T IT? WELL, A CONTROLLED JOURNEY ANYWAY.
WHAT DID YOU THINK?
WHAT DO I THINK? I THINK I NEED A DRINK.
PREFERABLY SOMETHING WITH ALCOHOL?
I THINK THE SIXTIES SUCKED, SO WHY RELIVE THEM NOW?
AND I THINK I WOULD LIKE TO LEAVE RIGHT--

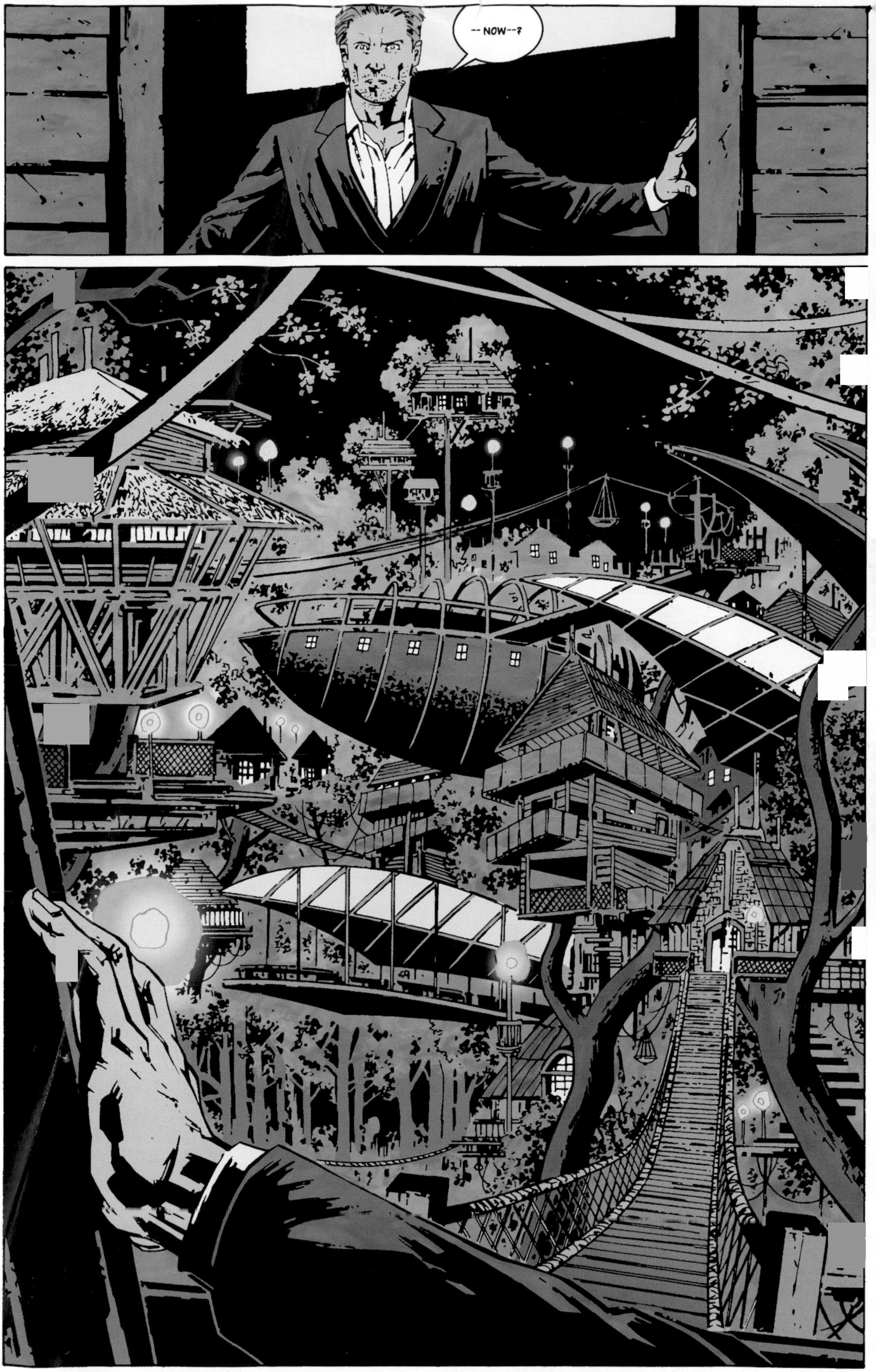
-- NOW--?

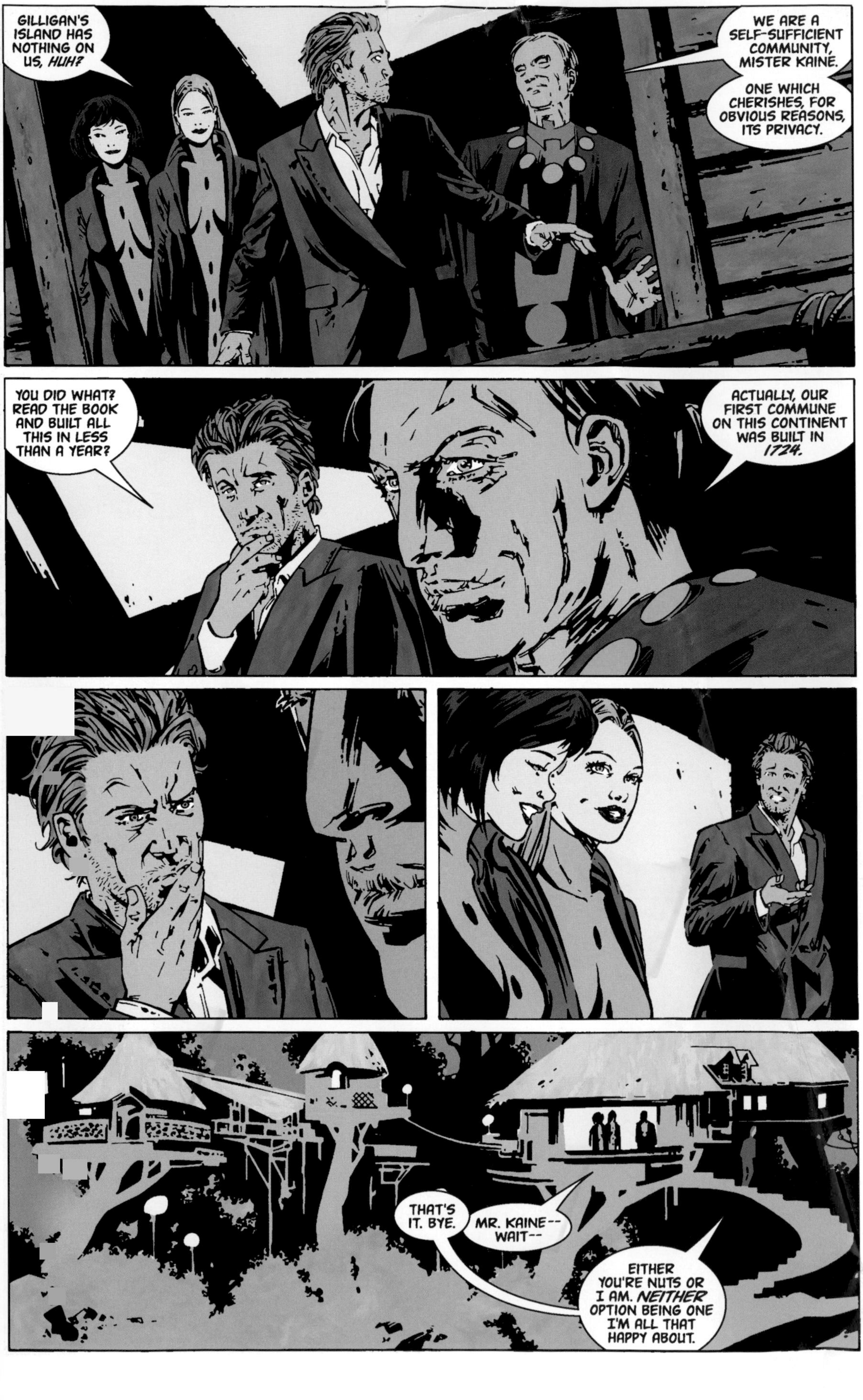
GILLIGAN'S ISLAND HAS NOTHING ON US, HUH?
WE ARE A SELF-SUFFICIENT COMMUNITY, MISTER KAINE.
ONE WHICH CHERISHES, FOR OBVIOUS REASONS, ITS PRIVACY.
YOU DID WHAT? READ THE BOOK AND BUILT ALL THIS IN LESS THAN A YEAR?
ACTUALLY, OUR FIRST COMMUNE ON THIS CONTINENT WAS BUILT IN 1724.
THAT'S IT. BYE.
MR. KAINE-- WAIT--
EITHER YOU'RE NUTS OR I AM. NEITHER OPTION BEING ONE I'M ALL THAT HAPPY ABOUT.

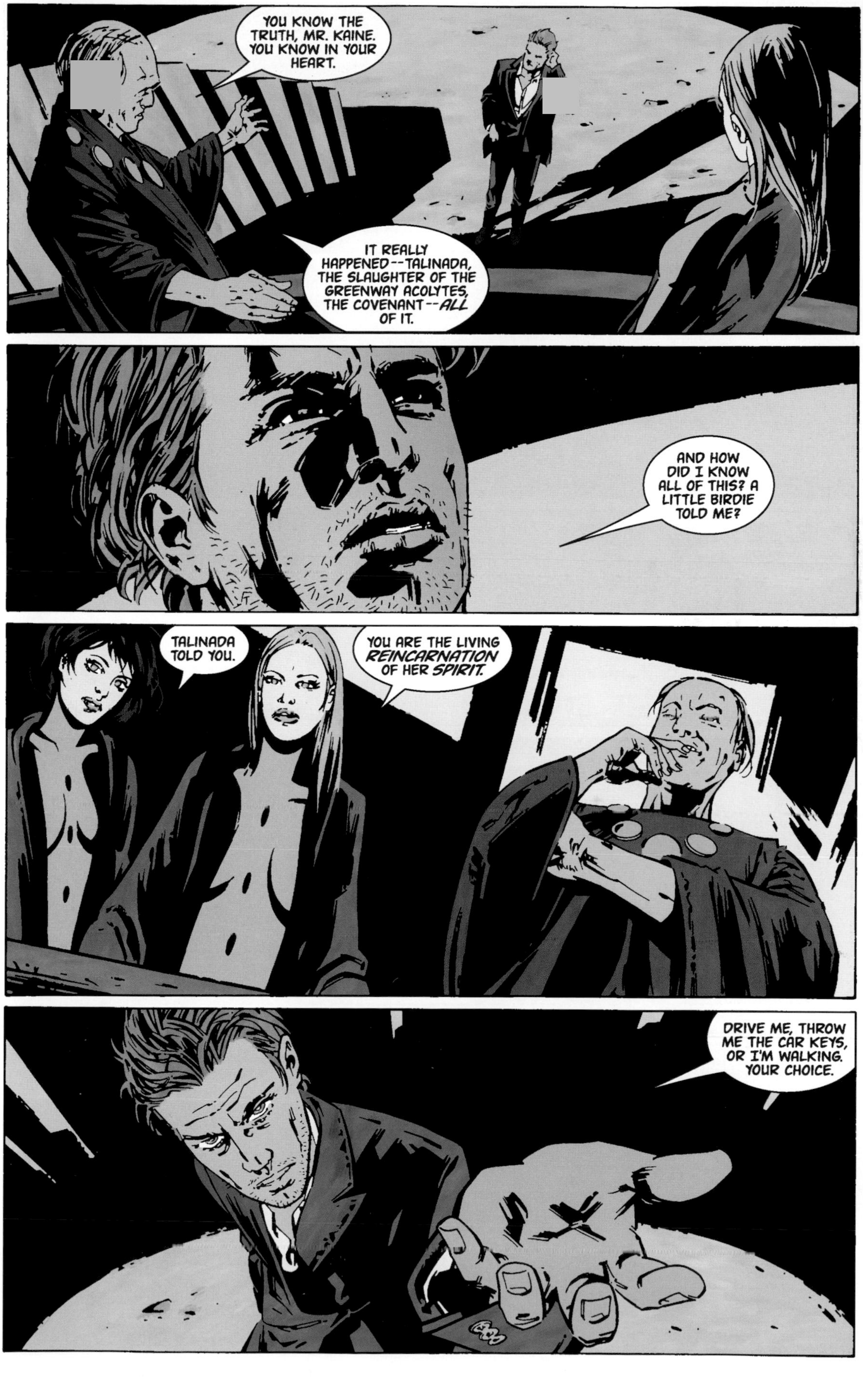
YOU KNOW THE TRUTH, MR. KAINE. YOU KNOW IN YOUR HEART.
IT REALLY HAPPENED--TALINADA, THE SLAUGHTER OF THE GREENWAY ACOLYTES, THE COVENANT--*ALL* OF IT.
AND HOW DID I KNOW ALL OF THIS? A LITTLE BIRDIE TOLD ME?
TALINADA TOLD YOU.
YOU ARE THE LIVING *REINCARNATION* OF HER *SPIRIT.*
DRIVE ME, THROW ME THE CAR KEYS, OR I'M WALKING. YOUR CHOICE.

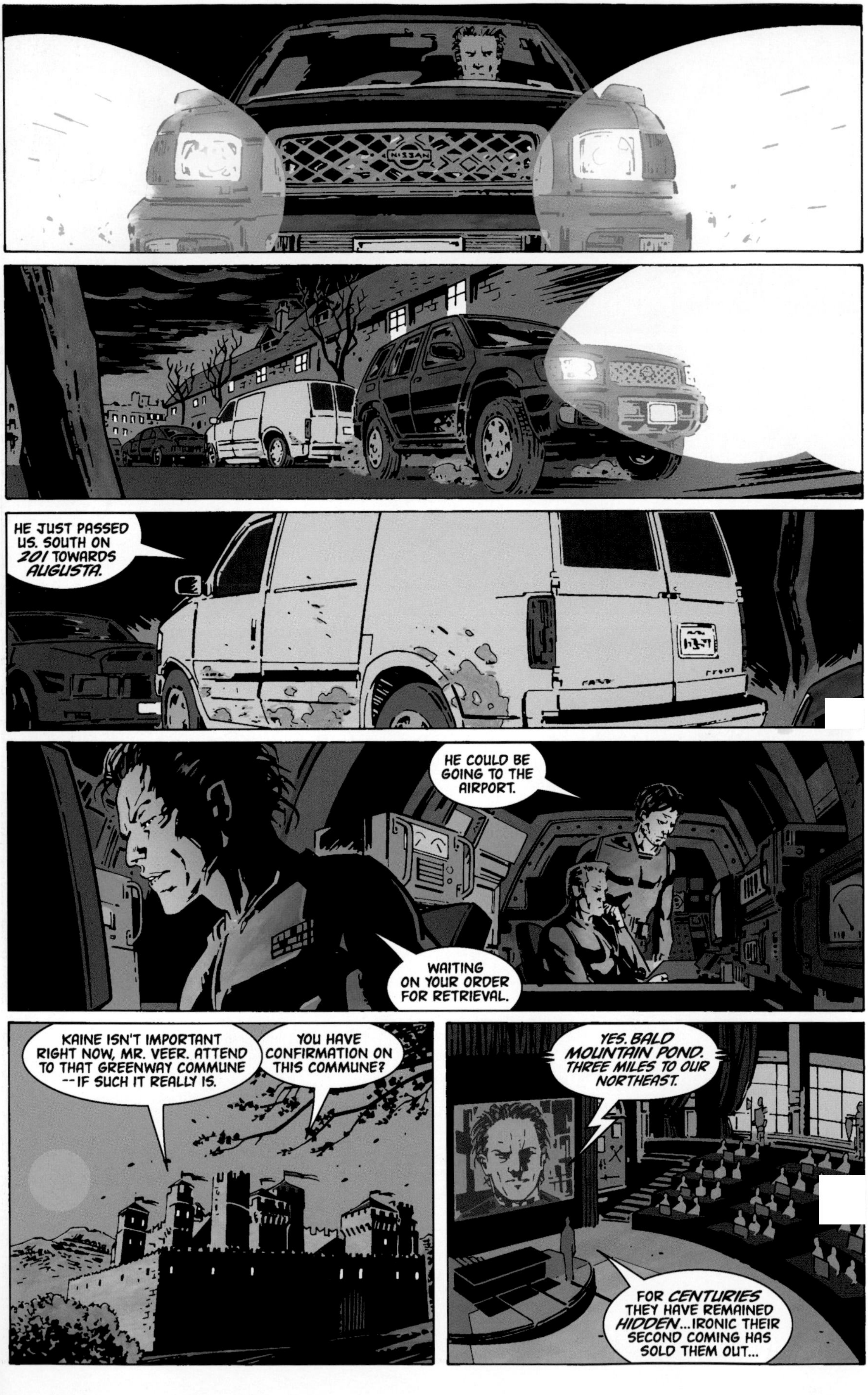
HE JUST PASSED US. SOUTH ON 201 TOWARDS AUGUSTA.
HE COULD BE GOING TO THE AIRPORT.
WAITING ON YOUR ORDER FOR RETRIEVAL.
KAINE ISN'T IMPORTANT RIGHT NOW, MR. VEER. ATTEND TO THAT GREENWAY COMMUNE --IF SUCH IT REALLY IS.
YOU HAVE CONFIRMATION ON THIS COMMUNE?
YES. BALD MOUNTAIN POND. THREE MILES TO OUR NORTHEAST.
FOR CENTURIES THEY HAVE REMAINED HIDDEN...IRONIC THEIR SECOND COMING HAS SOLD THEM OUT...

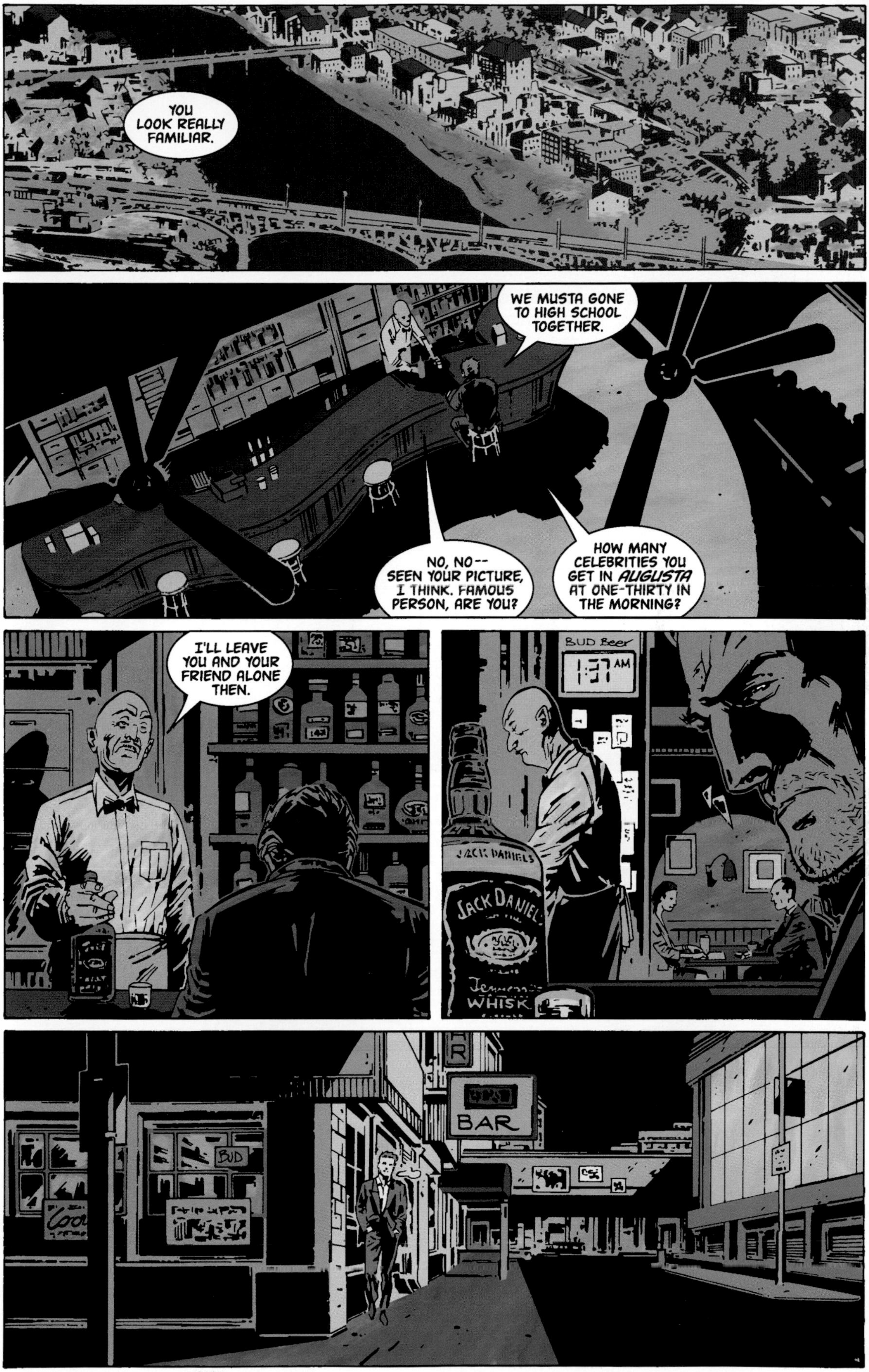
YOU LOOK REALLY FAMILIAR.
WE MUSTA GONE TO HIGH SCHOOL TOGETHER.
NO, NO-- SEEN YOUR PICTURE, I THINK. FAMOUS PERSON, ARE YOU?
HOW MANY CELEBRITIES YOU GET IN AUGUSTA AT ONE-THIRTY IN THE MORNING?
I'LL LEAVE YOU AND YOUR FRIEND ALONE THEN.
BUD Beer
1:37 AM
JACK DANIEL'S
WHISK
BAR
BUD

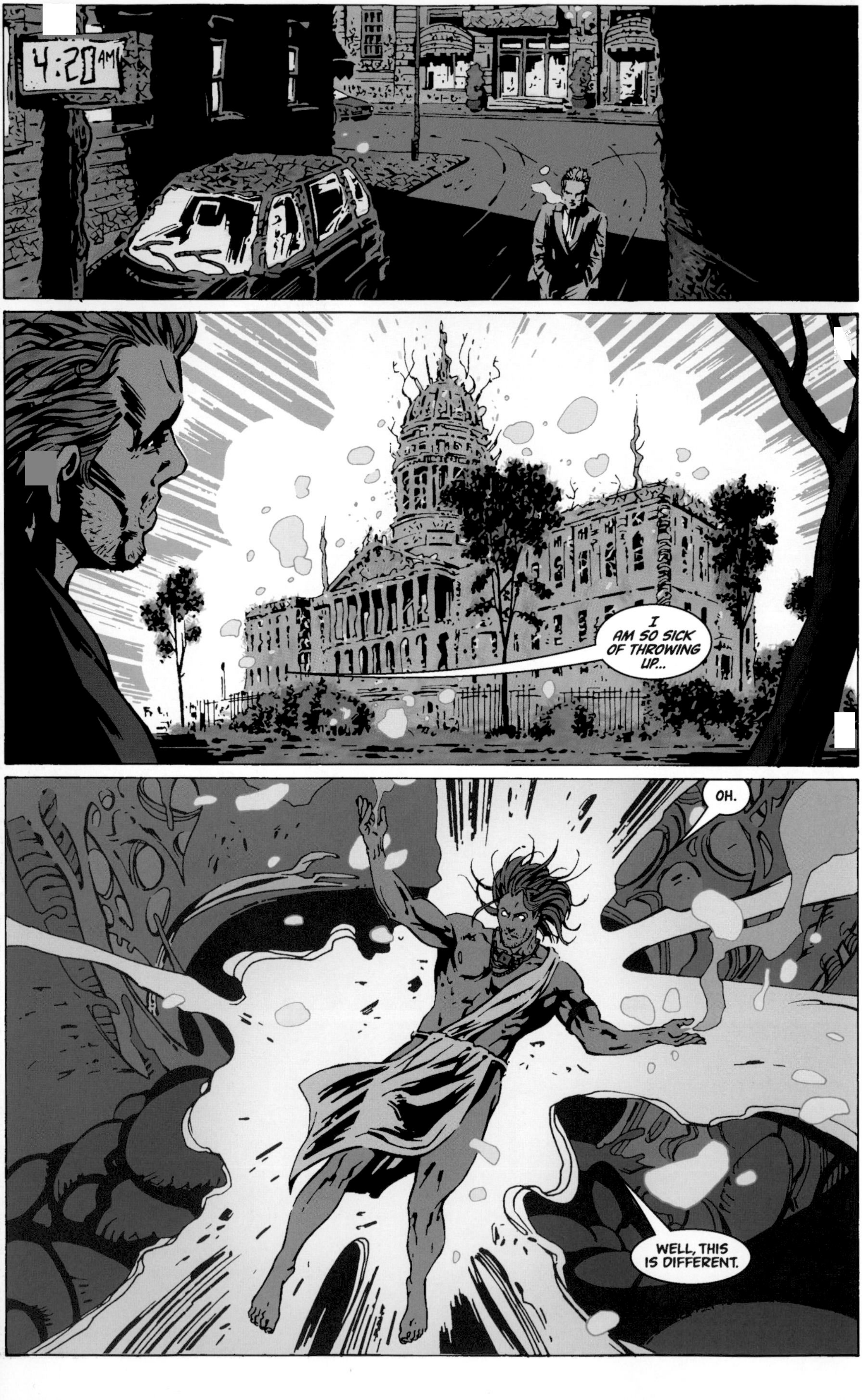
4:20AM
I AM SO SICK OF THROWING UP...
OH.
WELL, THIS IS DIFFERENT.

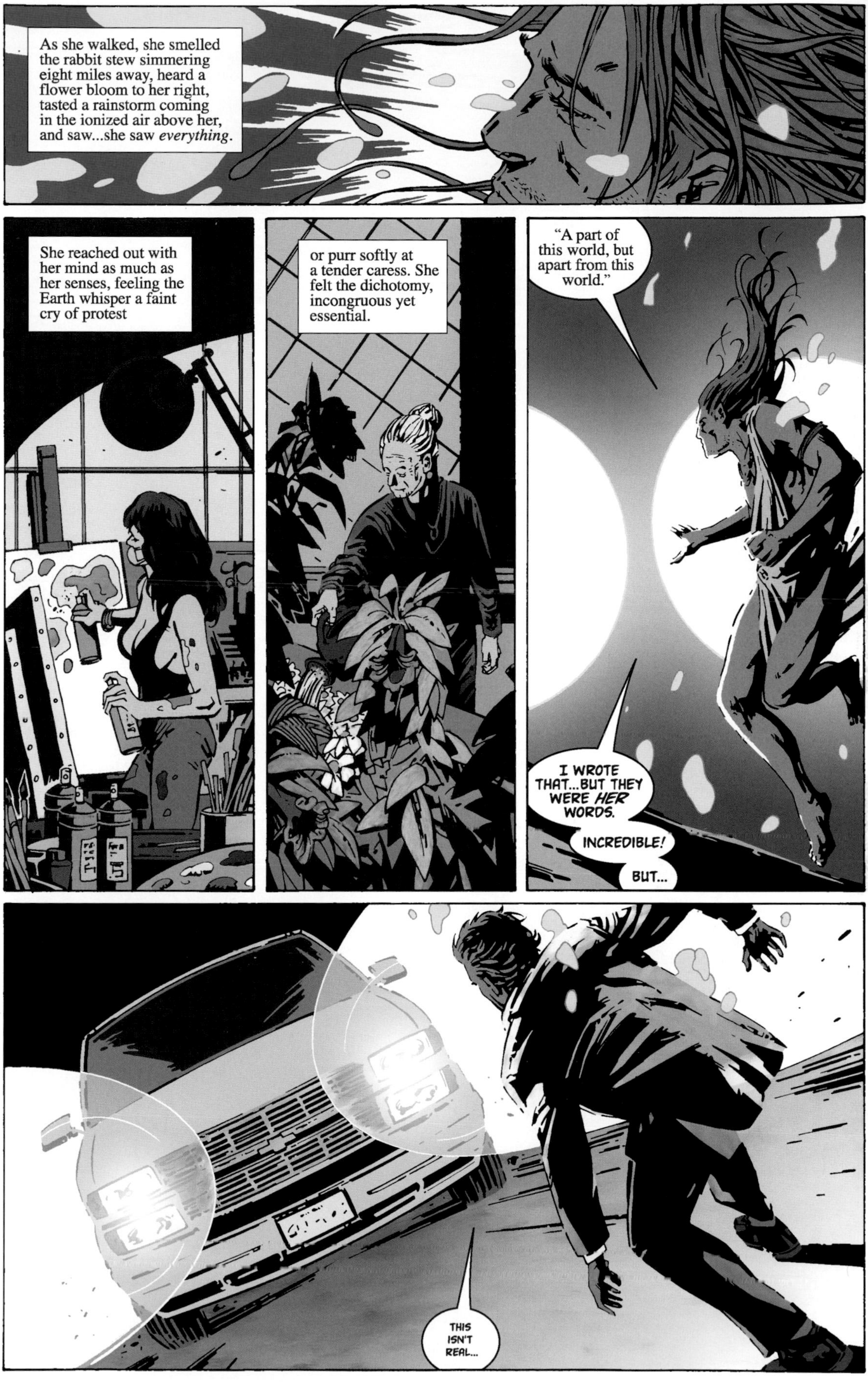
As she walked, she smelled the rabbit stew simmering eight miles away, heard a flower bloom to her right, tasted a rainstorm coming in the ionized air above her, and saw...she saw *everything*.
She reached out with her mind as much as her senses, feeling the Earth whisper a faint cry of protest
or purr softly at a tender caress. She felt the dichotomy, incongruous yet essential.
"A part of this world, but apart from this world."
I WROTE THAT...BUT THEY WERE *HER* WORDS.
INCREDIBLE!
BUT...
THIS ISN'T REAL...

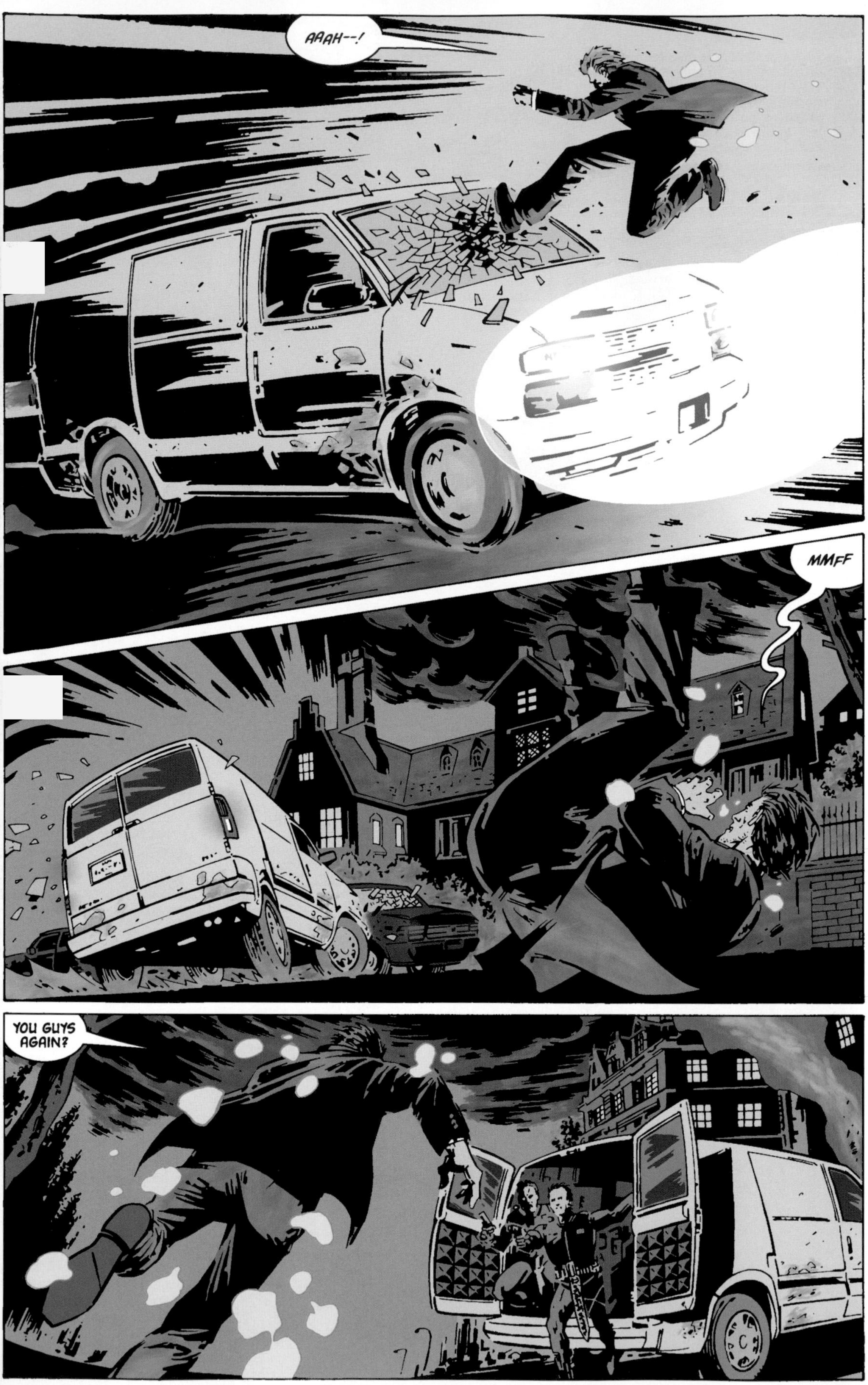
AAAH--!
MMFF
YOU GUYS AGAIN?

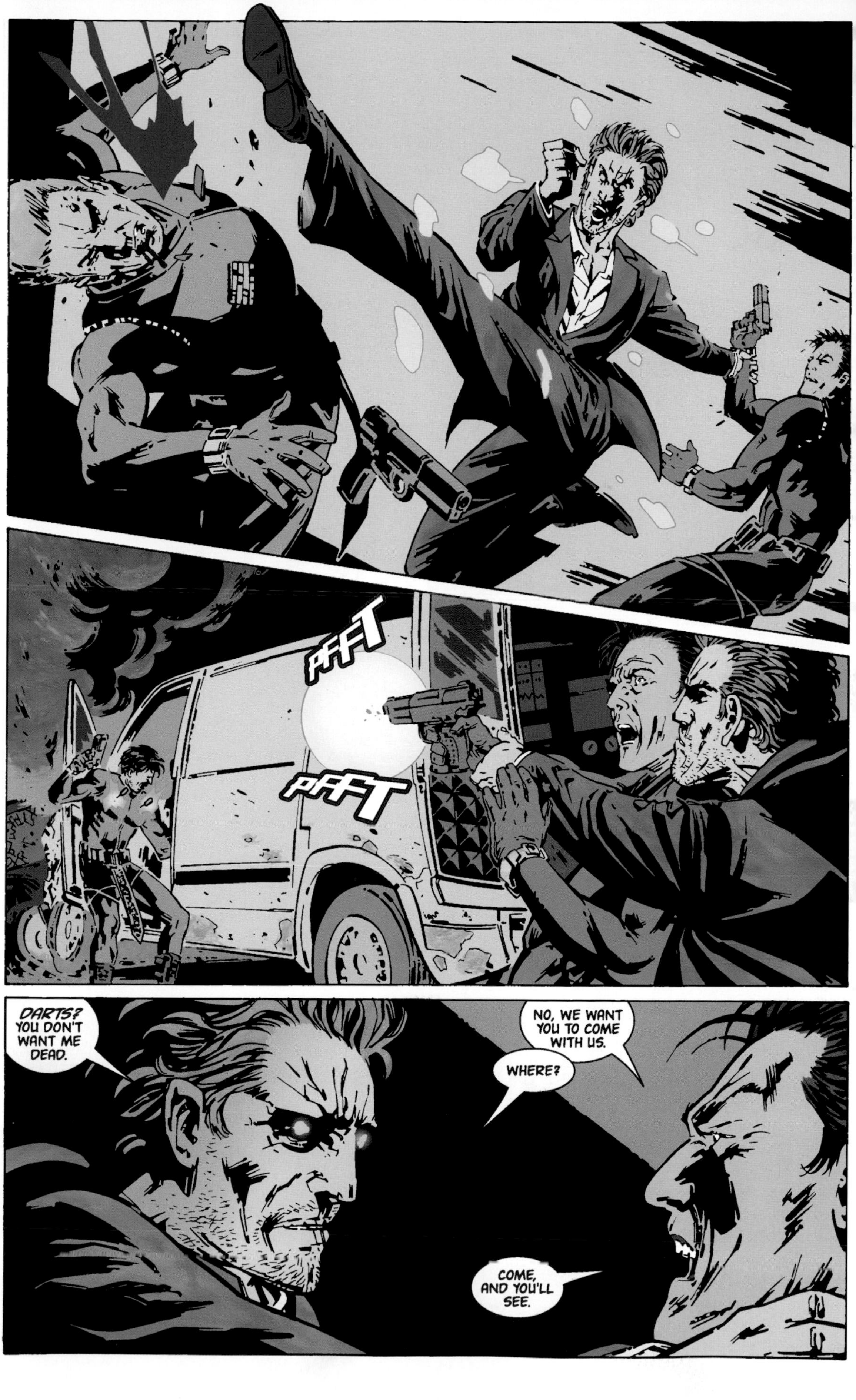

PFFT
PFFT
DARTS? YOU DON'T WANT ME DEAD.
NO, WE WANT YOU TO COME WITH US.
WHERE?
COME, AND YOU'LL SEE.

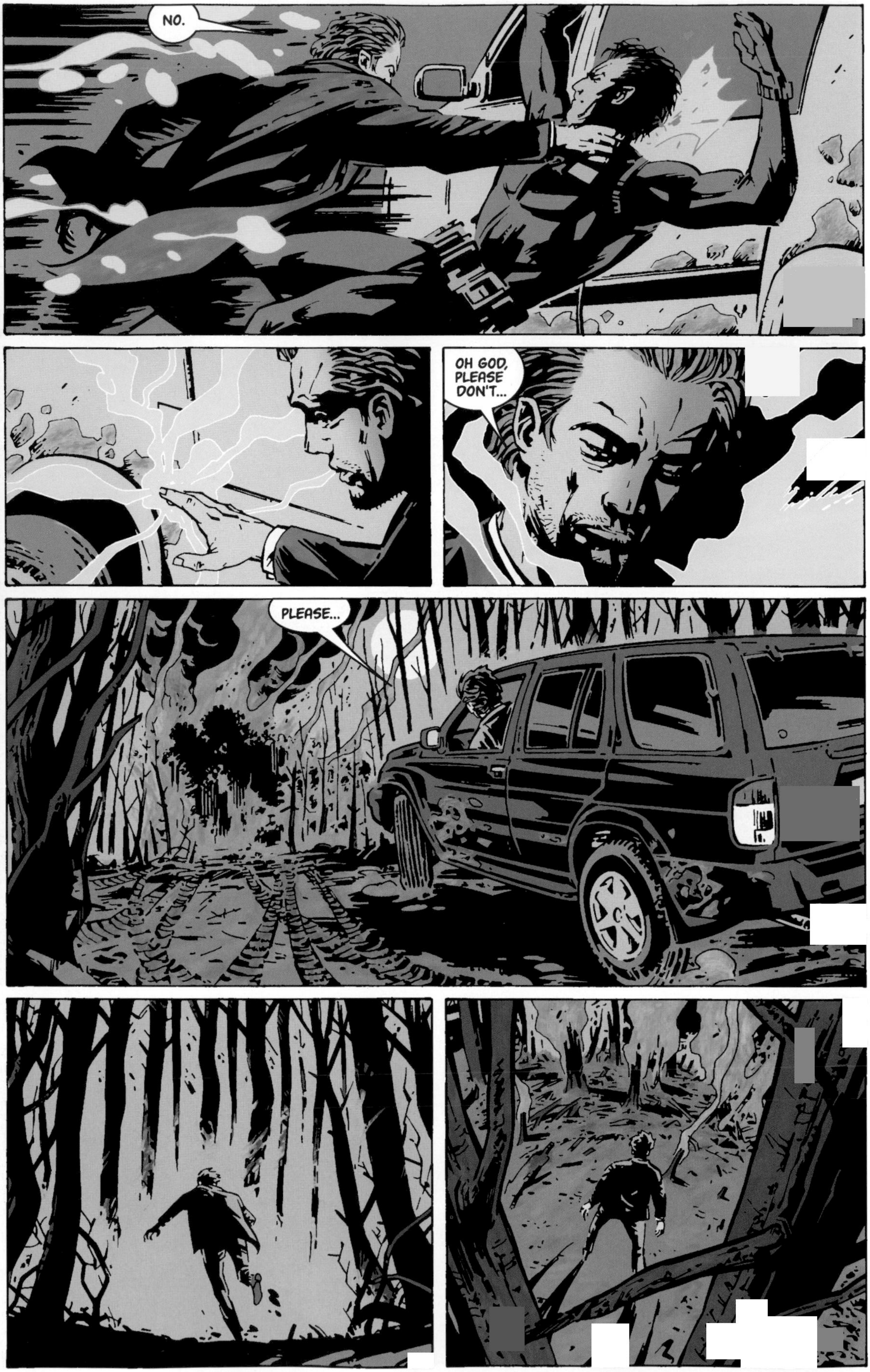
NO.
OH GOD, PLEASE DON'T...
PLEASE...

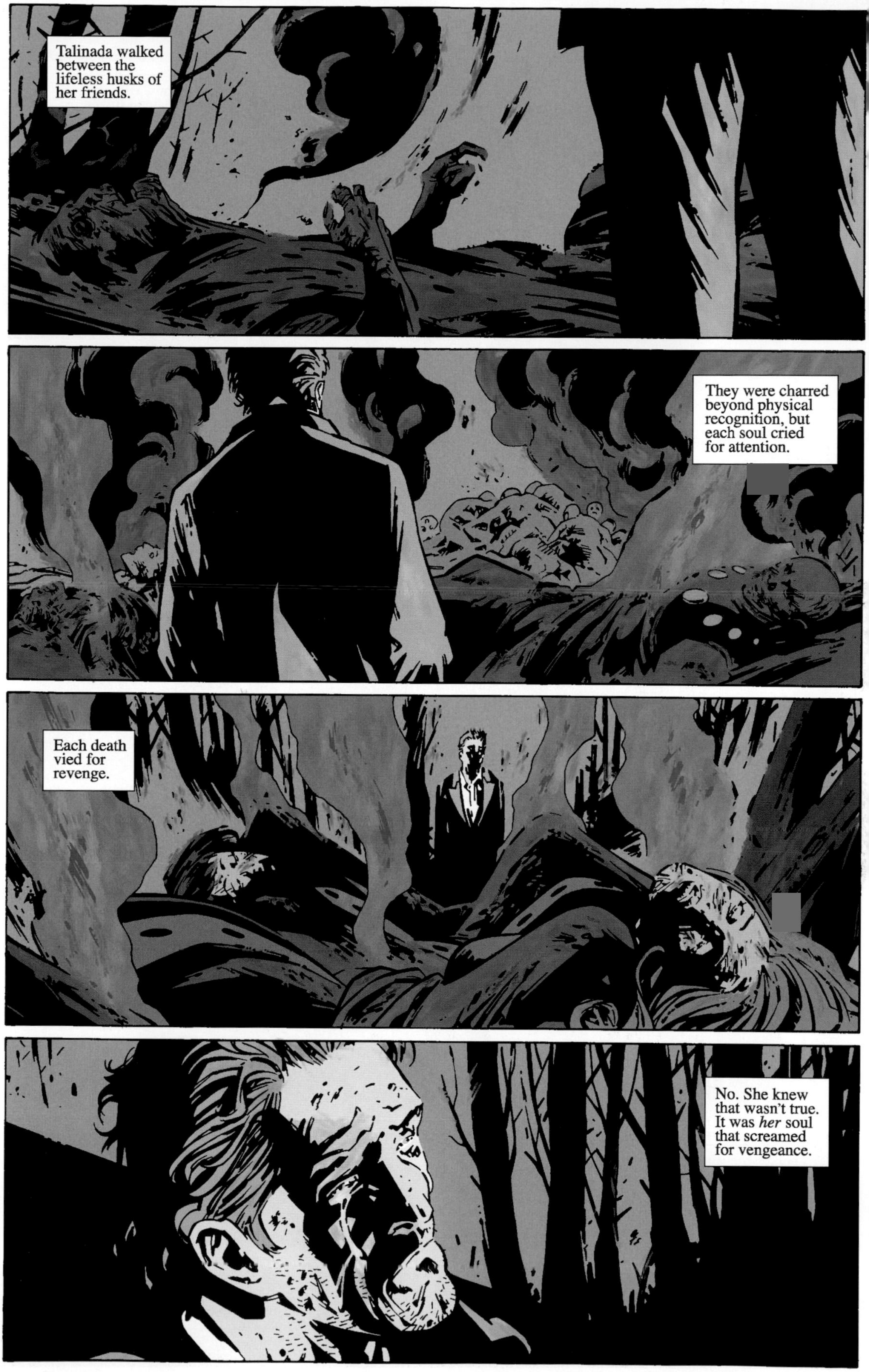
Talinada walked between the lifeless husks of her friends.
They were charred beyond physical recognition, but each soul cried for attention.
Each death vied for revenge.
No. She knew that wasn't true. It was *her* soul that screamed for vengeance.

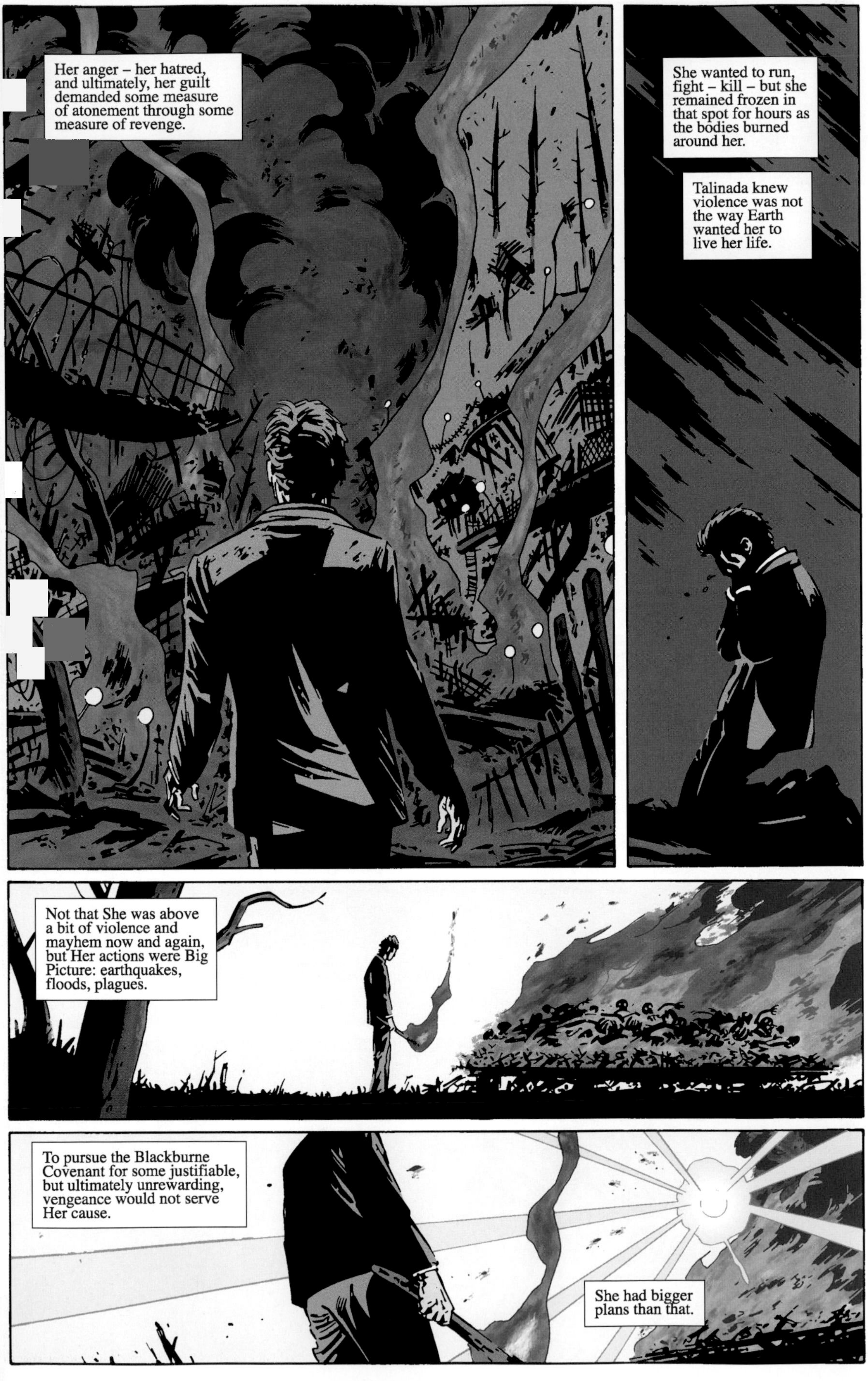
Her anger – her hatred, and ultimately, her guilt demanded some measure of atonement through some measure of revenge.
She wanted to run, fight – kill – but she remained frozen in that spot for hours as the bodies burned around her.
Talinada knew violence was not the way Earth wanted her to live her life.
Not that She was above a bit of violence and mayhem now and again, but Her actions were Big Picture: earthquakes, floods, plagues.
To pursue the Blackburne Covenant for some justifiable, but ultimately unrewarding, vengeance would not serve Her cause.
She had bigger plans than that.

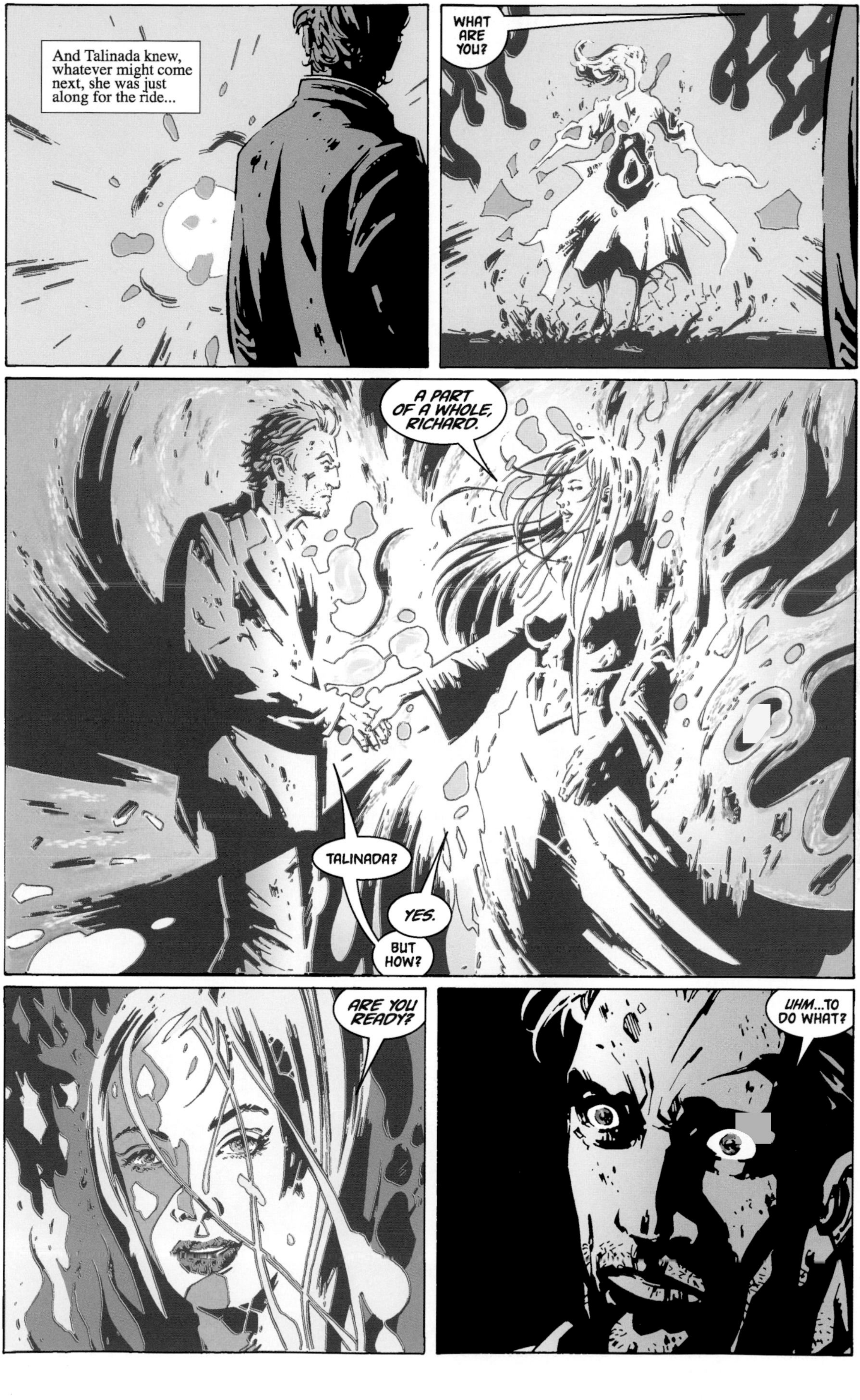
And Talinada knew, whatever might come next, she was just along for the ride...
WHAT ARE YOU?
A PART OF A WHOLE, RICHARD.
TALINADA?
YES.
BUT HOW?
ARE YOU READY?
UHM...TO DO WHAT?

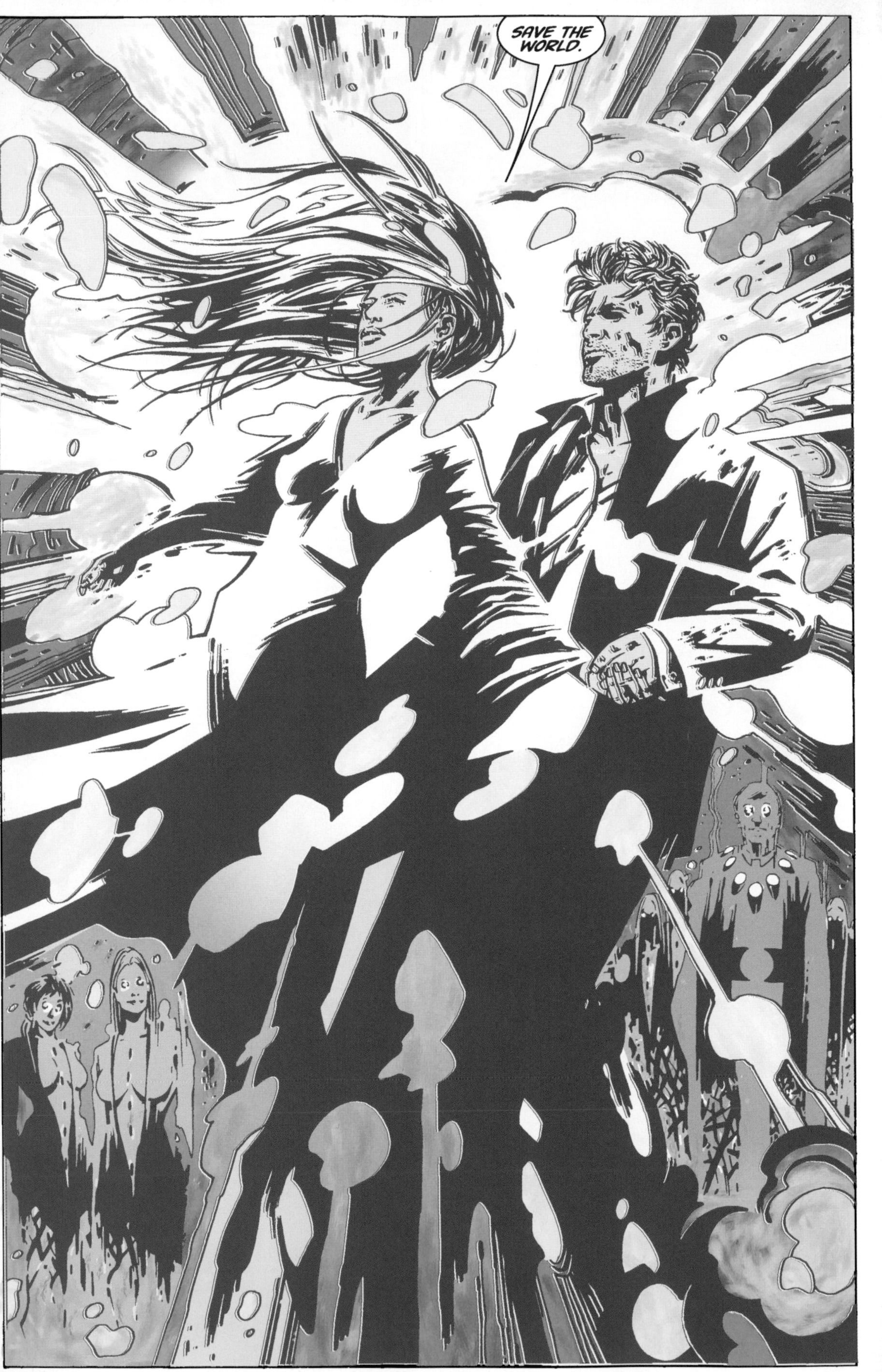
SAVE THE WORLD.

Act Four

SUICIDE–HOMICIDE–PESTICIDE

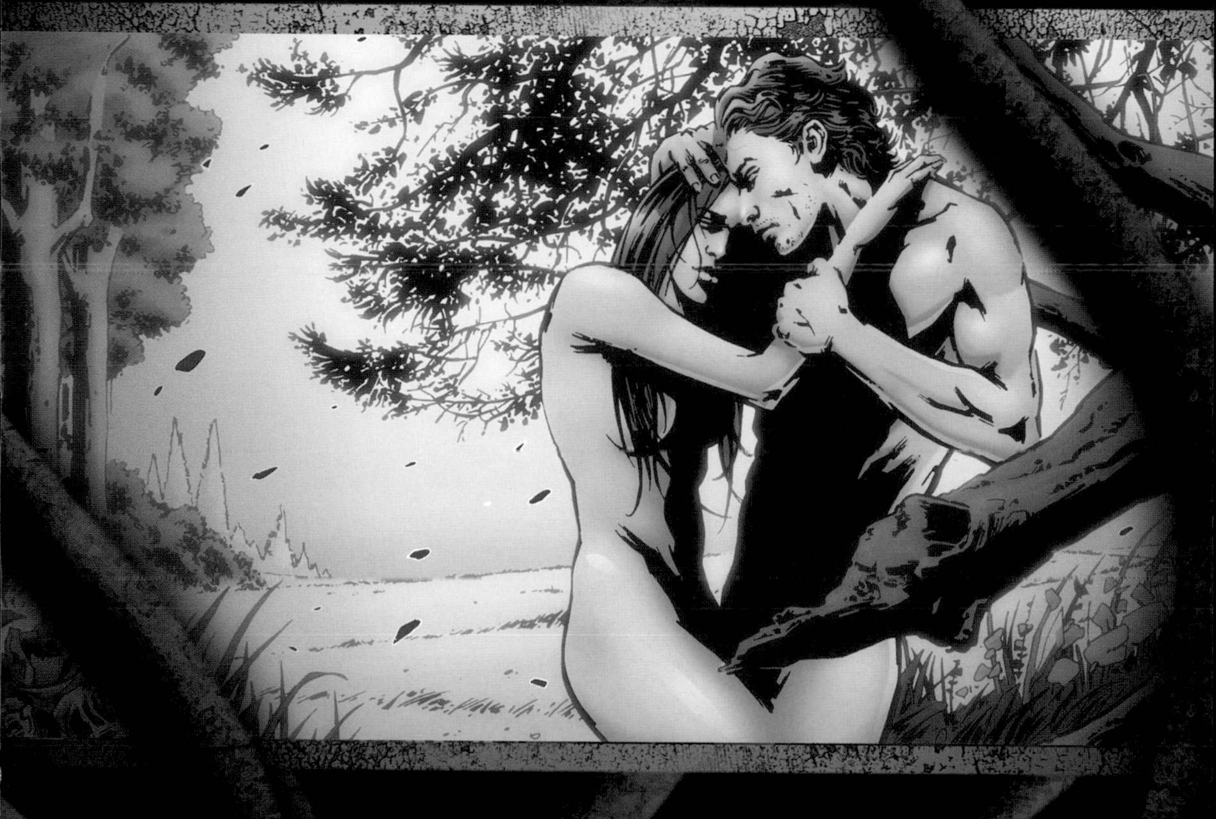

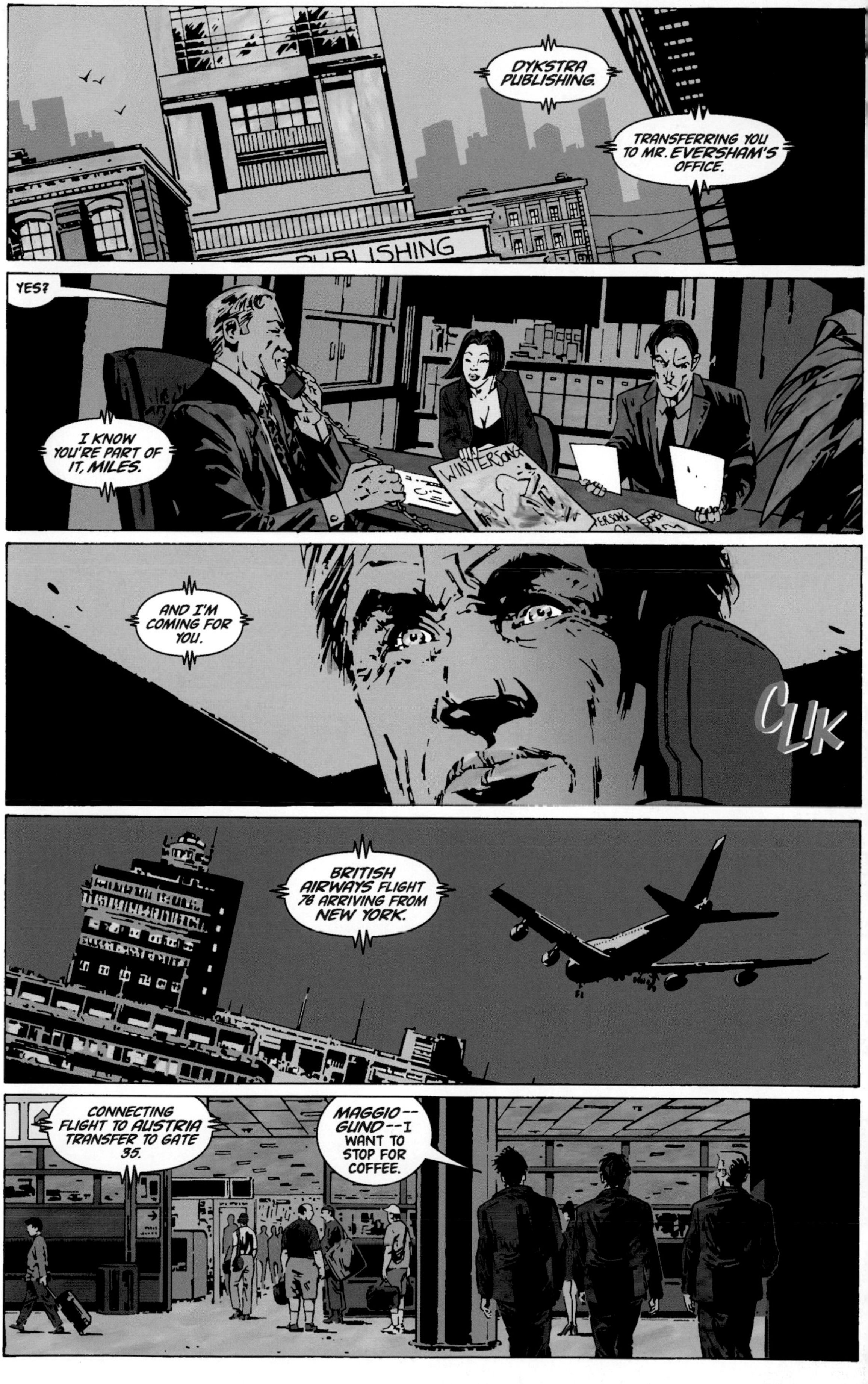
DYKSTRA PUBLISHING.
TRANSFERRING YOU TO MR. EVERSHAM'S OFFICE.
PUBLISHING
YES?
I KNOW YOU'RE PART OF IT, MILES.
WINTERSONG
AND I'M COMING FOR YOU.
CLIK
BRITISH AIRWAYS FLIGHT 76 ARRIVING FROM NEW YORK.
CONNECTING FLIGHT TO AUSTRIA TRANSFER TO GATE 35.
MAGGIO-- GUND--I WANT TO STOP FOR COFFEE.

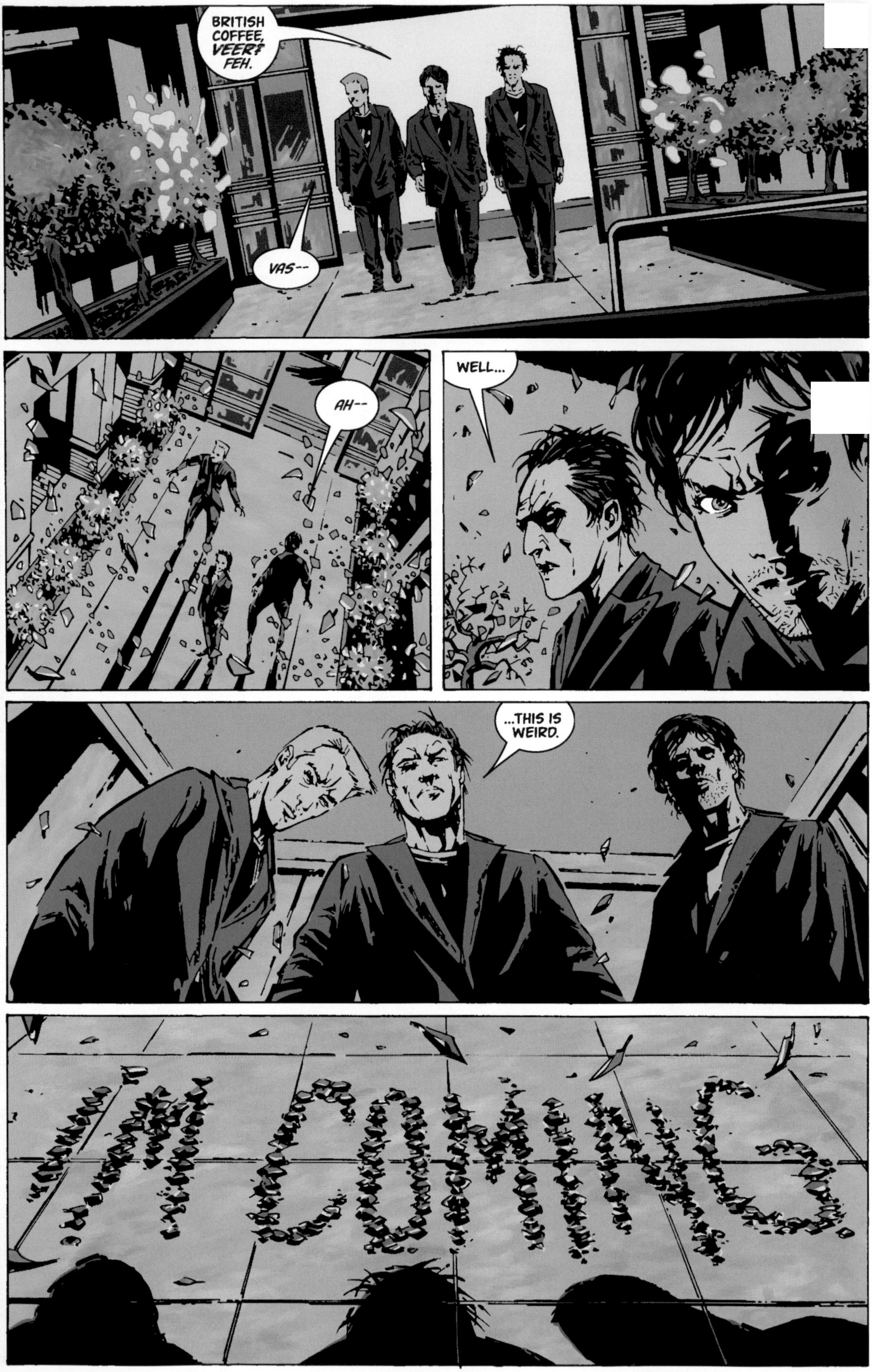
BRITISH COFFEE, VEER? FEH.
VAS--
AH--
WELL...
...THIS IS WEIRD.
I'M COMING

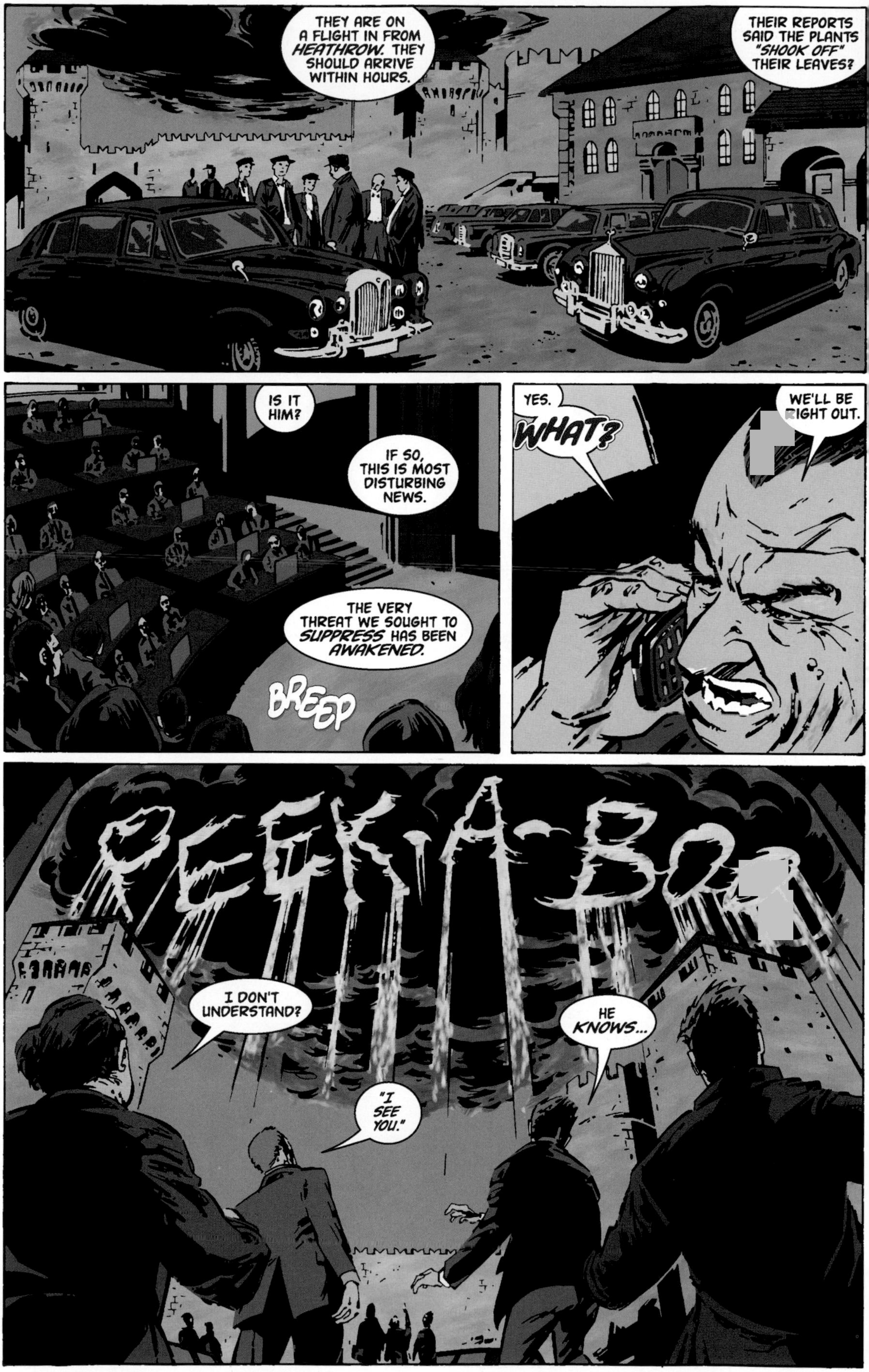
THEY ARE ON A FLIGHT IN FROM *HEATHROW.* THEY SHOULD ARRIVE WITHIN HOURS.
THEIR REPORTS SAID THE PLANTS *"SHOOK OFF"* THEIR LEAVES?
IS IT HIM?
IF SO, THIS IS MOST DISTURBING NEWS.
THE VERY THREAT WE SOUGHT TO *SUPPRESS* HAS BEEN *AWAKENED.*
BREEP
YES.
WHAT?
WE'LL BE RIGHT OUT.
PEEK-A-BO
I DON'T UNDERSTAND?
HE *KNOWS...*
"I SEE YOU."

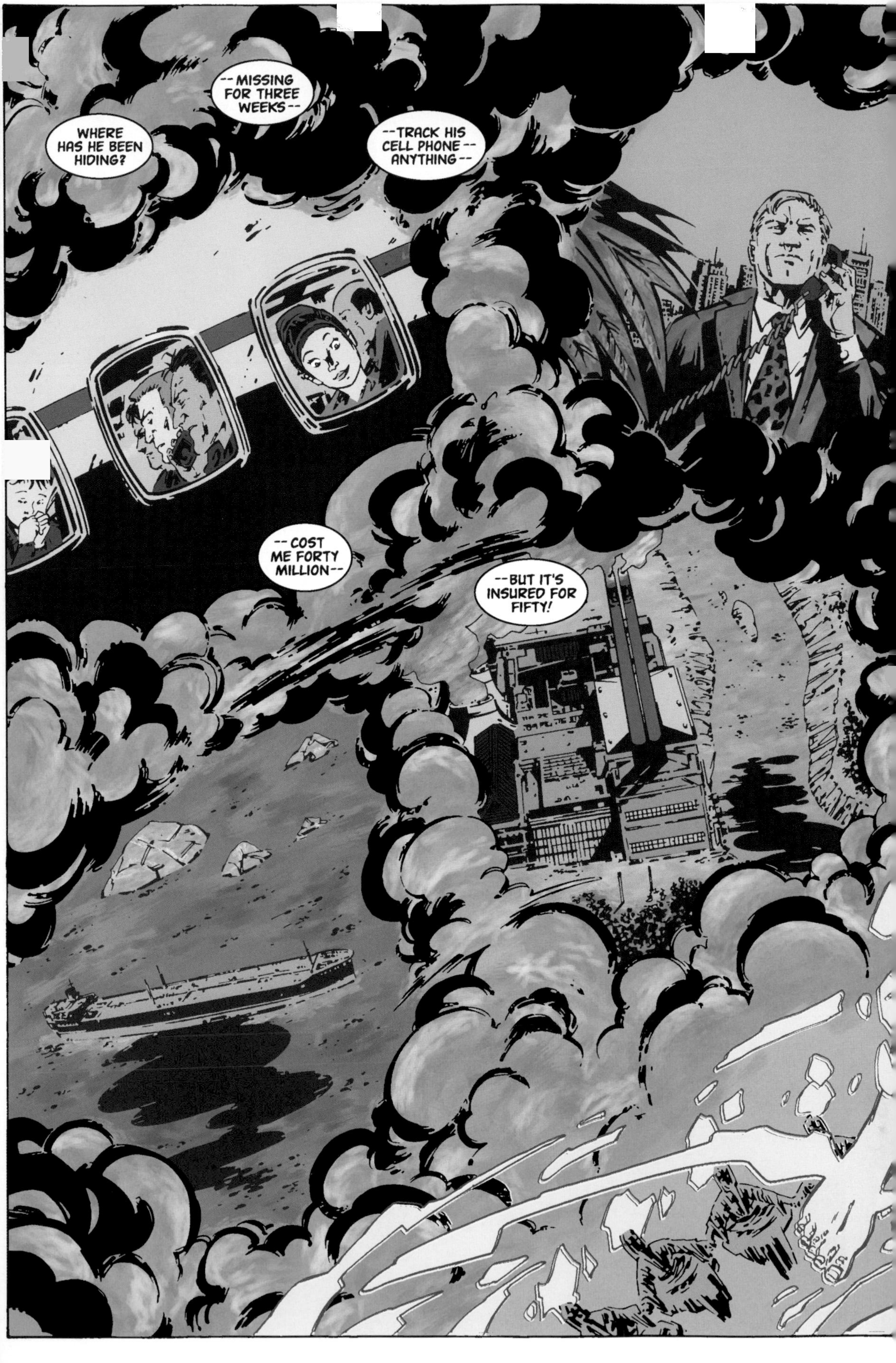
WHERE HAS HE BEEN HIDING?
--MISSING FOR THREE WEEKS--
--TRACK HIS CELL PHONE-- ANYTHING--
--COST ME FORTY MILLION--
--BUT IT'S INSURED FOR FIFTY!

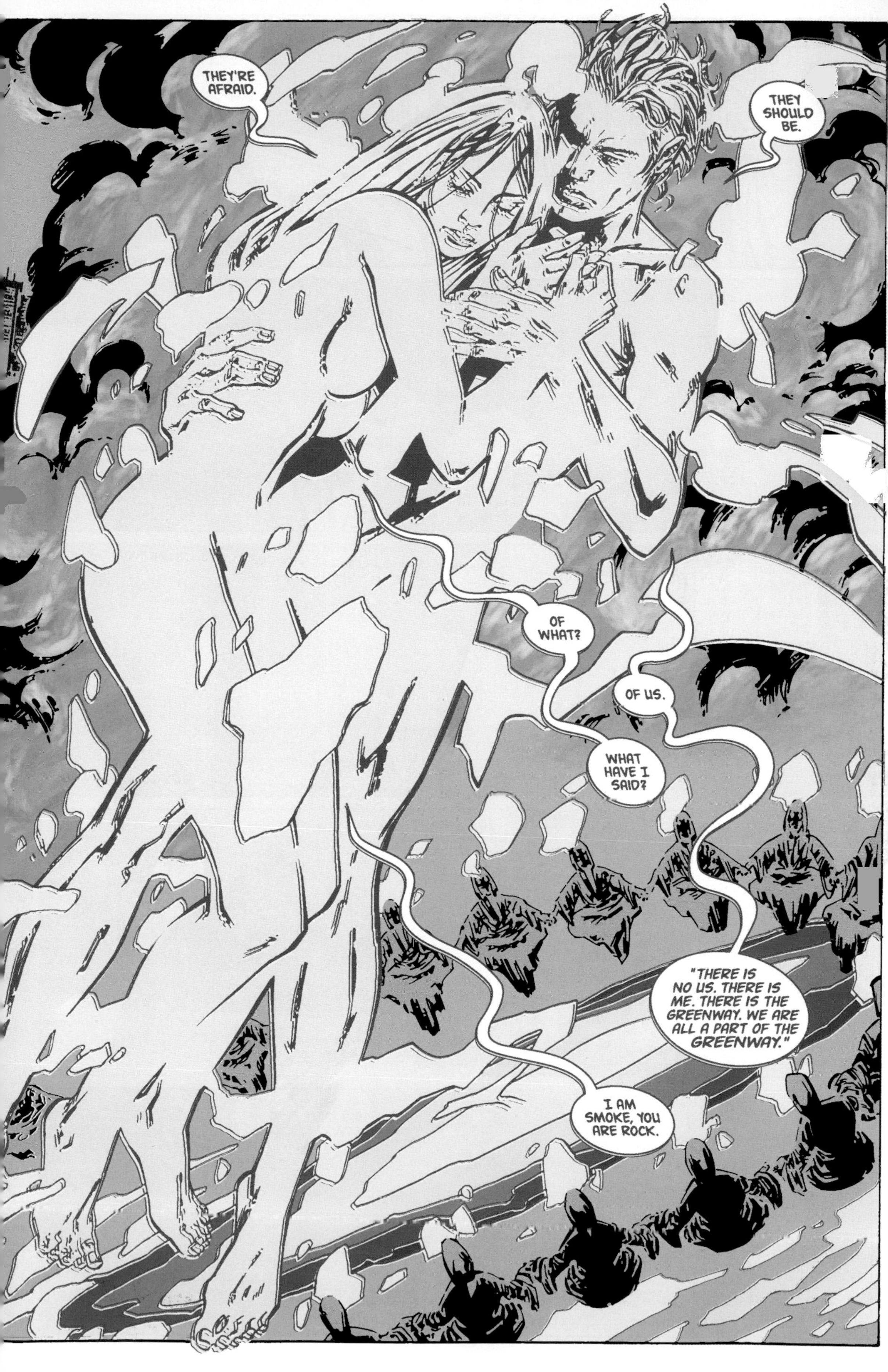
THEY'RE AFRAID.
THEY SHOULD BE.
OF WHAT?
OF US.
WHAT HAVE I SAID?
"THERE IS NO US. THERE IS ME. THERE IS THE GREENWAY. WE ARE ALL A PART OF THE GREENWAY."
I AM SMOKE, YOU ARE ROCK.

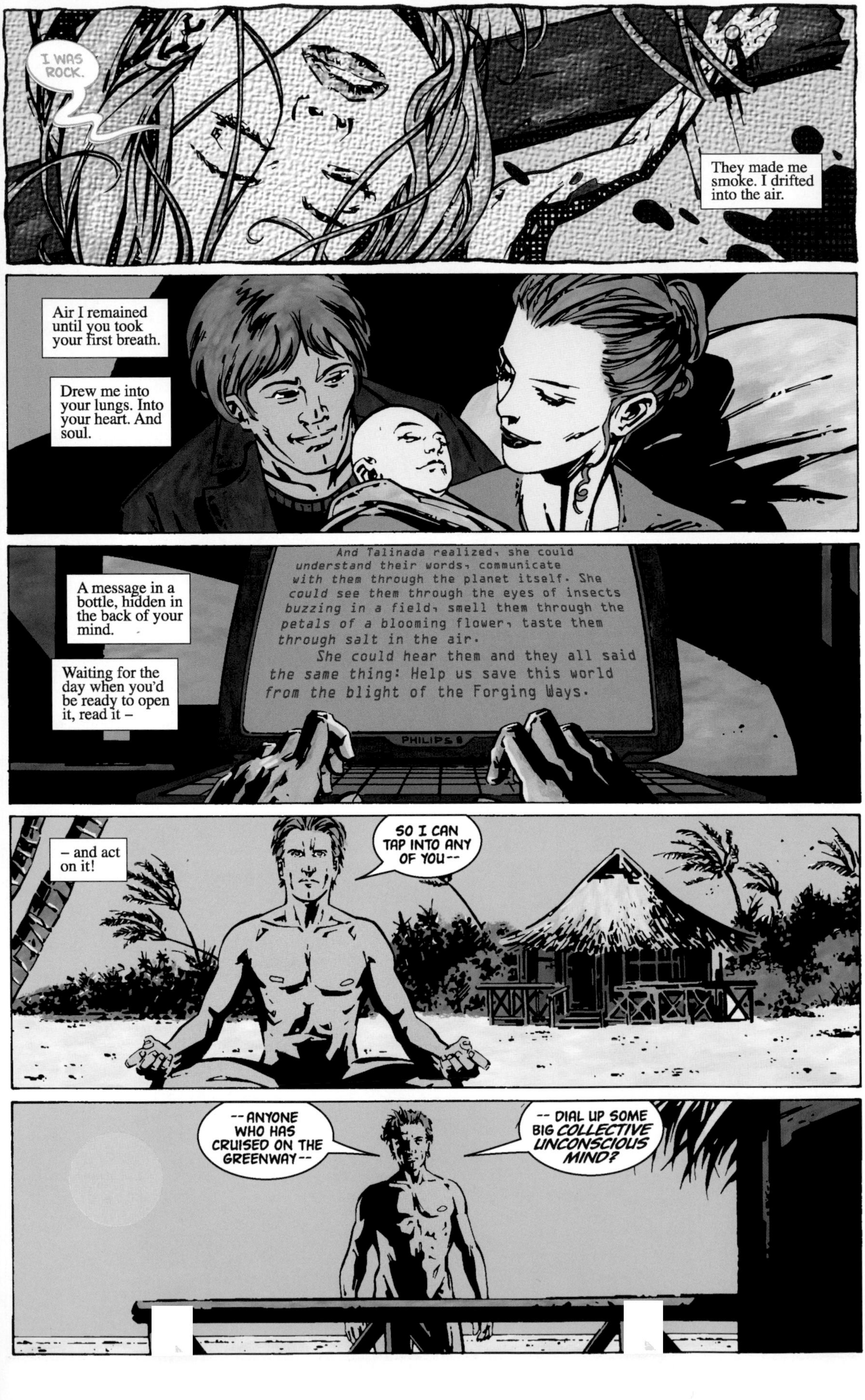
I WAS ROCK.
They made me smoke. I drifted into the air.
Air I remained until you took your first breath.
Drew me into your lungs. Into your heart. And soul.
A message in a bottle, hidden in the back of your mind.
Waiting for the day when you'd be ready to open it, read it –
And Talinada realized, she could understand their words, communicate with them through the planet itself. She could see them through the eyes of insects buzzing in a field, smell them through the petals of a blooming flower, taste them through salt in the air.
She could hear them and they all said the same thing: Help us save this world from the blight of the Forging Ways.
PHILIPS
– and act on it!
SO I CAN TAP INTO ANY OF YOU--
--ANYONE WHO HAS CRUISED ON THE GREENWAY--
-- DIAL UP SOME BIG COLLECTIVE UNCONSCIOUS MIND?

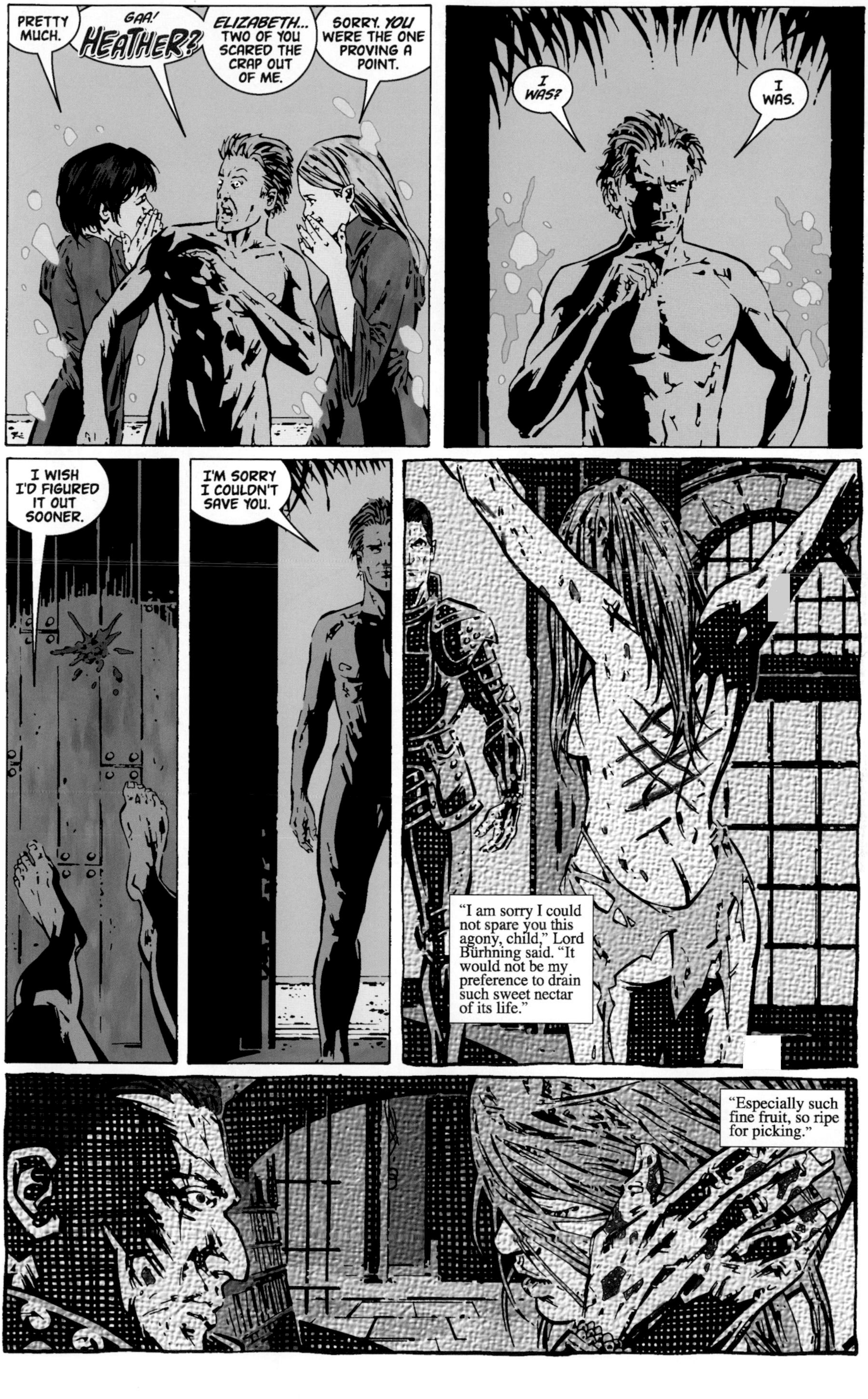
PRETTY MUCH.
GAA! HEATHER?
ELIZABETH... TWO OF YOU SCARED THE CRAP OUT OF ME.
SORRY. YOU WERE THE ONE PROVING A POINT.
I WAS?
I WAS.
I WISH I'D FIGURED IT OUT SOONER.
I'M SORRY I COULDN'T SAVE YOU.
"I am sorry I could not spare you this agony, child," Lord Bürhning said. "It would not be my preference to drain such sweet nectar of its life."
"Especially such fine fruit, so ripe for picking."

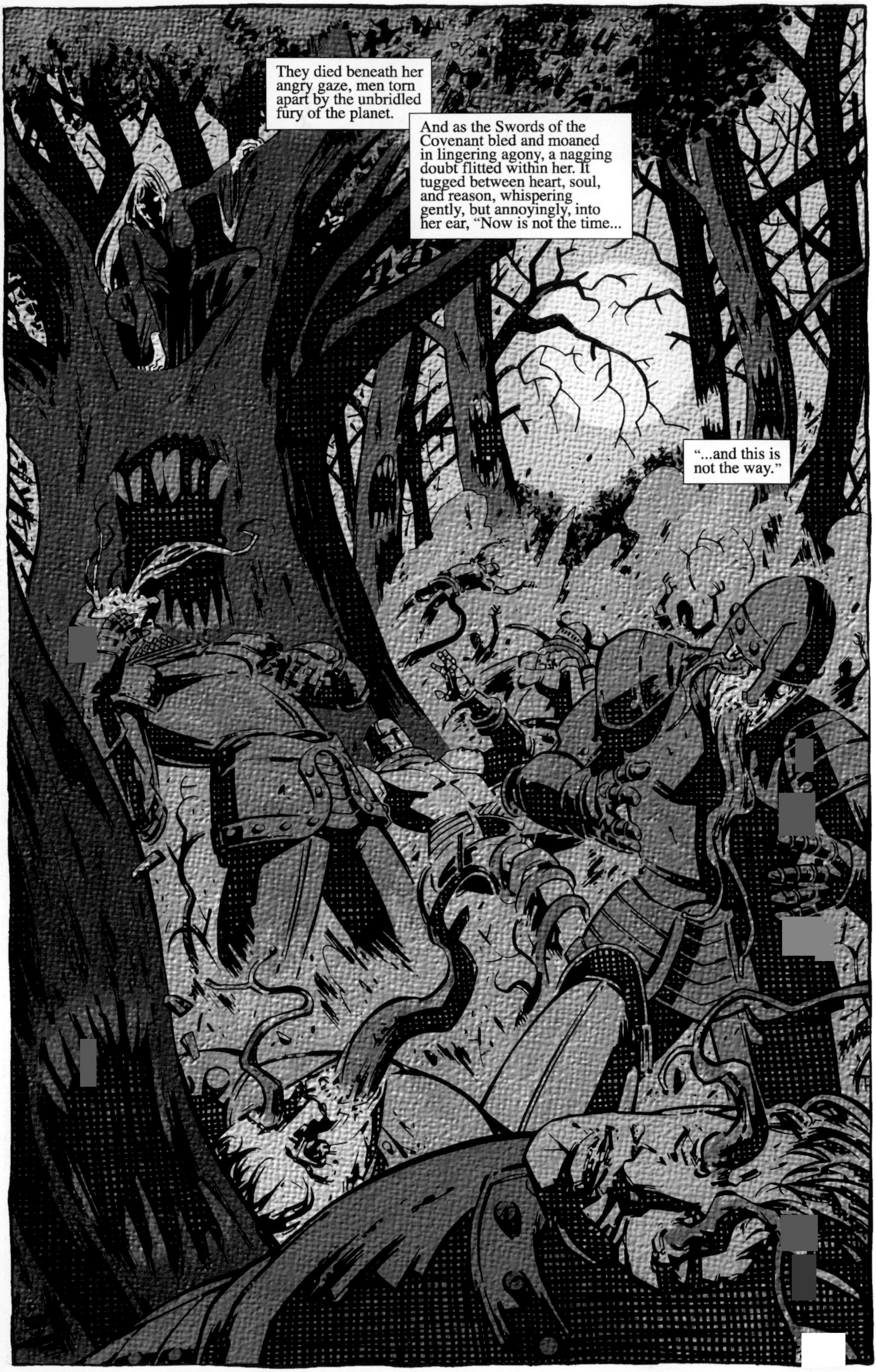
They died beneath her angry gaze, men torn apart by the unbridled fury of the planet.
And as the Swords of the Covenant bled and moaned in lingering agony, a nagging doubt flitted within her. It tugged between heart, soul, and reason, whispering gently, but annoyingly, into her ear, "Now is not the time...
"...and this is not the way."

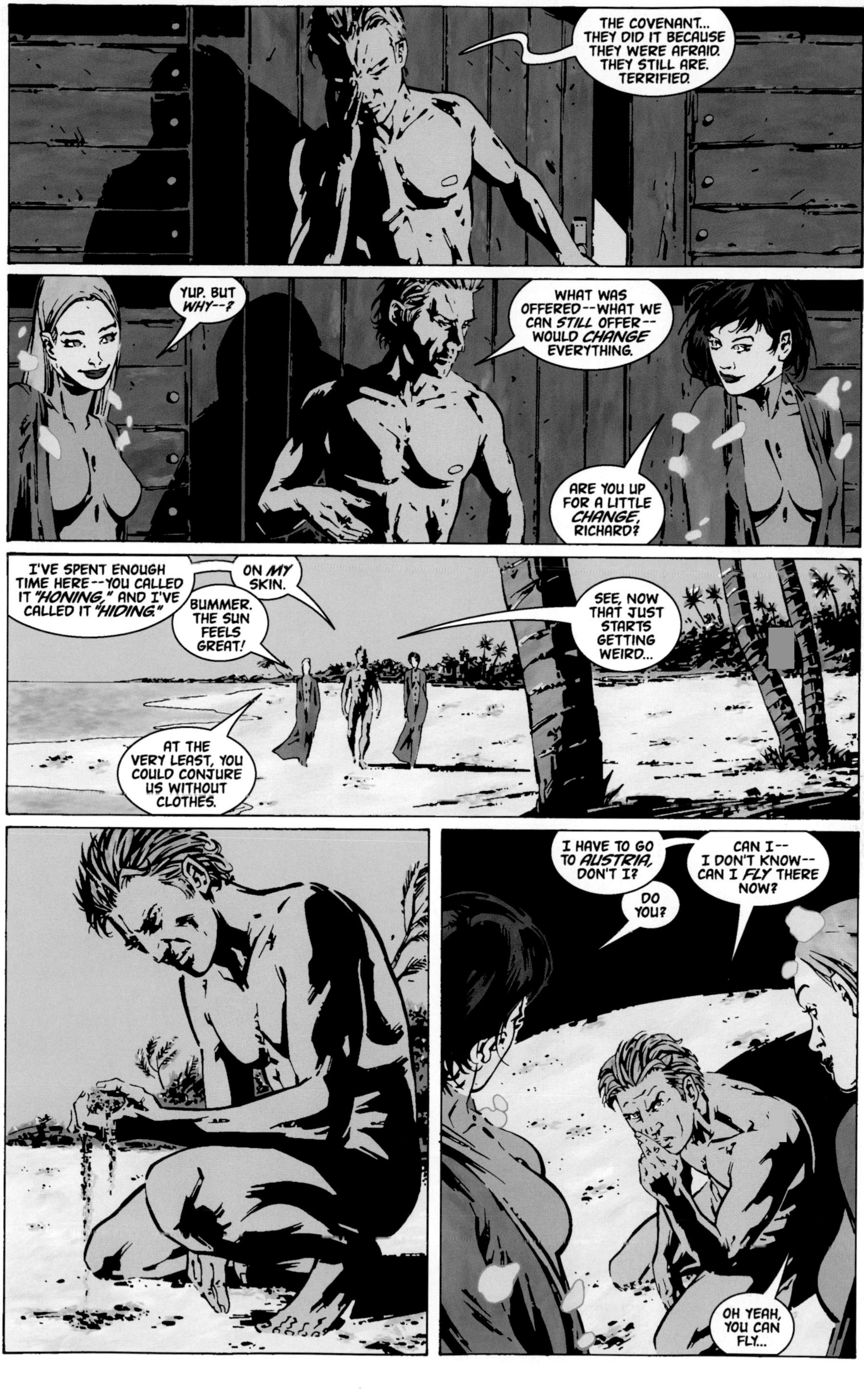
THE COVENANT... THEY DID IT BECAUSE THEY WERE AFRAID. THEY STILL ARE. TERRIFIED.
YUP. BUT WHY--?
WHAT WAS OFFERED--WHAT WE CAN STILL OFFER--WOULD CHANGE EVERYTHING.
ARE YOU UP FOR A LITTLE CHANGE, RICHARD?
I'VE SPENT ENOUGH TIME HERE--YOU CALLED IT "HONING," AND I'VE CALLED IT "HIDING."
BUMMER. THE SUN FEELS GREAT!
ON MY SKIN.
SEE, NOW THAT JUST STARTS GETTING WEIRD...
AT THE VERY LEAST, YOU COULD CONJURE US WITHOUT CLOTHES.
I HAVE TO GO TO AUSTRIA, DON'T I?
DO YOU?
CAN I-- I DON'T KNOW-- CAN I FLY THERE NOW?
OH YEAH, YOU CAN FLY...

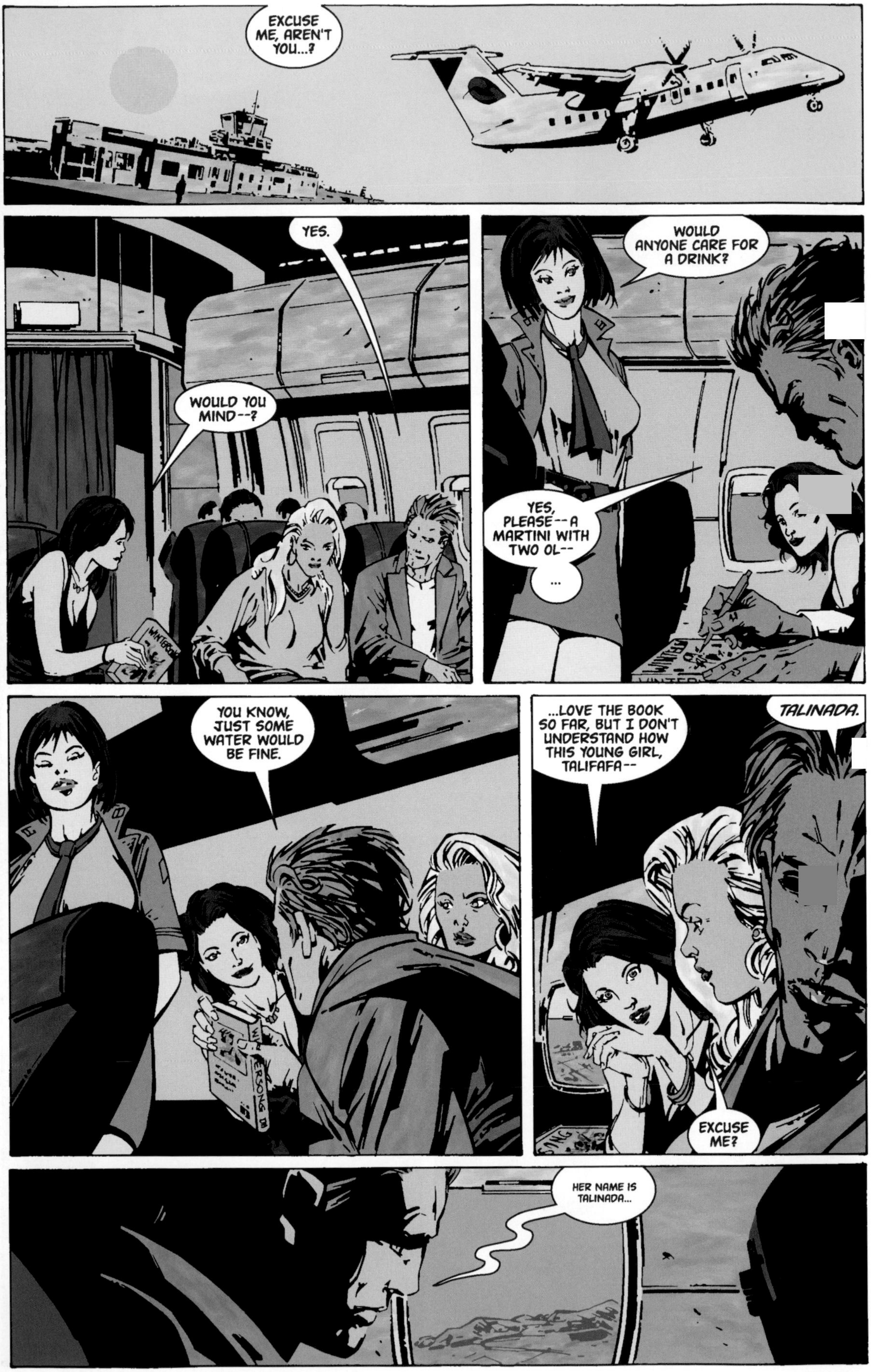
EXCUSE ME, AREN'T YOU...?
YES.
WOULD YOU MIND--?
WOULD ANYONE CARE FOR A DRINK?
YES, PLEASE--A MARTINI WITH TWO OL--
...
YOU KNOW, JUST SOME WATER WOULD BE FINE.
...LOVE THE BOOK SO FAR, BUT I DON'T UNDERSTAND HOW THIS YOUNG GIRL, TALIFAFA--
TALINADA.
EXCUSE ME?
HER NAME IS TALINADA...

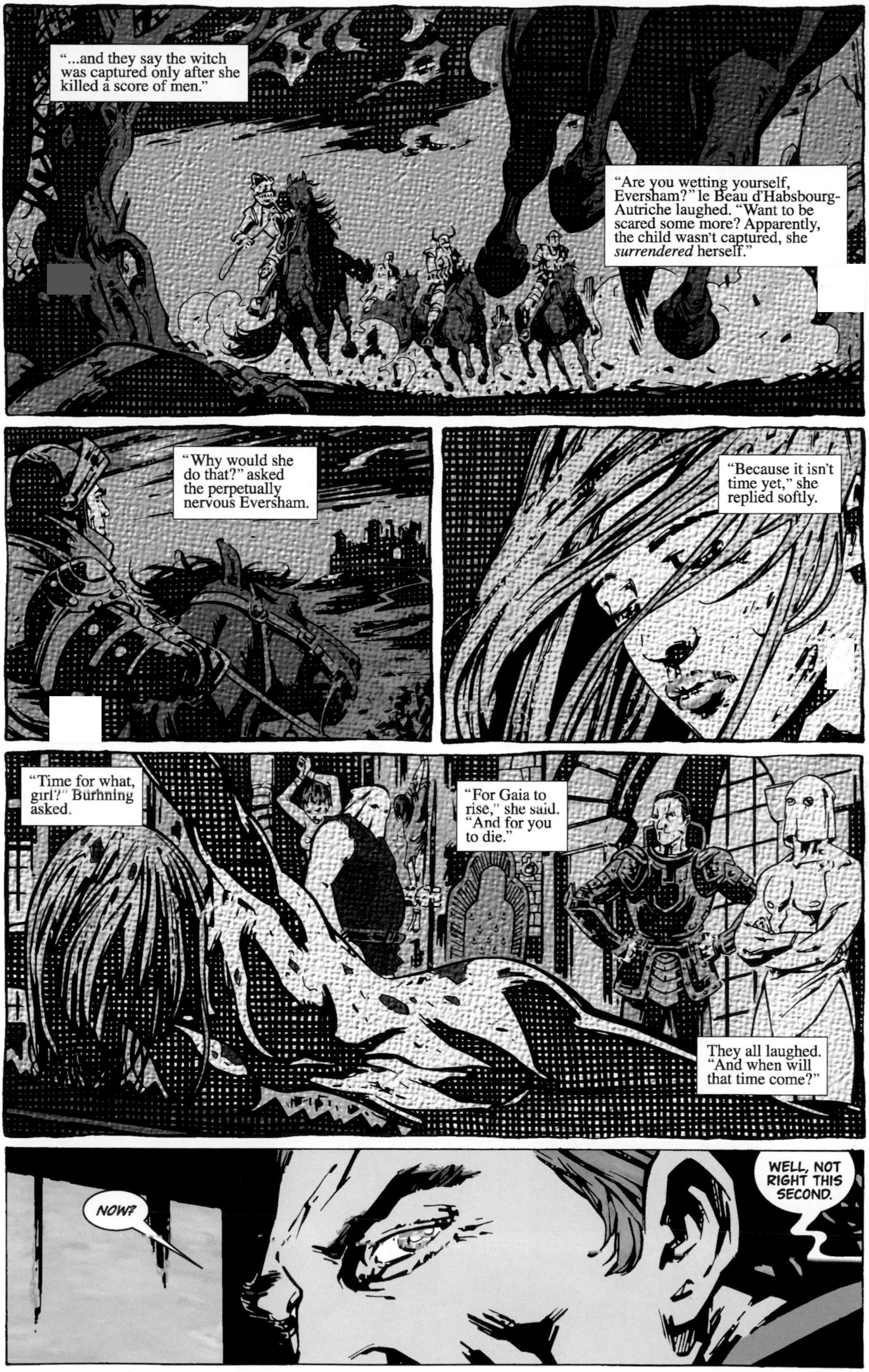
"...and they say the witch was captured only after she killed a score of men."
"Are you wetting yourself, Eversham?" le Beau d'Habsbourg-Autriche laughed. "Want to be scared some more? Apparently, the child wasn't captured, she *surrendered* herself."
"Why would she do that?" asked the perpetually nervous Eversham.
"Because it isn't time yet," she replied softly.
"Time for what, girl?" Burhning asked.
"For Gaia to rise," she said. "And for you to die."
They all laughed. "And when will that time come?"
NOW?
WELL, NOT RIGHT THIS SECOND.

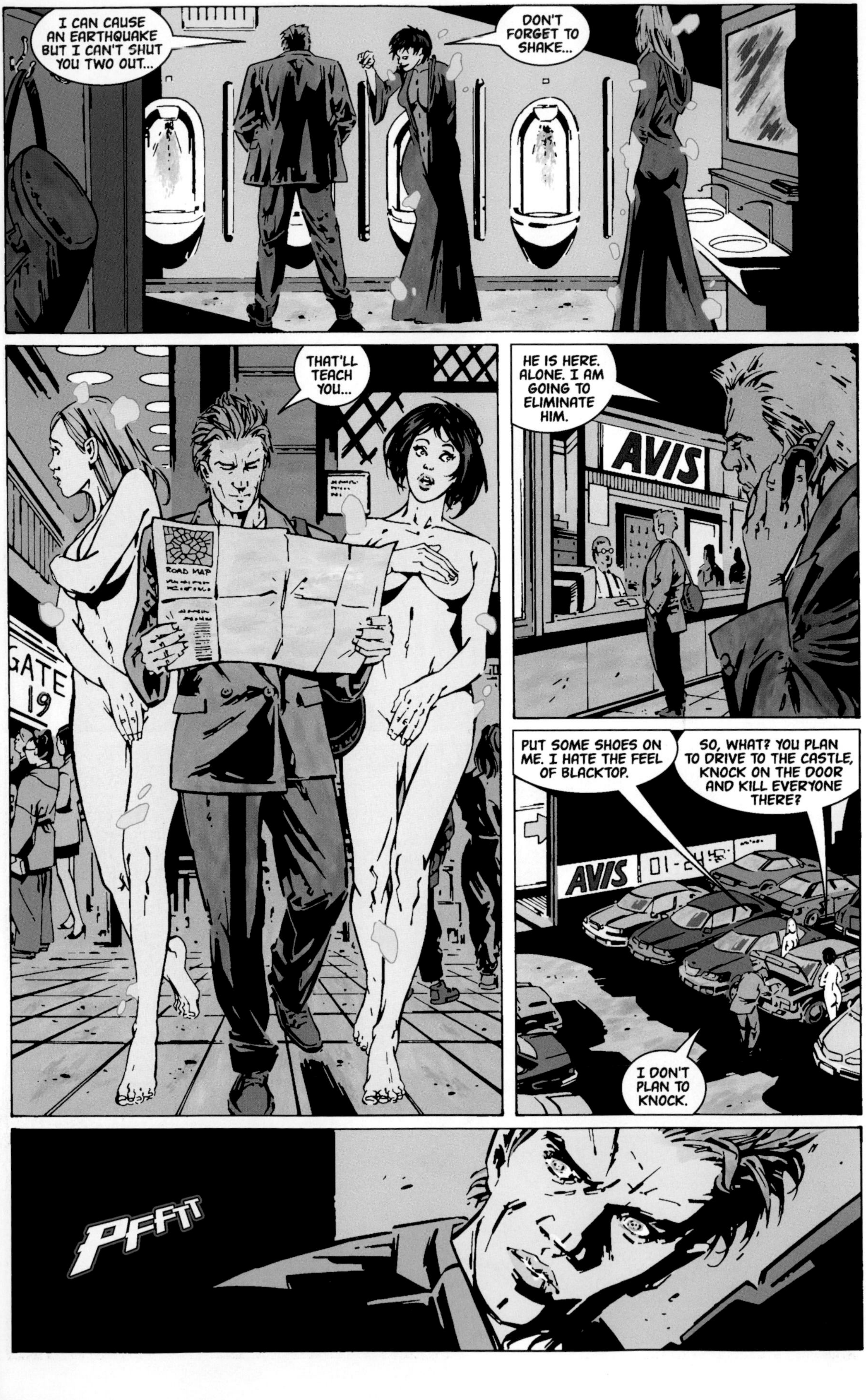
I CAN CAUSE AN EARTHQUAKE BUT I CAN'T SHUT YOU TWO OUT...
DON'T FORGET TO SHAKE...
THAT'LL TEACH YOU...
ROAD MAP
GATE 19
HE IS HERE. ALONE. I AM GOING TO ELIMINATE HIM.
AVIS
PUT SOME SHOES ON ME. I HATE THE FEEL OF BLACKTOP.
SO, WHAT? YOU PLAN TO DRIVE TO THE CASTLE, KNOCK ON THE DOOR AND KILL EVERYONE THERE?
AVIS
I DON'T PLAN TO KNOCK.
PFFTT

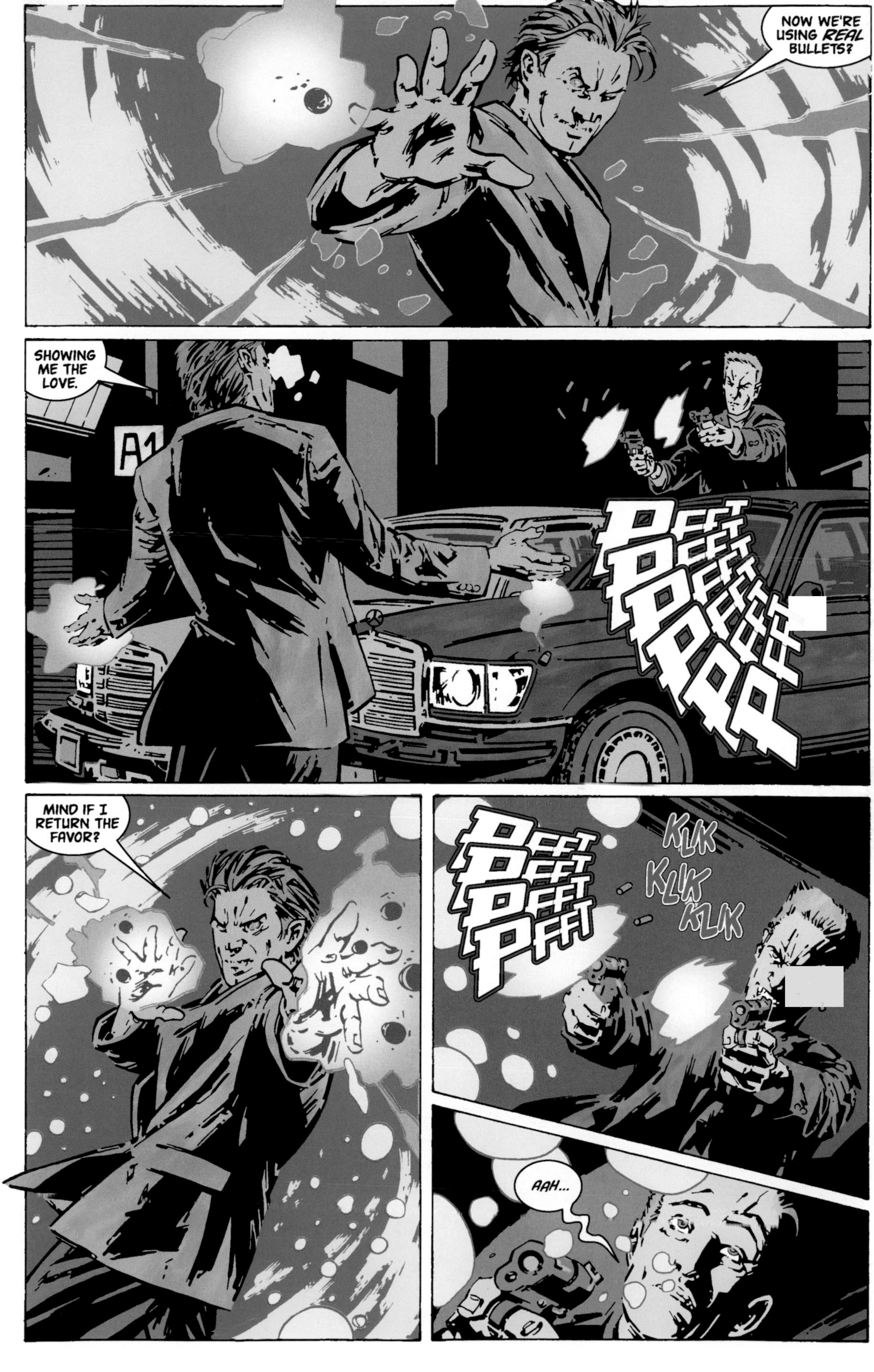
NOW WE'RE USING *REAL* BULLETS?
SHOWING ME THE LOVE.
A1
PFFT PFFT PFFT PFFT PFFT PFFT
MIND IF I RETURN THE FAVOR?
PFFT PFFT PFFT PFFT
KLIK KLIK KLIK
AAH...

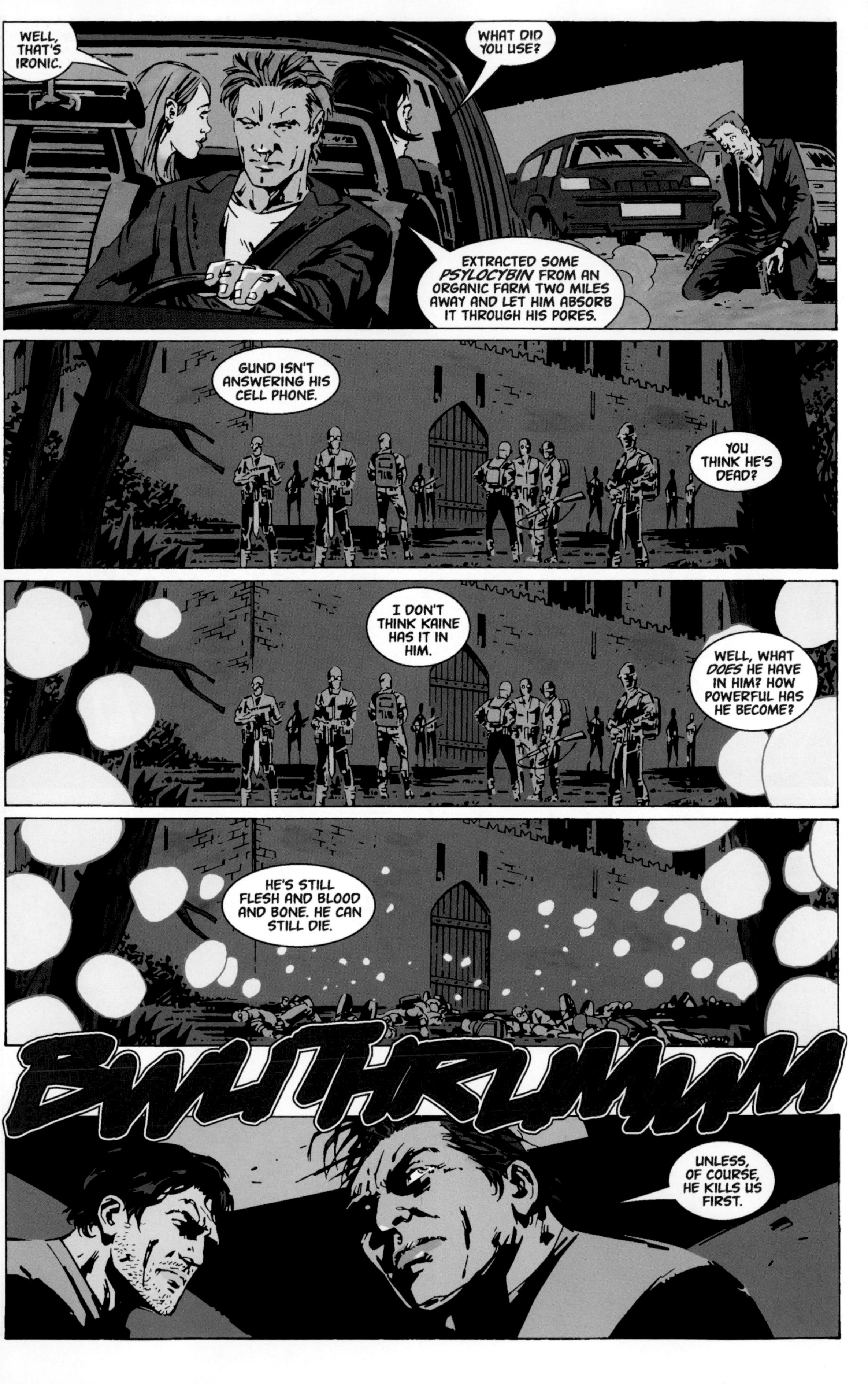
WELL, THAT'S IRONIC.
WHAT DID YOU USE?
EXTRACTED SOME *PSYLOCYBIN* FROM AN ORGANIC FARM TWO MILES AWAY AND LET HIM ABSORB IT THROUGH HIS PORES.
GUND ISN'T ANSWERING HIS CELL PHONE.
YOU THINK HE'S DEAD?
I DON'T THINK KAINE HAS IT IN HIM.
WELL, WHAT *DOES* HE HAVE IN HIM? HOW POWERFUL HAS HE BECOME?
HE'S STILL FLESH AND BLOOD AND BONE. HE CAN STILL DIE.
BWUTHRUMMM
UNLESS, OF COURSE, HE KILLS US FIRST.

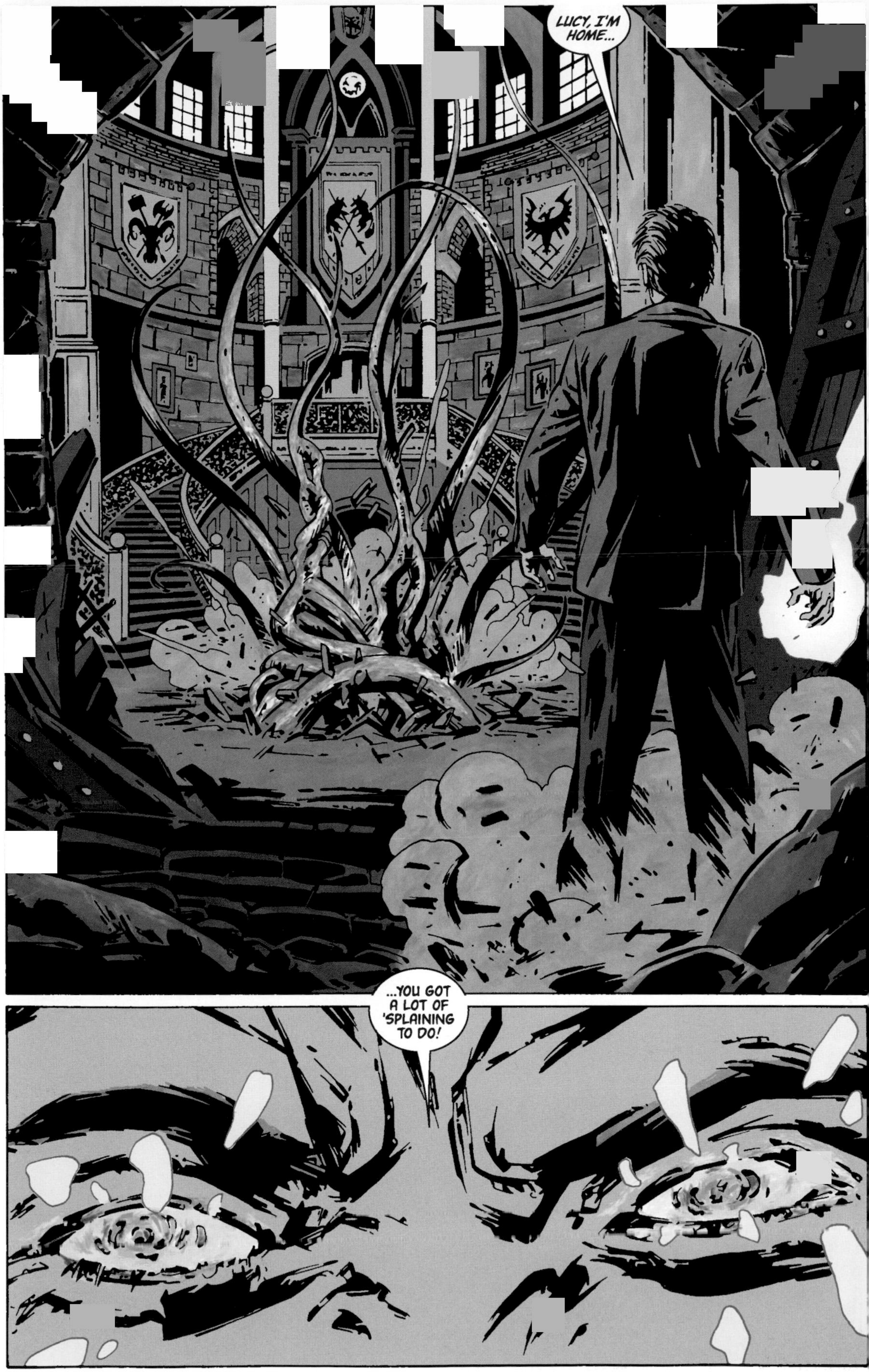
LUCY, I'M HOME...
...YOU GOT A LOT OF 'SPLAINING TO DO!

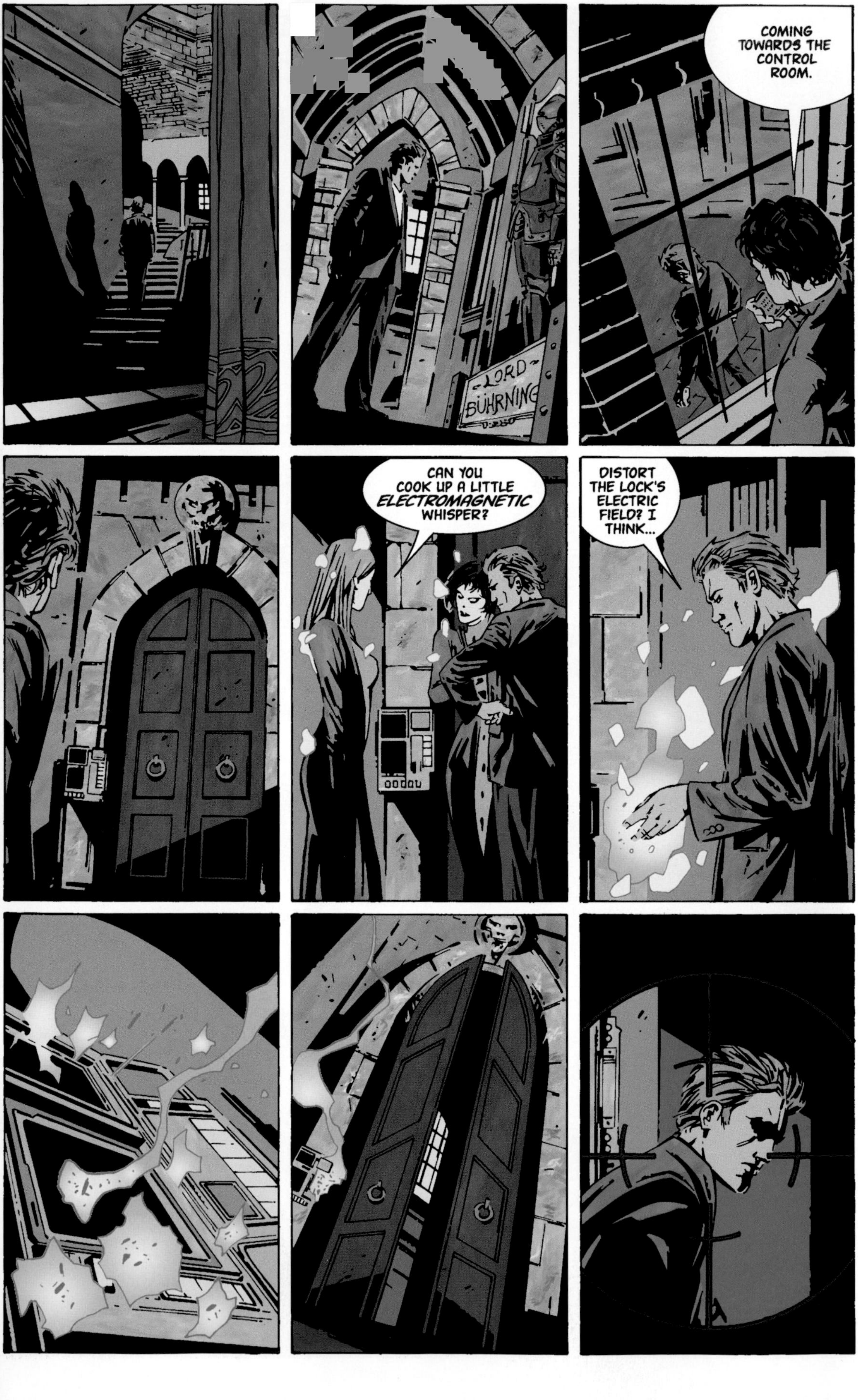
LORD
BÜHRNING
COMING TOWARDS THE CONTROL ROOM.
CAN YOU COOK UP A LITTLE *ELECTROMAGNETIC* WHISPER?
DISTORT THE LOCK'S ELECTRIC FIELD? I THINK...

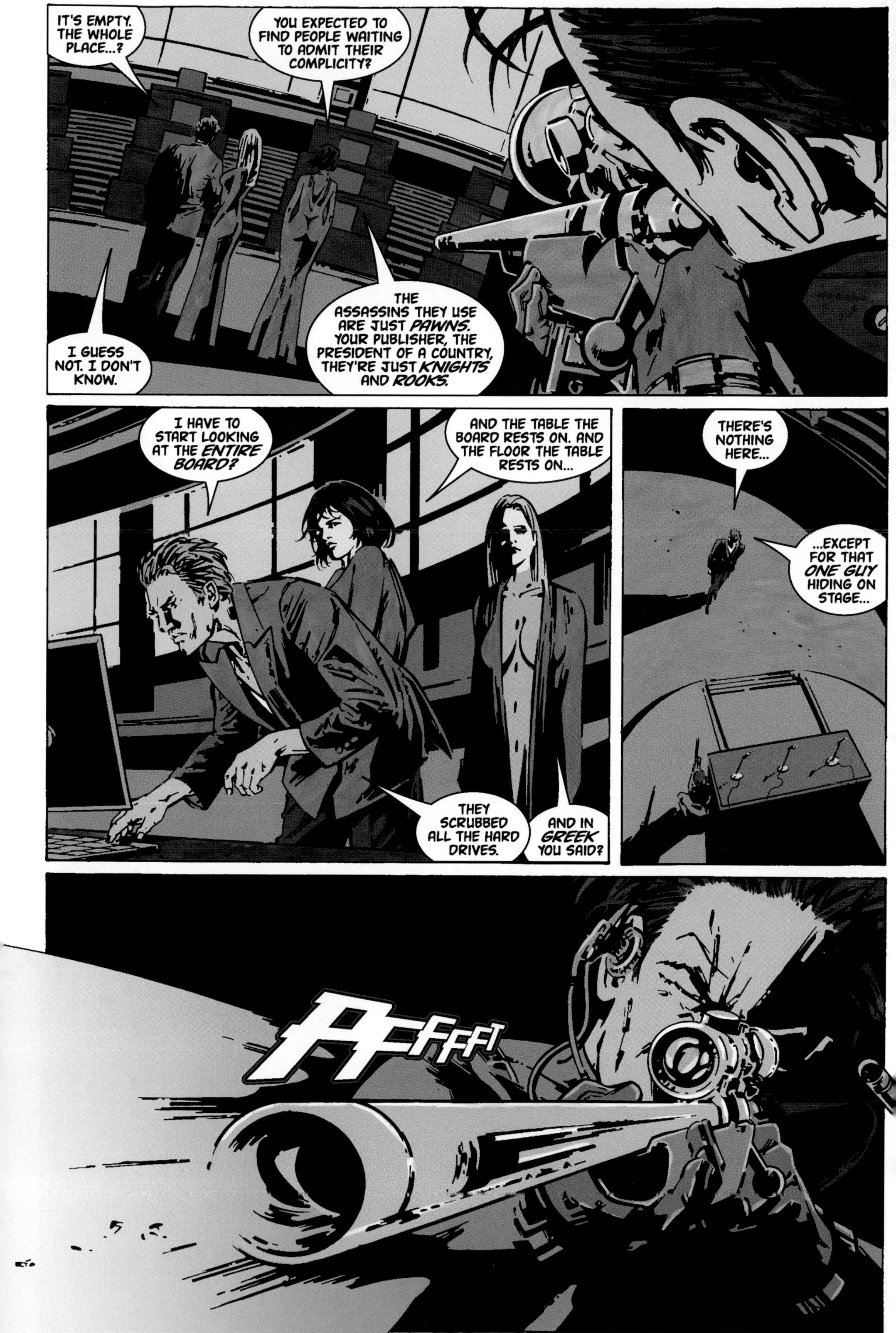
IT'S EMPTY. THE WHOLE PLACE...?
YOU EXPECTED TO FIND PEOPLE WAITING TO ADMIT THEIR COMPLICITY?
I GUESS NOT. I DON'T KNOW.
THE ASSASSINS THEY USE ARE JUST PAWNS. YOUR PUBLISHER, THE PRESIDENT OF A COUNTRY, THEY'RE JUST KNIGHTS AND ROOKS.
I HAVE TO START LOOKING AT THE ENTIRE BOARD?
AND THE TABLE THE BOARD RESTS ON. AND THE FLOOR THE TABLE RESTS ON...
THEY SCRUBBED ALL THE HARD DRIVES.
AND IN GREEK YOU SAID?
THERE'S NOTHING HERE...
...EXCEPT FOR THAT ONE GUY HIDING ON STAGE...
PFFFFT

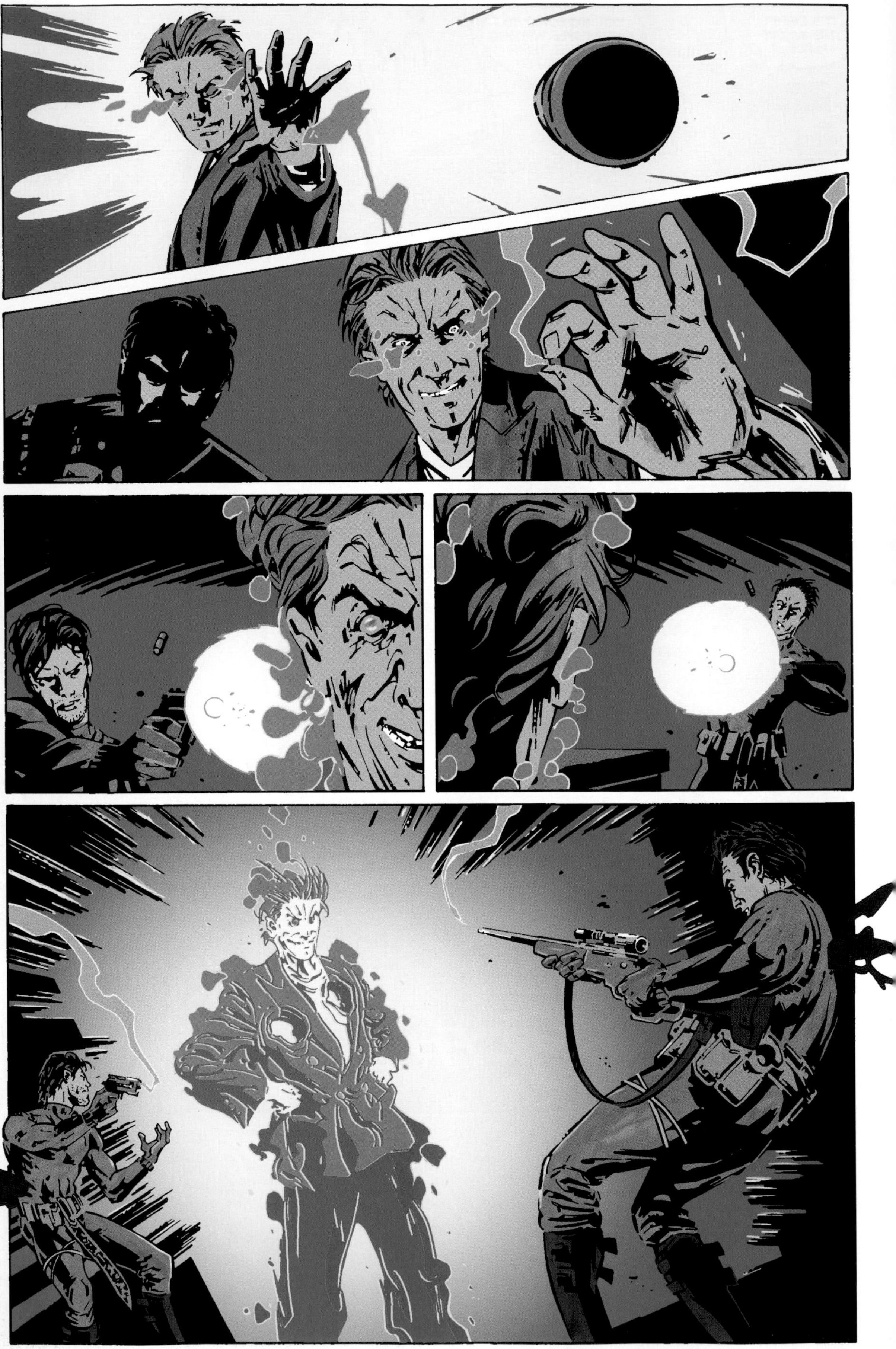

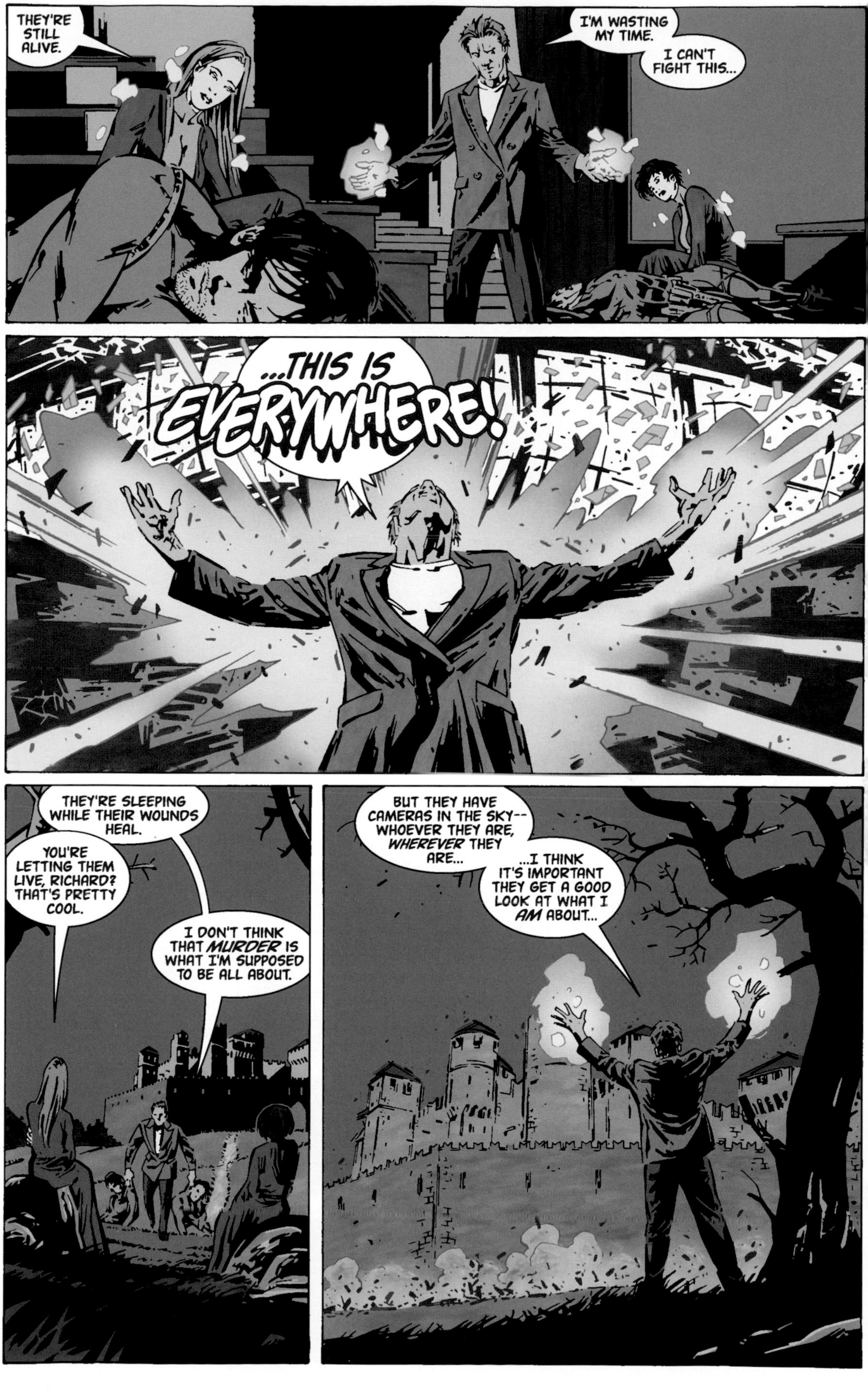
THEY'RE STILL ALIVE.
I'M WASTING MY TIME.
I CAN'T FIGHT THIS...
...THIS IS EVERYWHERE!
THEY'RE SLEEPING WHILE THEIR WOUNDS HEAL.
YOU'RE LETTING THEM LIVE, RICHARD? THAT'S PRETTY COOL.
I DON'T THINK THAT MURDER IS WHAT I'M SUPPOSED TO BE ALL ABOUT.
BUT THEY HAVE CAMERAS IN THE SKY-- WHOEVER THEY ARE, WHEREVER THEY ARE...
...I THINK IT'S IMPORTANT THEY GET A GOOD LOOK AT WHAT I AM ABOUT...

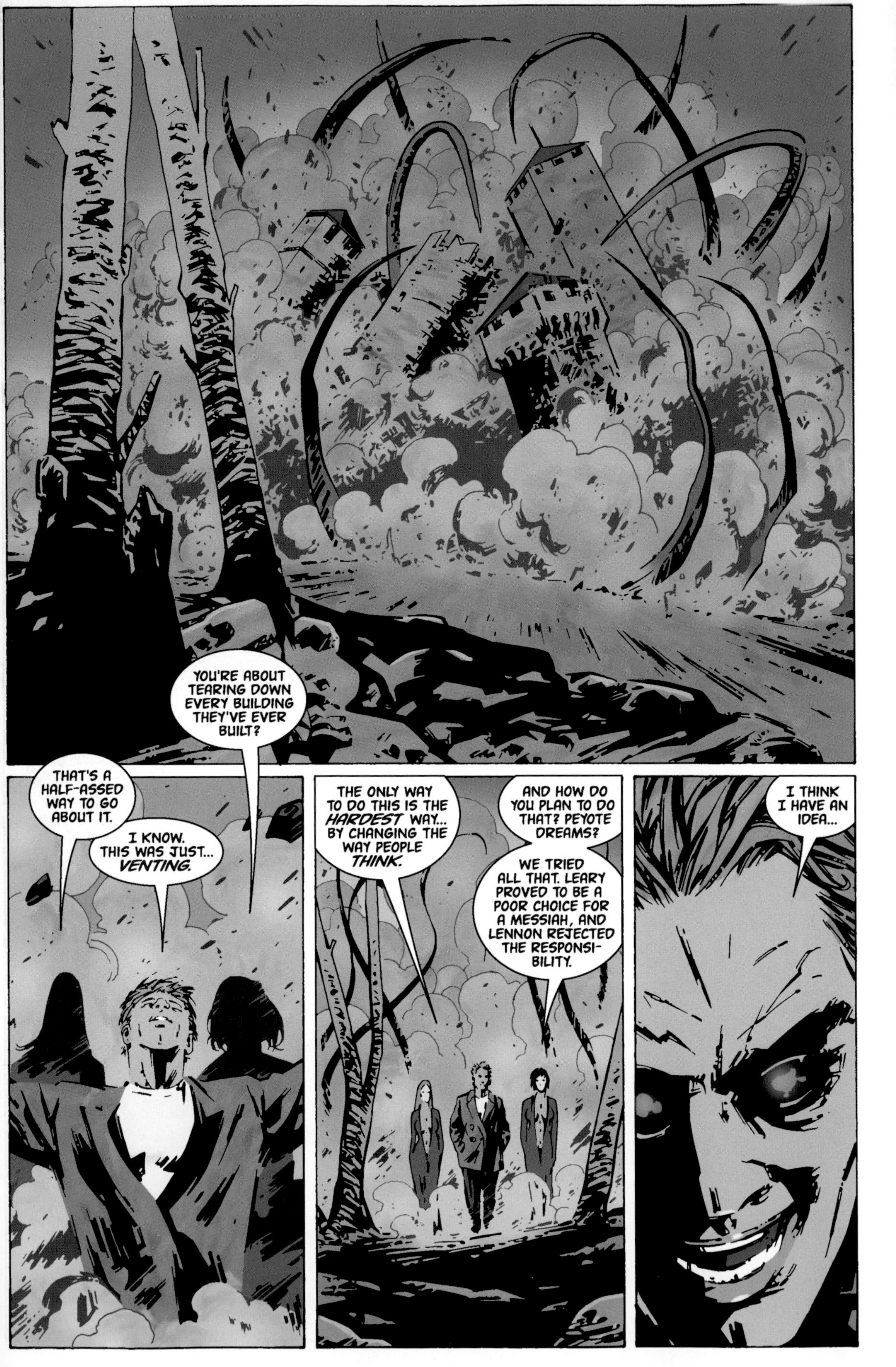
YOU'RE ABOUT TEARING DOWN EVERY BUILDING THEY'VE EVER BUILT?
THAT'S A HALF-ASSED WAY TO GO ABOUT IT.
I KNOW. THIS WAS JUST... VENTING.
THE ONLY WAY TO DO THIS IS THE HARDEST WAY... BY CHANGING THE WAY PEOPLE THINK.
AND HOW DO YOU PLAN TO DO THAT? PEYOTE DREAMS?
WE TRIED ALL THAT. LEARY PROVED TO BE A POOR CHOICE FOR A MESSIAH, AND LENNON REJECTED THE RESPONSI-BILITY.
I THINK I HAVE AN IDEA...

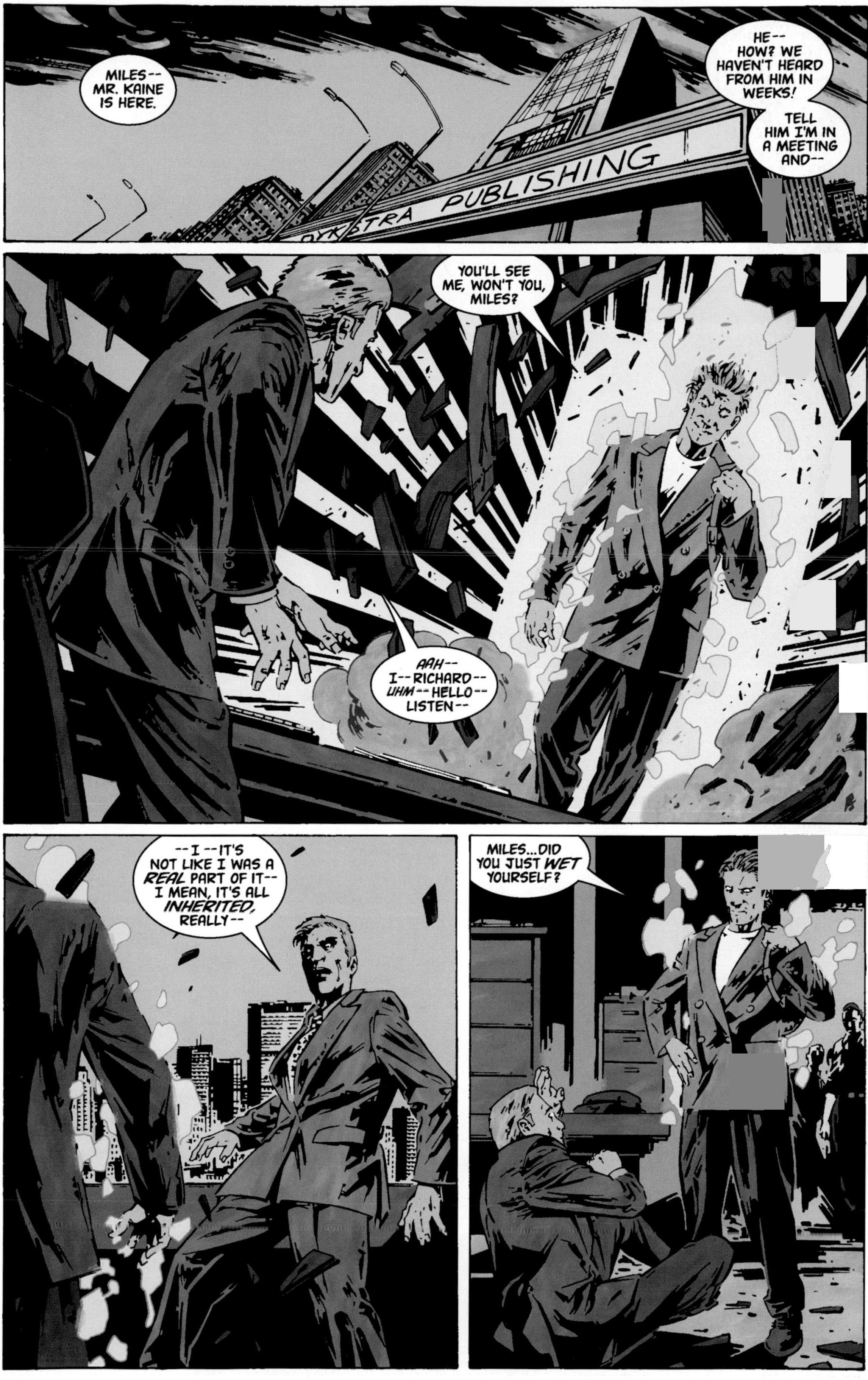
MILES-- MR. KAINE IS HERE.
HE-- HOW? WE HAVEN'T HEARD FROM HIM IN WEEKS!
TELL HIM I'M IN A MEETING AND--
DYKSTRA PUBLISHING
YOU'LL SEE ME, WON'T YOU, MILES?
AAH-- I--RICHARD-- UHM--HELLO-- LISTEN--
--I --IT'S NOT LIKE I WAS A REAL PART OF IT-- I MEAN, IT'S ALL INHERITED, REALLY--
MILES...DID YOU JUST WET YOURSELF?

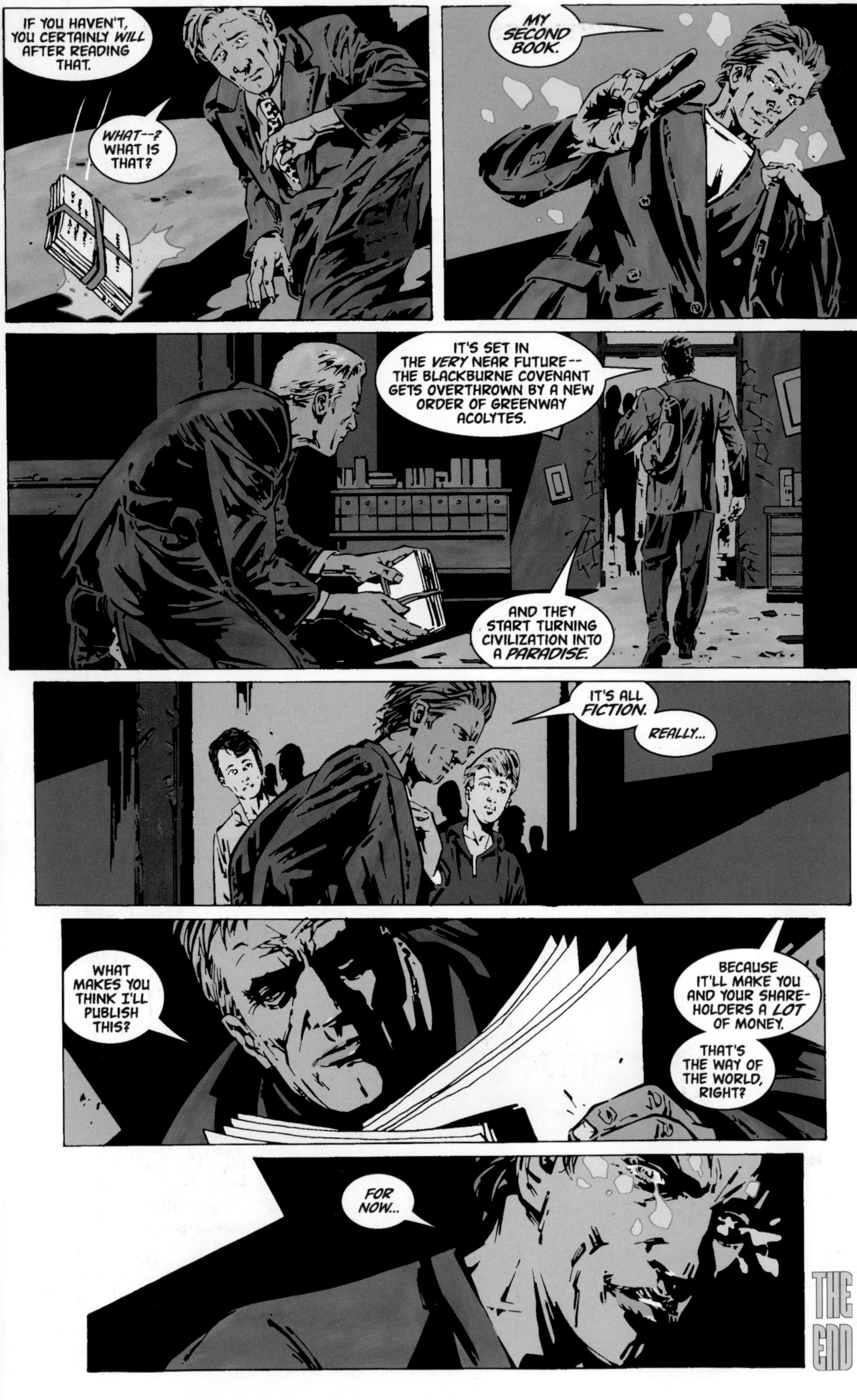
IF YOU HAVEN'T, YOU CERTAINLY *WILL* AFTER READING THAT.
WHAT--? WHAT IS THAT?
MY SECOND BOOK.
IT'S SET IN THE *VERY* NEAR FUTURE-- THE BLACKBURNE COVENANT GETS OVERTHROWN BY A NEW ORDER OF GREENWAY ACOLYTES.
AND THEY START TURNING CIVILIZATION INTO A *PARADISE*.
IT'S ALL *FICTION*.
REALLY...
WHAT MAKES YOU THINK I'LL PUBLISH THIS?
BECAUSE IT'LL MAKE YOU AND YOUR SHAREHOLDERS A *LOT* OF MONEY.
THAT'S THE WAY OF THE WORLD, RIGHT?
FOR NOW...
THE END

ALSO FROM DARK HORSE COMICS!

MIKE MIGNOLA'S
HELLBOY
WEIRD TALES
Volume One

HELLBOY: WEIRD TALES VOLUME ONE TPB

By Joe Casey, John Cassaday, Steve Lieber, Alex Maleev, Jason Pearson, Leinil Francis Yu, and many more! Cover by Mike Mignola.

Celebrating the release of the *Hellboy* motion picture, Dark Horse presents a lavish collection of stories featuring one of the greatest heroes of modern comics as drawn by the best artists in the comics industry, who've finally gotten their chance to play with Hellboy and the other fantastic characters created by Mike Mignola.

SC, 128 pgs, FC . . . . . . ISBN: 1-56971-622-6 . . . . . . $17.95

Mike Mignola
P. Craig Russell
Jill Thompson
Evan Dorkin
Paul Chadwick
Gary Gianni
and others
The Dark Horse Book of
HAUNTINGS

DARK HORSE BOOK OF HAUNTINGS

By Mike Mignola, P. Craig Russell, Paul Chadwick, Evan Dorkin, Jill Thompson, Various. Cover by Gary Gianni.

This hardcover book features original short stories by some of the most respected names in comics, including Mike Mignola's only new 2003 *Hellboy* adventure! This is the ultimate book for horror-comics enthusiasts and fans of fantastic artwork.

HC, 96pg, FC . . . . . . ISBN: 1-56971-958-6 . . . . . . $14.95

THE GOON
NOTHIN' BUT MISERY
by Eric Powell

THE GOON: NOTHIN' BUT MISERY TPB

By Eric Powell. Cover by Eric Powell.

An insane priest is building himself an army of the undead, and there's only one man to defend us: The Goon. Dark Horse kicks off our new bi-monthly Goon series with a collection of the series originally published by Albatross Exploding Funny Books, in color for the first time.

SC, 136pg, FC . . . . . . ISBN: 1-56971-998-5 . . . . . . $16.95

The DEVIL'S FOOTPRINTS
Paul Lee Brian Horton Dave Stewart

THE DEVIL'S FOOTPRINTS TPB

By Scott Allie, Paul Lee, Brian Horton, and Dave Stewart

After the mystic William Waite died, his son thought that the terror was over. But when the people closest to him begin to suffer from mysterious illnesses, including the loss of a baby, Brandon Waite must dig into his dead father's bag of tricks and jeopardize his own immortal soul.

SC, 144 pg, FC . . . . . . ISBN: 1-56971-933-0 . . . . . . $14.95

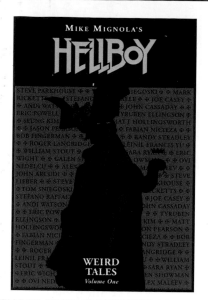

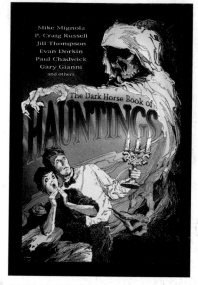

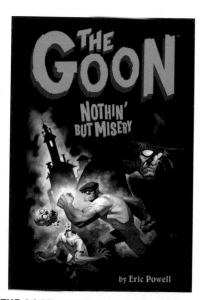

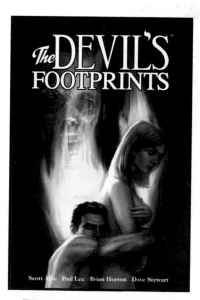

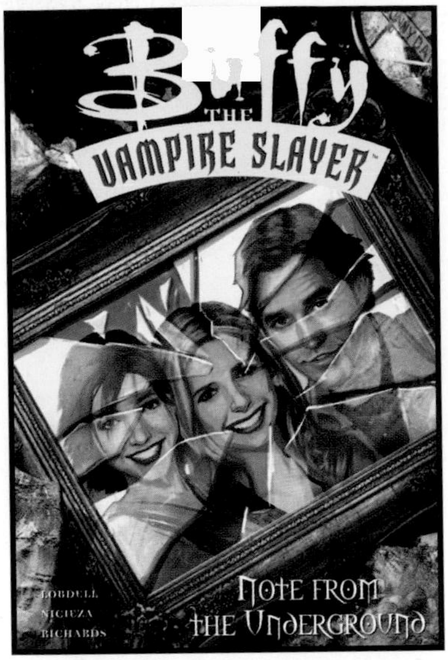
THE
VAMPIRE SLAYER
LOBDELL
NICIEZA
RICHARDS
NOTE FROM
THE UNDERGROUND

BUFFY THE VAMPIRE SLAYER:
NOTE FROM THE UNDERGROUND TPB

By Scott Lobdell, Fabian Nicieza, Cliff Richards and Will Conrad

Taking the series in a whole new direction, this volume collects Scott Lobdell's (*X-men*, *Highroads*) debut story arc with veteran Buffy scribe Fabian Nicieza! Joining established Buffy artist Cliff Richards, Lobdell, and Nicieza begin their run by wrapping up four years worth of stories, featuring many returning faces.

SC, 104pg, FC ...... ISBN: 1-56971-888-1 ...... $12.95

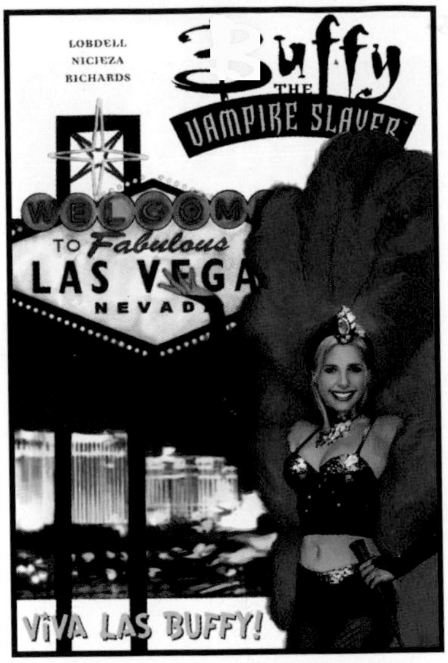
LOBDELL
NICIEZA
RICHARDS
THE
VAMPIRE SLAYER
TO Fabulous
LAS VEGA
NEVAD
VIVA LAS BUFFY!

BUFFY THE VAMPIRE SLAYER:
VIVA LAS BUFFY TPB

By Scott Lobdell, Fabian Nicieza, Cliff Richard, and Will Conrad

It's 1996, the summer before she arrived in Sunnydale, and Buffy Summers has just accepted her role as the Slayer. After the destruction of her high school, to sort out her life she flees to Las Vegas, where she discovers a coven of vampires has big plans for the strip.

SC, 96pg, FC ...... ISBN: 1-56971-980-2 ...... $12.95

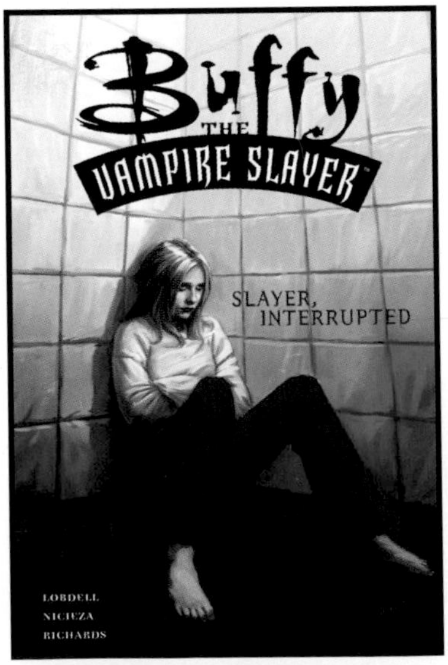
Buffy
THE
VAMPIRE SLAYER
SLAYER,
INTERRUPTED
LOBDELL
NICIEZA
RICHARDS

BUFFY THE VAMPIRE SLAYER:
SLAYER, INTERRUPTED TPB

By Scott Lobdell, Fabian Nicieza, Cliff Richards, and Will Conrad

Buffy burns down the school gym, runs off to Vegas, then fills her diary with tales of vampires and demons. Now her parents have had her committed to a mental institution, where she doesn't have to slay vampires night after night. But she discovers a sinister presence inside the institution.

SC, 96 pg, FC ...... ISBN: 1-59307-011-X $14.95

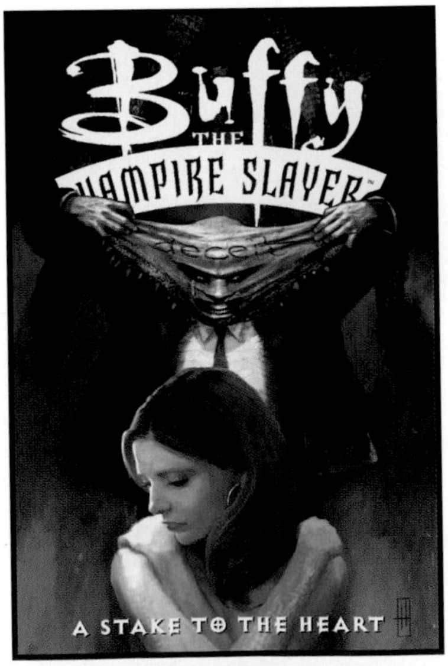
Buffy
THE
VAMPIRE SLAYER
A STAKE TO THE HEART

BUFFY THE VAMPIRE SLAYER:
A STAKE TO THE HEART TPB

By Fabian Nicieza, Cliff Richards, Will Conrad, and Brian Horton

Buffy faces the scariest thing of all: her parents' divorce. No vampire is safe when she takes her anger to the streets. Meanwhile, Angel watches over her, then accidentally unleashes upon Buffy and her family bizarre Malignancy Demons, each of which personifies and draws its power from particular bad feelings.

SC, 96 pg, FC ...... ISBN: 1-59307-012-8 ...... $12.95

PN
6728
.B53
N53
2004

Nicieza, Fabian

The Blackburne
Covenant